Geometry Connections
Version 3.1

Managing Editor

Leslie Dietiker
Phillip and Sala Burton Academic High School
San Francisco, CA

Contributing Editors

Elizabeth Ellen Coyner
Christian Brothers High School
Sacramento, CA

Lew Douglas
The College Preparatory School
Oakland, CA

David Gulick
Phillips Exeter Academy
Exeter, NH

Lara Lomac
Phillip and Sala Burton Academic
High School, San Francisco, CA

Damian Molinari
Phillip and Sala Burton Academic
High School, San Francisco, CA

Jason Murphy-Thomas
George Washington High School
San Francisco, CA

Leslie Nielsen
Isaaquah High School
Issaquah, WA

Karen O'Connell
San Lorenzo High School
San Lorenzo, CA

Ward Quincey
Gideon Hausner Jewish Day School
Palo Alto, CA

Barbara Shreve
San Lorenzo High School
San Lorenzo, CA

Michael Titelbaum
University of California
Berkeley, CA

Illustrator

Kevin Coffey
San Francisco, CA

Technical Assistants

Erica Andrews

Elizabeth Burke

Carrie Cai

Daniel Cohen

Elizabeth Fong

Rebecca Harlow

Michael Leong

Thomas Leong

Marcos Rojas

Susan Ryan

Program Directors

Leslie Dietiker
Phillip and Sala Burton Academic High School
San Francisco, CA

Brian Hoey
Christian Brothers High School
Sacramento, CA

Judy Kysh, Ph.D.
Departments of Mathematics and Education
San Francisco State University

Tom Sallee, Ph.D.
Department of Mathematics
University of California, Davis

Contributing Editor of the Parent Guide:

Karen Wootten, Managing Editor
Odenton, MD

Technical Manager of Parent Guide and Extra Practice:

Rebecca Harlow
Stanford University
Stanford, CA

Editor of Extra Practice:

Bob Petersen, Managing Editor
Rosemont High School
Sacramento, CA

Assessment Contributors:

John Cooper, Managing Editor
Del Oro High School
Loomis, CA

Leslie Dietiker
Phillip and Sala Burton Academic High School
San Francisco, CA

Lara Lomac
Phillip and Sala Burton Academic High School,
San Francisco, CA

Damian Molinari
Phillip and Sala Burton Academic High School,
San Francisco, CA

Barbara Shreve
San Lorenzo High School
San Lorenzo, CA

2 3 4 5 6 7 8 9   10 09 08 07 06   ISBN-10:   1-931287-59-7

Printed in the United States of America   Version 3.1   ISBN-13:   978-1-931287-59-3

A Note to Students:

Welcome to Geometry! This courses centers on the study of shapes. As you study geometry, you will be investigating new situations, discovering relationships, and figuring out what strategies can be used to solve problems. Learning to think this way is useful in mathematical contexts and other courses, as well as in situations outside the classroom.

In meeting the challenges of geometry, you will not be working alone. During this course you will collaborate with other students as a member of a study team. Working in a team means speaking up and interacting with others. You will explain your ideas, listen to what others have to say, and ask questions if there is something you do not understand. In geometry, a single problem can often be solved more than one way. You will see problems in different ways than your teammates do. Each of you has something to contribute while you work on the lessons in this course.

Together, your team will complete problems and activities that will help you discover new mathematical ideas and methods. Your teacher will support you as you work, but will not take away your opportunity to think and investigate for yourself. The ideas in the course will be revisited several times and connected to other topics. If something is not clear to you the first time you work with it, don't worry—you will have more chances to build your understanding as the course continues.

Learning math this way has a significant advantage: as long as you actively participate, make sure everyone in your study team is involved, and ask good questions, you will find yourself understanding mathematics at a deeper level than ever before. By the end of this course, you will have an understanding of a variety of geometric principles and properties that govern the world around us. You will see how these principles and properties interweave so that you can use them together to solve new problems. With your teammates, you will meet mathematical challenges you would not have known how to approach before.

In addition to the support provided by your teacher and your study team, CPM has also created online resources to help you, including help with homework, a parent guide, and extra practice. You will find these resources and more at www.cpm.org.

We wish you well and are confident that you will enjoy learning geometry!

Sincerely,
The CPM Team

Geometry
Connections
Table of Contents

Student Edition

Chapter 3 Justification and Similarity

133

Chapter 4 Trigonometry and Probability

185

CHAPTER 7   Proof and Quadrilaterals

This chapter opens with a set of explorations designed to introduce you to new geometric topics that you will explore further in Chapters 8 through 12. You will learn about the special properties of a circle, explore three-dimensional shapes, and use a hinged mirror to learn more about a rhombus.

Section 7.2 then builds upon your work from Chapters 3 through 6. Using congruent triangles, you will explore the relationships of the sides and diagonals of a parallelogram, kite, trapezoid, rectangle, and rhombus. As you explore new geometric properties, you will formalize your understanding of proof.

This chapter ends with an exploration of coordinate geometry.

Guiding Questions

Think about these questions throughout this chapter:

What's the connection?

How can I prove it?

Is it convincing?

What tools can I use?

In this chapter, you will learn:

➤ The relationships of the sides, angles, and diagonals of special quadrilaterals, such as parallelograms, rectangles, kites, and rhombi (plural of rhombus).

➤ How to write a convincing proof in a variety of formats, such as a flowchart or two-column proof.

➤ How to find the midpoint of a line segment.

➤ How to use algebraic tools to explore quadrilaterals on coordinate axes.

Chapter Outline

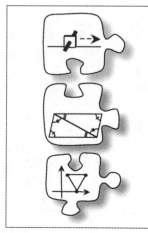

Section 7.1   This section contains four large **investigations** introducing you to geometry topics that will be explored further in Chapters 8 through 12.

Section 7.2   While **investigating** what congruent triangles can inform you about the sides, angles, and diagonals of a quadrilateral, you will develop an understanding of proof.

Section 7.3   This section begins a focus on coordinate geometry, the study of geometry on coordinate axes. During this section, you will use familiar algebraic tools (such as slope) to make and justify conclusions about shapes.

7.1.1 Does it roll smoothly?

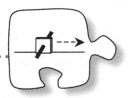

Properties of a Circle

In Chapters 1 through 6, you studied many different types of two-dimensional shapes, explored how they could be related, and developed tools to measure their lengths and areas. In Chapters 7 through 12, you will examine ways to extend these ideas to new shapes (such as polygons and circles) and will thoroughly **investigate** what we can learn about three-dimensional shapes.

To start, Section 7.1 contains four key **investigations** that will touch upon the big ideas of these chapters. As you explore these lessons, take note of what mathematical tools from Chapters 1 through 6 you are using and think about what new directions this course will take. Generate "What if…" questions that can be answered later once new tools are developed.

Since much of the focus of Chapters 7 through 12 is on the study of circles, this lesson will first explore the properties of a circle. What makes a circle special? Today you are going to answer that question and, at the same time, explore other shapes with surprisingly similar qualities.

7-1. THE INVENTION OF THE WHEEL

One of the most important human inventions was the wheel. Many archeologists estimate that the wheel was probably first invented about 10,000 years ago in Asia. It was an important tool that enabled humans to transport very heavy objects long distances. Most people agree that impressive structures, such as the Egyptian pyramids, could not have been built without the help of wheels.

a. One of the earliest types of "wheels" used were actually logs. Ancient civilizations laid multiple logs on the ground, parallel to each other, under a heavy item that needed to be moved. As long as the logs had the same thickness (called **diameter**) and the road was even, the heavy object had a smooth ride. What is special about a circle that allows it to be used in this way? In other words, why do circles enable this heavy object to roll smoothly?

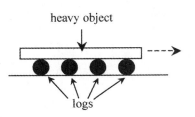

b. What happens to a point on a wheel as it turns? For example, as the wheel at right rolls along the line, what is the path of point P? Imagine a piece of gum stuck to a tire as it rolls. On your paper, draw the motion of point P. If you need help, find a coin or other round object and test this situation.

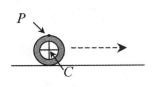

Problem continues on next page →

7-1.   *Problem continued from previous page.*

c.   Now turn your attention to the center of the wheel (labeled *C* in the diagram above). As the wheel rolls along the line, what is the path of point *C*? Describe its motion. Why does that happen?

7-2.   DO CIRCLES MAKE THE BEST WHEELS?

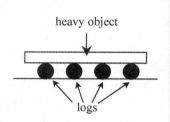

heavy object

logs

As you read in problem 7-1, ancient civilizations used circular logs to roll heavy objects. However, are circles the only shape they could have chosen? Are there any other shapes that could rotate between a flat road and a heavy object in a similar fashion?

Examine the shapes below. Would logs of any of these shapes be able to roll heavy objects in a similar fashion? Be prepared to defend your conclusion!

a.   b.   c.   d.

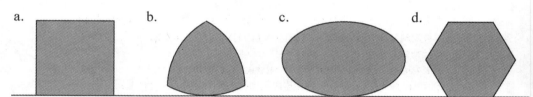

7-3.   Stanley says that he has a tricycle with square wheels and claims that it can ride as smoothly as a tricycle with circular wheels! Rosita does not believe him. Analyze this possibility with your team as you answer the questions below.

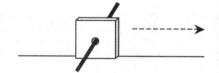

a.   Is Stanley's claim possible? Describe what it would be like to ride a tricycle with square tires. What type of motion would the rider experience? Why does this happen?

b.   When Rosita challenged him, Stanley confessed that he needed a special road so that the square wheels would be able to rotate smoothly and would keep Stanley at a constant height. What would his road need to look like? Draw an example on your paper.

c.   How would Stanley need to change his road to be able to ride a tricycle with rectangular (but non-square) wheels? Draw an example on your paper.

d.   Read the Math Notes box for this lesson to see a picture of Stanley and his tricycle. Then explain why the square wheel needed a modified road to ride smoothly, while the circular wheel did not. What is different between the two shapes?

7-4. REULEAUX CURVES

Reuleaux curves (pronounced "roo **low**") are special because they have a constant diameter. That means that as a Reuleaux curve rotates, its height remains constant. Although the diagram at right is an example of a Reuleaux curve based on an equilateral triangle, these special curves can be based on any polygon with an odd number of sides, including scalene triangles and pentagons.

    a.   What happens to the center (point C) as the Reuleaux wheel at right rolls?

    b.   Since logs with a Reuleaux curve shape can also smoothly roll heavy objects, why are these shapes not used for bicycle wheels? In other words, what is the difference between a circle and a Reuleaux curve?

7-5.   A big focus of Chapters 7 through 12 is on circles. What did you learn about circles today? Did you learn anything about other shapes that was new or that surprised you? Write a Learning Log entry explaining what you learned about the shapes of wheels. Title this entry "Shapes of Wheels" and include today's date.

LOOKING DEEPER

MATH NOTES

Square Tires

As the picture at right shows, square wheels are possible if the road is specially curved to accommodate the change in the radius of the wheel as it rotates. An example is shown below.

On a level surface

On a curved surface

The picture above shows Stan Wagon riding his special square-wheeled tricycle. This tricycle is on display at Macalester College in St. Paul, Minnesota. *Reprinted with permission.*

7-6.   **Examine** △ABC and △DEF at right.

   a.   Assume the triangles are not drawn to
        scale. Using the information provided
        in each diagram, write a mathematical
        statement describing the relationship
        between the two triangles. **Justify**
        your conclusion.

   b.   Find AC and DF.

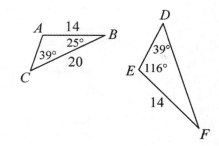

7-7.   Use the relationships in the diagram at right to find
         the values of each variable. Name which geometric
         relationships you used.

7-8.   A rectangle has one side of length 11 mm and a
         diagonal of 61 mm. Draw a diagram of this rectangle
         and find its width and area.

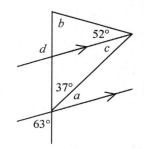

7-9.   Troy is thinking of a shape. He says that it has four sides and that no sides have equal
         length. He also says that no sides are parallel. What is the best name for his shape?

7-10.   Solve each system of equations below, if possible. If it is not possible, explain what
         the lack of an algebraic solution tells you about the graphs of the equations. Write
         each solution in the form (x, y). Show all work.

   a. $y = -2x - 1$ b. $y = x^2 + 1$

        $y = \frac{1}{2}x - 16$ $y = -x^2$

7.1.2 What can I build with a circle?

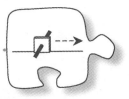

Building a Tetrahedron

In later chapters, you will learn more about polygons, circles, and 3-dimensional shapes. Later **investigations** will require that you remember key concepts you have already learned about triangles, parallel lines, and other angle relationships. Today you will have the opportunity to review some of the geometry you have learned while also beginning to think about what you will be studying in the future.

As you work with your team, consider the following focus questions:

Is there more than one way?

How can you be sure that is true?

What else can we try?

7-11.   IS THERE MORE TO THIS CIRCLE?

Circles can be folded to create many different shapes. Today, you will work with a circle and use properties of other shapes to develop a three-dimensional shape. Be sure to have **reasons** for each conclusion you make as you work. Each person in your team should start by obtaining a copy of a circle from your teacher and cutting it out.

a.   Fold the circle in half to create a crease that lies on a line of symmetry of the circle. Unfold the circle and then fold it in half again to create a new crease that is perpendicular to the first crease. Unfold your paper back to the full circle. How could you convince someone else that your creases are perpendicular? What is another name for the line segment represented by each crease?

b.   On the circle, label the endpoints of one diameter A and B. Fold the circle so that point A touches the center of the circle and create a new crease. Then label the endpoints of this crease C and D. What appears to be the relationship between $\overline{AB}$ and $\overline{CD}$? Discuss and **justify** with your team. Be ready to share your **reasons** with the class.

c.   Now fold the circle twice to form creases $\overline{BC}$ and $\overline{BD}$ and use scissors to cut out $\triangle BCD$. What type of triangle is $\triangle BCD$? How can you be sure? Be ready to convince the class.

7-12.   ADDING DEPTH

Your equilateral triangle should now be flat (also called two-dimensional). **Two-dimensional** shapes have length and width, but not depth (or "thickness").

a.   Label the vertices of △*BCD* if the labels were cut off. Then, with the unmarked side of the triangle facedown, fold and crease the triangle so that *B* touches the midpoint of $\overline{CD}$. Keep it in the folded position.

What does the resulting shape appear to be? What smaller shapes do you see inside the larger shape? **Justify** that your ideas are correct (for example, if you think that lines are parallel, you must provide evidence).

b.   Open your shape again so that you have the large equilateral triangle in front of you. How does the length of a side of the large triangle compare to the length of the side of the small triangle formed by the crease? How many of the small triangles would fit inside the large triangle? In what ways are the small and large triangles related?

c.   Repeat the fold in part (a) so that *C* touches the midpoint of $\overline{BD}$. Unfold the triangle and fold again so that *D* touches the midpoint of $\overline{BC}$. Create a three-dimensional shape by bringing points *B*, *C*, and *D* together. (A **three-dimensional** shape has length, width, and depth.) Use tape to hold your shape together.

d.   Three-dimensional shapes formed with polygons have **faces** and **edges**, as well as **vertices**. Faces are the flat surfaces of the shape, while edges are the line segments formed when two faces meet. Vertices are the points where edges intersect. Discuss with your team how to use these words to describe your new shape. Then write a complete description. If you think you know the name of this shape, include it in your description.

7-13.   Your team should now have 4 three-dimensional shapes (called **tetrahedra**). (If you are working in a smaller team, you should quickly fold more shapes so that you have a total of four.

a.   Put four tetrahedra together to make an enlarged tetrahedron like the one pictured at right. Is the larger tetrahedron similar to the small tetrahedron? How can you tell?

b.   To determine the edges and faces of the new shape, pretend that it is solid. How many edges does a tetrahedron have? Are all of the edges the same length? How does the length of an edge of the team shape compare with the length of an edge of one of the small shapes?

c.   How many faces of the small tetrahedral would it take to cover the face of the large tetrahedron? Remember to count gaps as part of a face. Does the area of the tetrahedron change in the same way as the length?

Enlarged tetrahedron   Original

Geometry Connections

METHODS AND MEANINGS

Parts of a Circle

A **circle** is the set of all points that are the same distance from a fixed central point, C. This text will use the notation $\odot C$ to name a circle with **center** at point C.

The distance from the center to the points on the circle is called the **radius** (usually denoted r), while the line segment drawn through the center of the circle with both endpoints on the circle is called a **diameter** (denoted d).

Notice that a diameter of a circle is always twice as long as the radius.

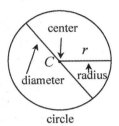

Review & Preview

7-14.   What is the relationship of $\triangle ABC$ and $\triangle GHJ$ at right? **Justify** your conclusion.

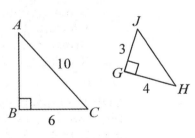

7-15.   The area of the trapezoid at right is 56 un². What is h? Show all work.

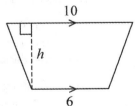

7-16.   **Examine** the geometric relationships in each of the diagrams below. For each one, write and solve an equation to find the value of the variable. Name any geometric property or conjecture that you used.

a.

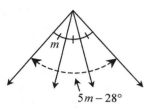

$5m - 28°$

b.

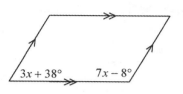

$3x + 38°$ $7x - 8°$

c. $\triangle ABC$ below is equilateral.

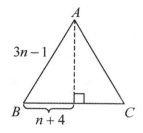

$3n - 1$

B $n + 4$ C

d. C is the center of the circle below.
$AB = 11x - 1$ and $CD = 3x + 12$

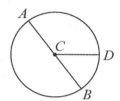

7-17.   In the Shape Factory, you created many shapes by rotating triangles about the midpoint of its sides. (Remember that the **midpoint** is the point exactly halfway between the endpoints of the line segment.) However, what if you rotate a trapezoid instead?

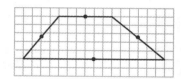

Carefully draw the trapezoid above on graph paper, along with the given midpoints. Then rotate the trapezoid 180° about one of the midpoints and **examine** the resulting shape formed by both trapezoids (the original and its image). Continue this process with each of the other midpoints, until you discover all the shapes that can be formed by a trapezoid and its image when rotated 180° about the midpoint of one of its sides.

7-18.   On graph paper, plot the points $A(-5, 7)$ and $B(3, 1)$.

a.   Find AB (the length of $\overline{AB}$).

b.   Locate the midpoint of $\overline{AB}$ and label it C. What are the coordinates of C?

c.   Find AC. Can you do this without using the Pythagorean Theorem?

7.1.3 What's the shortest distance?

Shortest Distance Problems

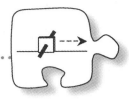

Questions such as, "What length will result in the largest area?" or "When was the car traveling the slowest?" concern *optimization*. To **optimize** a quantity is to find the "best" possibility. Calculus is often used to solve optimization problems, but sometimes geometric tools offer surprisingly simple and elegant solutions.

7-19.   INTERIOR DESIGN

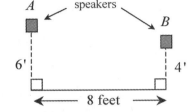

Laura needs your help. She needs to order expensive wire to connect her stereo to her built-in speakers and would like your help to save her money.

She plans to place her stereo somewhere on a cabinet that is 8 feet wide. Speaker A is located 6 feet above one end of the cabinet, while speaker B is located 4 feet above the other end. She will need wire to connect the stereo to speaker A, and additional wire to connect the stereo to speaker B.

Where should she place her stereo so that she needs the least amount of wire?

Your Task: Before you discuss this with your team, make your own guess. What does your intuition tell you? Then, using the Lesson 7.1.3 Resource Page, work with your team to determine where on the cabinet the stereo should be placed. How can you be sure that you found the best answer? In other words, how do you know that the amount of wire you found is the least amount possible?

Discussion Points

What is this problem about? What are you supposed to find?

What is a reasonable estimate of the total length of speaker wire?

What mathematical tools could be helpful to solve this problem?

Further Guidance

7-20. To help solve problem 7-19, first collect some data.

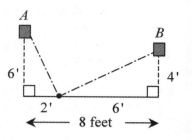

a. Calculate the total length of wire needed if the stereo is placed 2 feet from the left edge of the cabinet (the edge below Speaker A), as shown in the diagram at right.

b. Now calculate the total length of wire needed if the stereo is placed 3 feet from the same edge. Does this placement require more or less wire than that from part (a)?

c. Continue testing placements for the stereo and create a table with your results. Where should the stereo be placed to minimize the amount of wire?

7-21. This problem reminds Bradley of problem 3-93, *You Are Getting Sleepy...*, in which you and a partner created two triangles by standing and gazing into a mirror. He remembered that the only way two people could see each others' eyes in the mirror was when the triangles were similar. **Examine** your solution to problem 7-19. Are the two triangles created by the speaker wires similar? **Justify** your conclusion.

7-22. Bradley enjoyed solving problem 7-19 so much that he decided to create other "shortest distance" problems. For each situation below, first predict where the shortest path lies using visualization and intuition. Then find a way to determine whether the path you chose is, in fact, the shortest.

a. In this first puzzle, Bradley decided to test what would happen on the side of a cylinder, such as a soup can. On a can provided by your teacher, find points *A* and *B* labeled on the outside of the can. With your team, determine the shortest path from point *A* to point *B* along the surface of the can. (In other words, no part of your path can go inside the can.) Describe how you found your solution.

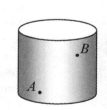

b. What if the shape is a cube? Using a cube provided by your teacher, predict which path would be the shortest path from opposite corners of the cube (labeled points *C* and *D* in the diagram at right). Then test your prediction. Describe how you found the shortest path.

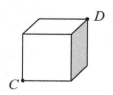

7-23.   MAKING CONNECTIONS

As Bradley looked over his answer from
problem 7-19, he couldn't help but wonder
if there is a way to change this problem
into a straight-line problem like those in
problem 7-22.

a.   On the Lesson 7.1.3 Resource Page, reflect
one of the speakers so that when the two
speakers are connected with a straight line,
the line passes through the horizontal
cabinet.

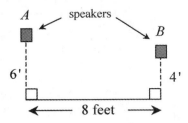

b.   When the speakers from part (a) are connected
with a straight line, two triangles are formed.
How are the two triangles related? **Justify**
your conclusion.

c.   Use the fact that the triangles are similar to find
where the stereo should be placed. Did your
answer match that from problem 7-19?

7-24.   TAKE THE SHOT

While playing a game of pool,
"Montana Mike" needed to hit
the last remaining ball into
pocket A, as shown in the
diagram below. However, to
show off, he decided to make
the ball first hit at least one of
the rails of the table.

Your Task: On the Lesson 7.1.3
Resource Page provided by your
teacher, determine where Mike
could bounce the ball off a rail so
that it will land in pocket A. Work
with your team to find as many
possible locations as you can.
Can you find a way he could hit
the ball so that it would rebound
twice before entering pocket A?

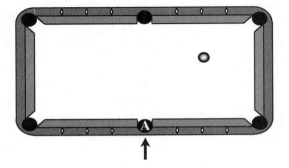

Be ready to share your solutions with the class.

7-25. Look over your work from problems 7-19 to 7-24. What mathematical ideas did you use? What connections, if any, did you find? Can any other problems you have seen so far be solved using a straight line? Describe the mathematical ideas you developed during this lesson in your Learning Log. Title this entry "Shortest Distance" and include today's date.

METHODS AND **M**EANINGS

Congruent Triangles → Congruent Corresponding Parts

As you learned in Chapter 3, if two shapes are congruent, then they have exactly the same shape and the same size. This means that if you know two triangles are congruent, you can state that corresponding parts are congruent. This can be also stated with the arrow diagram:

$$\cong \triangle s \rightarrow \cong \text{ parts}$$

For example, if $\triangle ABC \cong \triangle PQR$, then it follows that $\angle A \cong \angle P$, $\angle B \cong \angle Q$, and $\angle C \cong \angle R$. Also, $\overline{AB} \cong \overline{PQ}$, $\overline{AC} \cong \overline{PR}$, and $\overline{BC} \cong \overline{QR}$.

7-26. $\triangle XYZ$ is reflected across $\overline{XZ}$, as shown at right.

a. How can you **justify** that the points Y, Z, and Y' all lie on a straight line?

b. What is the relationship between $\triangle XYZ$ and $\triangle XY'Z$? Why?

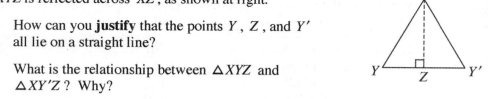

c. Read the Math Notes box for this lesson. Then make all the statements you can about the corresponding parts of these two triangles.

7-27. Remember that a midpoint of a line segment is the point that divides the segment into two segments of equal length. On graph paper, plot the points $P(0, 3)$ and $Q(0, 11)$. Where is the midpoint M if $PM = MQ$? Explain how you found your answer.

7-28.   Recall the three similarity shortcuts for triangles: SSS ~, SAS ~ and AA ~. For each pair of triangles below, decide whether the triangles are congruent and/or similar. **Justify** each conclusion.

a.

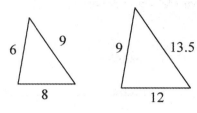

b.

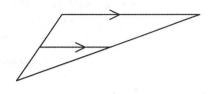

c.

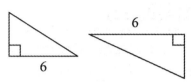

d.

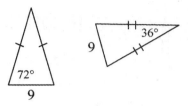

7-29.   On graph paper, plot and connect the points $A(1, 1)$, $B(2, 3)$, $C(5, 3)$, and $D(4, 1)$ to form quadrilateral $ABCD$.

a.   What is the best name for quadrilateral $ABCD$? **Justify** your answer.

b.   Find and compare $m\angle DAB$ and $m\angle BCD$. What is their relationship?

c.   Find the equations of diagonals $\overline{AC}$ and $\overline{BD}$. Are the diagonals perpendicular?

d.   Find the point where diagonals $\overline{AC}$ and $\overline{BD}$ intersect.

7-30.   Solve each system of equations below, if possible. If it is not possible, explain what having "no solution" tells you about the graphs of the equations. Write each solution in the form (x, y). Show all work.

a. $y = -\frac{1}{3}x + 7$

$y = -\frac{1}{3}x - 2$

b. $y = 2x + 3$

$y = x^2 - 2x + 3$

7-31.   How long is the longest line segment that will fit inside a square of area 50 square units? Show all work.

7-32.   Graph and connect the points $G(-2, 2)$, $H(3, 2)$, $I(6, 6)$, and $J(1, 6)$ to form *GHIJ*.

    a.   What specific type of shape is quadrilateral *GHIJ*? **Justify** your conclusion.

    b.   Find the equations of the diagonals $\overline{GI}$ and $\overline{HJ}$.

    c.   Compare the slopes of the diagonals. How do the diagonals of a rhombus appear to be related?

    d.   Find J' if quadrilateral *GHIJ* is rotated 90° clockwise (↻) about the origin.

    e.   Find the area of quadrilateral *GHIJ*.

7-33.   **Examine** the relationships in the diagrams below. For each one, write an equation and solve for the given variable(s). Show all work.

    a.

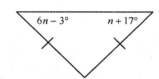

    b.

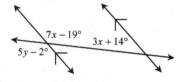

    c.

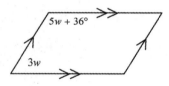

    d.

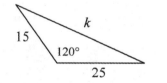

7-34.   Find the perimeter of the shape at right. Show all work.

7-35.   Three spinners are shown at right. If each spinner is randomly spun and if spinners #2 and #3 are each equally divided, find the following probabilities.

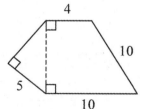

    a.   P(spinning *A*, *C*, and *E*)

    b.   P(spinning at least one vowel)

7.1.4 How can I create it?

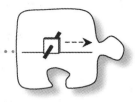

Using Symmetry to Study Polygons

In Chapter 1, you used a hinged mirror to study the special angles associated with regular polygons. In particular, you **investigated** what happens as the angle formed by the sides of the mirror is changed. Today, you will use a hinged mirror to determine if there is more than one way to build each regular polygon using the principals of symmetry. And what about other types of polygons? What can a hinged mirror help you understand about them?

As your work with your study team, keep these focus questions in mind:

Is there another way?

What types of symmetry can I find?

What does symmetry tell me about the polygon?

7-36. THE HINGED MIRROR TEAM CHALLENGE

Obtain a hinged mirror, a piece of unlined colored paper, and a protractor from your teacher.

With your team, spend five minutes reviewing how to use the mirror to create regular polygons. (Remember that a **regular polygon** has equal sides and angles). Once everyone remembers how the hinged mirror works, select a team member to read the directions of the task below.

Your Task: Below are four challenges for your team. Each requires you to find a creative way to position the mirror in relation to the colored paper. You can tackle the challenges in any order, but you must work together as a team on each. Whenever you successfully create a shape, do not forget to measure the angle formed by the mirror, as well as draw a diagram on your paper of the core region in front of the mirror. If your team decides that a shape is impossible to create with the hinged mirror, explain why.

- Create a regular hexagon.

- Create an equilateral triangle at least <u>two</u> different ways.

- Create a rhombus that is <u>not</u> a square.

- Create a circle.

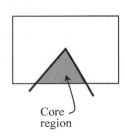

Core region

7-37.   ANALYSIS

How can symmetry help you to learn more about shapes? Discuss each question
below with the class.

a.   One way to create a regular hexagon with a hinged
      mirror is with six triangles, as shown in the diagram at
      right. (Note: the gray lines represent reflections of the
      bottom edges of the mirrors and the edge of the paper,
      while the core region is shaded.)

      What is special about each of the triangles in the diagram? What is the
      relationship between the triangles? Support your conclusions. Would it be
      possible to create a regular hexagon with 12 triangles? Explain.

b.   If you have not done so already, create an equilateral triangle so that the core
      region in front of the mirror is a right triangle. Draw a diagram of the result
      that shows the different reflected triangles like the one above. What special
      type of right triangle is the core region? Can all regular polygons be created
      with a right triangle in a similar fashion?

c.   In problem 7-36, your team formed a rhombus that is not a square. On your
      paper, draw a diagram like the one above that shows how you did it. How can
      you be sure your resulting shape is a rhombus? Using what you know about the
      angle of the mirror, explain what must be true about the diagonals of a
      rhombus.

7-38.   Use what you learned today to answer the questions below.

a.   **Examine** the regular octagon at right. What is
      the measure of angle θ ? Explain how you know.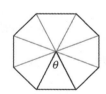

b.   Quadrilateral *ABCD* at right is a
      rhombus. If $BD = 10$ units and
      $AC = 18$ units, then what is the
      perimeter of *ABCD*? Show all work.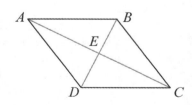

METHODS AND MEANINGS

Regular Polygons

A polygon is **regular** if all its sides are congruent and its angles have equal measure. An equilateral triangle and a square are each regular polygons since they are both *equilateral* and *equiangular*. See the diagrams of common regular polygons below.

Equilateral Triangle   Square   Regular Hexagon   Regular Octagon   Regular Decagon

Review & Preview

7-39.   Felipe set his hinged mirror so that its angle was 36° and the core region was isosceles, as shown at right.

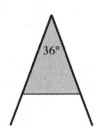

a.   How many sides did his resulting polygon have? Show how you know.

b.   What is another name for this polygon?

7-40.   In problem 7-37 you learned that the diagonals of a rhombus are perpendicular bisectors. If *ABCD* is a rhombus with side length 15 mm and if *BD* = 24 mm, then find the length of the other diagonal, $\overline{AC}$. Draw a diagram and show all work.

7-41.   Joanne claims that (2, 4) is the midpoint of the segment connecting the points (–3, 5) and (7, 3). Is she correct? Explain how you know.

7-42.   If $\triangle ABC \cong \triangle DEC$, which of the statements below must be true? **Justify** your conclusion. Note: More than one statement may be true.

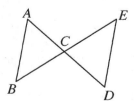

a. $\overline{AC} \cong \overline{DC}$ b. $m\angle B = m\angle D$ c. $\overline{AB} \parallel \overline{DE}$

d. $AD = BE$ e.   None of these are true.

7-43.   On graph paper, graph the points *A*(2, 9), *B*(4, 3), and *C*(9, 6). Which point (*A* or *C*) is closer to point *B*? **Justify** your conclusion.

7.2.1 What can congruent triangles tell me?

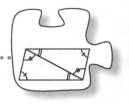

Special Quadrilaterals and Proof

In earlier chapters you studied the relationships between the sides and angles of a triangle, and solved problems involving congruent and similar triangles. Now you are going to expand your study of shapes to quadrilaterals. What can triangles tell you about parallelograms and other special quadrilaterals?

By the end of this lesson, you should be able to answer these questions:

> What are the relationships between the sides, angles,
> and diagonals of a parallelogram?

> How are congruent triangles useful?

7-44. Carla is thinking about parallelograms, and wondering if there are as many special properties for parallelograms as there are for triangles. She remembers that is it possible to create a shape that looks like a parallelogram by rotating a triangle about the midpoint of one of its sides.

    a.   Carefully trace the triangle at right onto tracing paper. Be sure to copy the angle markings as well. Then rotate the triangle to make a shape that looks like a parallelogram.

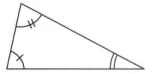

    b.   Is Carla's shape truly a parallelogram? Use the angles to convince your teammates that the opposites sides must be parallel. Then write a convincing argument.

    c.   What else can the congruent triangles tell you about a parallelogram? Look for any relationships you can find between the angles and sides of a parallelogram.

    d.   Does this work for all parallelograms? That is, does the diagonal of a parallelogram always split the shape into two congruent triangles? Draw the parallelogram at right on your paper. Knowing only that the opposite sides of a parallelogram are parallel, create a flowchart to show that the triangles are congruent.

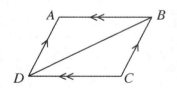

7-45.   CHANGING A FLOWCHART INTO A PROOF

The flowchart you created for part (d) of problem 7-44 shows how you can conclude that if a quadrilateral is a parallelogram, then its each of its diagonals splits the quadrilateral into two congruent triangles.

However, to be convincing, the facts that you listed in your flowchart need to have **justification**. This shows the reader how you know the facts are true and helps to **prove** your conclusion.

Therefore, with the class or your team, decide how to add reasons to each statement (bubble) in your flowchart. You may need to add more bubbles to your flowchart to add **justification** and to make your proof more convincing.

7-46.   Kip is confused. He put his two triangles from problem 7-44 together as shown at right, but he didn't get a parallelogram.

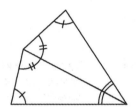

a.   What shape did he make? **Justify** your conclusion.

b.   What transformation(s) did Kip use to form his shape?

c.   What do the congruent triangles tell you about the angles of this shape?

7-47.   KITES

Kip shared his findings about his kite with his teammate, Carla, who wants to learn more about the diagonals of a kite. Carla quickly sketched the kite at right onto her paper with a diagonal showing the two congruent triangles.

a.   **EXPLORE:** Trace this diagram onto tracing paper and carefully add the other diagonal. Then, with your team, consider how the diagonals may be related. Use tracing paper to help you explore the relationships between the diagonals. If you make an observation you think is true, move on to part (b) and write a conjecture.

b.   **CONJECTURE:** If you have not already done so, write a conjecture based on your observations in part (a).

Problem continues on next page →

7-47.   *Problem continued from previous page.*

c.   **PROVE:** When she drew the second diagonal, Carla noticed that four new triangles appeared. "If any of these triangles are congruent, then they may be able to help us prove our conjecture from part (b)," she said.

Examine △*ABC* below. Are △*ACD* and △*BCD* congruent? Create a flowchart proof like the one from problem 7-45 to **justify** your conclusion.

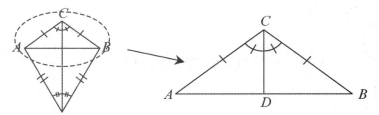

d.   Now extend your proof from part (c) to prove your conjecture from part (b).

7-48.   Reflect on all of the interesting facts about parallelograms and kites you have proven during this lesson. Obtain a Theorem Toolkit (Lesson 7.2.1A Resource Page) from your teacher or from www.cpm.org. In it, record each **theorem** (proven conjecture) that you have proven about the sides, angles, and diagonals of a parallelogram. Do the same for a kite. Be sure your diagrams contain appropriate markings to represent equal parts.

(M)ETHODS AND MEANINGS

Reflexive Property of Equality

MATH NOTES

In problem 7-44, you used the fact that two triangles formed by the diagonal of a parallelogram share a side of the same length to help show that the triangles were congruent.

The **Reflexive Property of Equality** states that the measure of any side or angle is equal to itself. For example, in the parallelogram at right, $\overline{BD} \cong \overline{DB}$ because of the Reflexive Property.

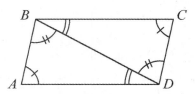

7-49.   Use the information given for each diagram below to solve for *x*. Show all work.

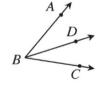

a. $\overrightarrow{BD}$ bisects $\measuredangle ABC$. (Remember that this means it divides the angle into two equal parts.) If $m\measuredangle ABD = 5x - 10°$ and $m\measuredangle ABC = 65°$, solve for *x*.

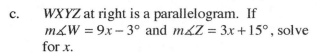

b.   Point *M* is a midpoint of $\overline{EF}$. If $EM = 4x - 2$ and $MF = 3x + 9$, solve for *x*.

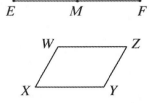

c.   *WXYZ* at right is a parallelogram. If $m\measuredangle W = 9x - 3°$ and $m\measuredangle Z = 3x + 15°$, solve for *x*.

7-50.   Jamal used a hinged mirror to create a regular polygon like he did in Lesson 7.1.4.

a.   If his hinged mirror formed a 72° angle and the core region in front of the mirror was isosceles, how many sides did his polygon have?

b.   Now Jamal has decided to create a regular polygon with 9 sides, called a **nonagon**. If his core region is again isosceles, what angle is formed by his mirror?

7-51.   Sandra wants to park her car so that she is the shortest distance possible from the entrances of both the Art Museum and the Public Library. Locate where on the street she should park so that her total distance directly to each building is the shortest.

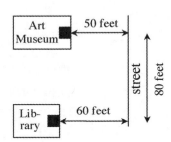

7-52.   Use the geometric relationships in the diagrams below to solve for *x*.

a.
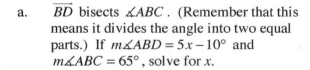

b.
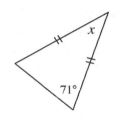

7-53.　Which pairs of triangles below are congruent and/or similar? For each part, explain how you know. Note: The diagrams are not necessarily drawn to scale.

a.
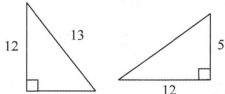

b.
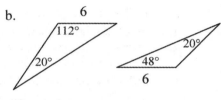

c.
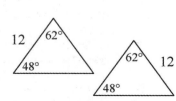

d.
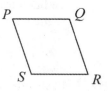

7.2.2 What is special about a rhombus?

Properties of Rhombi

In Lesson 7.2.1, you learned that congruent triangles can be a useful tool to discover new information about parallelograms and kites. But what about other quadrilaterals? Today you will use congruent triangles to **investigate** and prove special properties of rhombi (the plural of rhombus). At the same time, you will continue to develop your ability to make conjectures and prove them convincingly.

7-54.　Audrey has a favorite quadrilateral – the rhombus. Even though a rhombus is defined as having four congruent sides, she suspects that the sides of a rhombus have other special properties.

　　a.　**EXPLORE:** Draw a rhombus like the one at right on your paper. Mark the side lengths equal.

　　b.　**CONJECTURE:** What else might be special about the sides of a rhombus? Write a conjecture.

　　c.　**PROVE:** Audrey knows congruent triangles can help prove other properties about quadrilaterals. She starts by adding a diagonal $\overline{PR}$ to her diagram so that two triangles are formed. Add this diagonal to your diagram and prove that the triangles are congruent. Then use a flowchart with **reasons** to show your logic. Be prepared to share your flowchart with the class.

　　d.　How can the triangles from part (c) help you prove your conjecture from part (b) above? Discuss with the class how to extend your flowchart to convince others. Be sure to **justify** any new statements with reasons.

7-55.   Now that you know the opposite sides of a rhombus are parallel, what else can you prove about a rhombus? Consider this as you answer the questions below.

a.   **EXPLORE:** Remember that in Lesson 7.1.4, you explored the shapes that could be formed with a hinged mirror. During this activity, you used symmetry to form a rhombus. Think about what you know about the reflected triangles in the diagram. What do you think is true about the diagonals $\overline{SQ}$ and $\overline{PR}$? What is special about $\overline{ST}$ and $\overline{QT}$? What about $\overline{PT}$ and $\overline{RT}$?

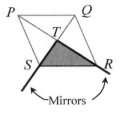

b.   **CONJECTURE:** Use your observations from part (a) to write a conjecture on the relationship of the diagonals of a rhombus.

c.   **PROVE:** Write a flowchart proof that proves your conjecture from part (b). Remember that to be convincing, you need to **justify** each statement with a reason. To help guide your discussion, consider the questions below.

   • Which triangles should you use? Find two triangles that involve the lengths $\overline{ST}$, $\overline{QT}$, $\overline{PT}$ and $\overline{RT}$.

   • How can you prove these triangles are congruent? Create a flowchart proof with **reasons** to prove these triangles must be congruent.

   • How can you use the congruent triangles to prove your conjecture from part (b)? Extend your flowchart proof to include this **reasoning** and prove your conjecture.

7-56.   There are often many ways to prove a conjecture. You have rotated triangles to create parallelograms and used congruent parts of congruent triangles to **justify** that opposite sides are parallel. But is there another way?

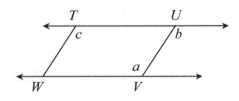

Ansel wants to prove the conjecture "*If a quadrilateral is a parallelogram, then opposite angles are congruent.*" He started by drawing parallelogram *TUVW* at right. Copy and complete his flowchart. Make sure that each statement has a **reason**.

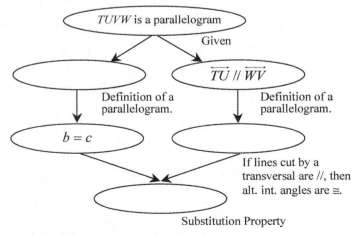

7-57.   Think about the new facts you have proven about
         rhombi during this lesson. On your Theorem Toolkit
         (Lesson 7.2.1A Resource Page), record each new
         theorem you have proven about the angles and
         diagonals of a rhombus. Include clearly labeled
         diagrams to illustrate your findings.

7-58.   Point *M* is the midpoint of $\overline{AB}$ and *B* is
         the midpoint of $\overline{AC}$. What are the values
         of *x* and *y*? Show all work and **reasoning**.

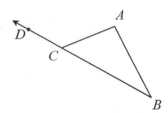

7-59.   In the diagram at right, ∡*DCA* is referred to as an
         exterior angle of △*ABC* because it lies outside the
         triangle and is formed by extending a side of the
         triangle.

    a.   If *m*∡*CAB* = 46° and *m*∡*ABC* = 37°, what is
         m∡*DCA*? Show all work.

    b.   If *m*∡*DCA* = 135° and *m*∡*ABC* = 43°, then what is *m*∡*CAB*?

7-60.   On graph paper, graph quadrilateral *MNPQ* if *M*(–3, 6), *N*(2, 8), *P*(1, 5), and *Q*(–4, 3).

    a.   What shape is *MNPQ*? Show how you know.

    b.   Reflect *MNPQ* across the *x*-axis to find *M′N′P′Q′*. What are the coordinates
         of *P′*?

7-61.   Jester started to prove that the triangles at right are congruent. He is <u>only</u> told <u>that</u> point *E* is the midpoint of segments $\overline{AC}$ and $\overline{BD}$.

Copy and complete his flowchart below. Be sure that a **reason** is provided for every statement.

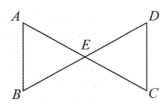

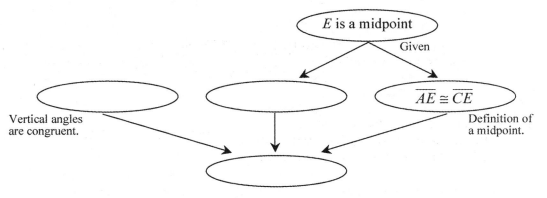

E is a midpoint

Given

Vertical angles are congruent.

$\overline{AE} \cong \overline{CE}$

Definition of a midpoint.

7-62.   On graph paper, graph and shade the solutions for the inequality below.

$$y < -\tfrac{2}{3}x + 5$$

7.2.3   What else can be proved?

More Proof with Congruent Triangles

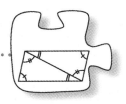

In Lessons 7.2.1 and 7.2.2, you used congruent triangles to learn more about parallelograms, kites, and rhombi. You now possess the tools to do the work of a geometrician: to discover and prove new properties about the sides and angles of shapes.

As you **investigate** these shapes, focus on proving your ideas. Remember to ask yourself and your teammates questions such as, "*Why does that work?*" and "*Is it always true?*" Decide whether your argument is convincing and work with your team to provide all of the necessary **justification**.

7-63.   Carla decided to turn her attention to
rectangles. Knowing that a rectangle is
defined as a quadrilateral with four
right angles, she drew the diagram at
right.

After some exploration, she conjectured
that all rectangles are also parallelograms.
Help her prove that her rectangle *ABCD*
must be a parallelogram. That is, prove
that the opposite sides must be parallel.
Then add this theorem to your Theorem
Toolkit (your Lesson 7.2.1A Resource
Page).

7-64.   For each diagram below, find the value of *x*, if possible. If the triangles are
congruent, state which triangle congruence property was used. If the triangles are not
congruent or if there is not enough information, state, "Cannot be determined."

a.   *ABC* below is a triangle.

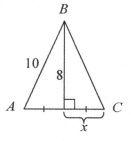

b.

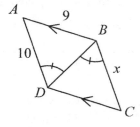

c.

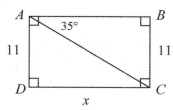

d. $\overline{AC}$ and $\overline{BD}$ are straight line
segments.

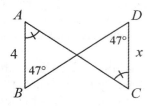

7-65.   With the class or your team, create a flowchart to prove your answer to part (b) of
problem 7-64. That is, prove that $\overline{AD} \cong \overline{CB}$. Be sure to include a diagram for your
proof and **reasons** for every statement. Make sure your argument is convincing and
has no "holes."

METHODS AND **M**EANINGS

Definitions of Quadrilaterals

When proving properties of shapes, it is necessary to know exactly how a shape is defined. Below are the definitions of several quadrilaterals that you will study in this chapter and the chapters that follow.

Quadrilateral: A closed four-sided polygon.

Kite: A quadrilateral with two distinct pairs of consecutive congruent sides.

Trapezoid: A quadrilateral with at least one pair of parallel sides.

Parallelogram: A quadrilateral with two pairs of parallel sides.

Rhombus: A quadrilateral with four sides of equal length.

Rectangle: A quadrilateral with four right angles.

Square: A quadrilateral with four sides of equal length and four right angles.

7-66.   Identify if each pair of triangles below is congruent or not. Remember that the diagram may not be drawn to scale. **Justify** your conclusion.

a.

b.

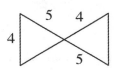

c.

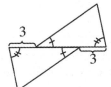

d.

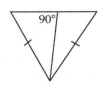

7-67.   **Examine** the information provided in each diagram below. Decide if each figure is possible or not. If the figure is not possible, explain why.

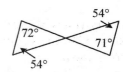

a.
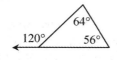

b.
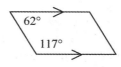

c.
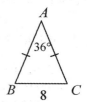

7-68.   Tromika wants to find the area of the isosceles triangle at right.

a.   She decided to start by drawing a height from vertex A to side $\overline{BC}$ as shown below. Will the two smaller triangles be congruent? In other words, is $\triangle ABD \cong \triangle ACD$? Why or why not?

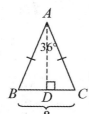

b.   What is $m\angle DAB$? BD?

c.   Find AD. Show how you got your answer.

d.   Find the area of $\triangle ABC$.

7-69.   On graph paper, graph quadrilateral $ABCD$ if $A(0, 0)$, $B(6, 0)$, $C(8, 6)$, and $D(2, 6)$.

a.   What is the best name for $ABCD$? **Justify** your answer.

b.   Find the equation of the lines containing each diagonal. That is, find the equations of lines $\overleftrightarrow{AC}$ and $\overleftrightarrow{BD}$.

7-70.   For each diagram below, solve for x. Show all work.

a.

b.
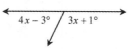

c.
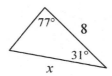

d.

7.2.4 What else can I prove?

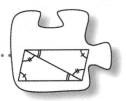

More Properties of Quadrilaterals

Today you will work with your team to apply what you have learned to other shapes. Remember to ask yourself and your teammates questions such as, *"Why does that work?"* and *"Is it always true?"* Decide whether your argument is convincing and work with your team to provide all of the necessary **justification**. By the end of this lesson, you should have a well-crafted mathematical argument proving something new about a familiar quadrilateral.

7-71.   WHAT ELSE CAN CONGRUENT TRIANGLES TELL US?

Your Task: For each situation below, determine how congruent triangles can tell you more information about the shape. Then prove your conjecture using a flowchart. Be sure to provide a **reason** for each statement. For example, stating "$m\angle A = m\angle B$" is not enough. You must give a convincing reason, such as *"Because vertical angles are equal"* or *"Because it is given in the diagram."* Use your triangle congruence properties to help prove that the triangles are congruent.

Later, your teacher will select one of these flowcharts for you to place on a poster. On your poster, include a diagram and all of your statements and reasons. Clearly state what you are proving and help the people who look at your poster understand your logic and **reasoning**.

a.   In Chapter 1, you used symmetry of an isosceles triangle to show that the base angles must be congruent. But what if you only know that the base angles are congruent? Does the triangle have to be isosceles?

Assume that you know that the two base angles of $\triangle ABC$ are congruent. With your team, decide how to split $\triangle ABC$ into two triangles that you can show are congruent to show that $AB = CB$.

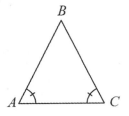

b.   What can congruent triangles tell us about the diagonals and angles of a rhombus? **Examine** the diagram of the rhombus at right. With your team, decide how to prove that the diagonals of a rhombus bisect the angles. That is, prove that $\angle ABD \cong \angle CBD$.

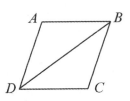

Problem continues on next page →

7-71. *Problem continued from previous page.*

c.   What can congruent triangles tell us about the diagonals of a rectangle? **Examine** the rectangle at right. Using the fact that the opposite sides of a rectangle are parallel (which you proved in problem 7-63), prove that the diagonals of the rectangle are congruent. That is, prove that $AC = BD$.

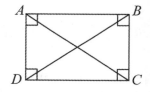

MATH NOTES

ETHODS AND MEANINGS

Diagonals of a Rhombus

A **rhombus** is defined as a quadrilateral with four sides of equal length. In addition, you proved in problem 7-55 that the diagonals of a rhombus are perpendicular bisectors of each other.

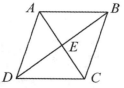

For example, in the rhombus at right, E is a midpoint of both $\overline{AC}$ and $\overline{DB}$. Therefore, $AE = CE$ and $DE = BE$. Also, $m\angle AEB = m\angle BEC = m\angle CED = m\angle DEA = 90°$.

In addition, you proved in problem 7-71 that the diagonals bisect the angles of the rhombus. For example, in the diagram above, $m\angle DAE = m\angle BAE$.

Review & Preview

7-72.   Use Tromika's method from problem 7-68 to find the area of an equilateral triangle with side length 12 units. Show all work.

7-73.   The guidelines set forth by the National Kitchen & Bath Association recommends that the perimeter of the triangle connecting the refrigerator (F), stove, and sink of a kitchen be 26 feet or less. Lashayia is planning to renovate her kitchen and has chosen the design at right. (Note: All measurements are in feet.) Does her design conform to the National Kitchen and Bath Association's guidelines? Show how you got your answer.

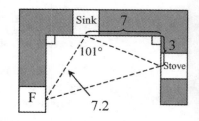

Geometry Connections

7-74.   For each figure below, determine if the two smaller triangles in each figure are congruent. If so, explain why and solve for *x*. If not, explain why not.

a.

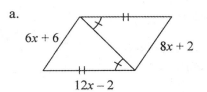

$6x + 6$

$8x + 2$

$12x - 2$

b.

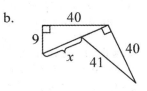

40

9

x

41

40

7-75.   The diagonals of a rhombus are 6 units and 8 units long. What is the area of the rhombus? Draw a diagram and show all reasoning.

7-76.   A hotel in Las Vegas is famous for its large-scale model of the Eiffel Tower. The model, built to scale, is 128 meters tall and 41 meters wide at its base. If the real tower is 324 meters tall, how wide is the base of the real Eiffel Tower?

7.2.5 How else can I write it?

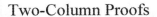

Two-Column Proofs

Today you will continue to work with constructing a convincing argument, otherwise known as writing a proof. You will use what you know about flowchart proofs to write a convincing argument using another format, called a "two-column" proof.

7-77.   The following pairs of triangles are not necessarily congruent even though they appear to be. Use the information provided in the diagram to show why. **Justify** your statements.

a.

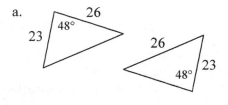

26

23

48°

26

23

48°

b.

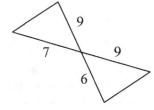

9

7

9

6

7-78.   Write a flowchart to prove that if *E* is the midpoint of $\overline{AD}$ and $\angle A$ and $\angle D$ are both right angles, then $\overline{AB} \cong \overline{DC}$.

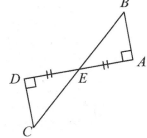

7-79.   Another way to organize a proof is called a **two-column proof**. Instead of using arrows to indicate the order of logical reasoning, this style of proof lists statements and reasons in a linear order.

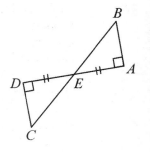

The proof from problem 7-78 has been converted to a two-column proof below. Copy and complete the proof on your paper using your statements and **reasons** from problem 7-78.

If: E is the midpoint of $\overline{AD}$ and $\angle A$ and $\angle D$ are both right angles,
Prove: $\overline{AB} \cong \overline{DC}$

Statements	Reasons (This statement is true because…)
E is the midpoint of $\overline{AD}$ and $\angle A$ and $\angle D$ are both right angles	Given
$\angle A \cong \angle D$	Angles with the same measure are congruent.
	Definition of a midpoint
$\angle DEC \cong \angle AEB$	

7-80.   Examine the posters of flowchart proofs from problem 7-71. Convert each flowchart proof to a two-column proof. Remember that one column must contain the statements of fact while the other must provide the **reason** (or **justification**) explaining why that fact must be true.

7-81. So far in Section 7.2, you have proven many special properties of quadrilaterals and other shapes. When a conjecture is proven, it is called a **theorem**. For example, once you proved the relationship between the sides of a right triangle, you were able to refer to that relationship as the Pythagorean Theorem. Find your Theorem Toolkit (Lesson 7.2.1A Resource Page) and make sure it contains all of the theorems you and your classmates have proven so far about various quadrilaterals. Be sure that your records include diagrams for each statement.

7-82. Reflect on the new proof format you learned today. Compare it to the flowchart proof format that you have used earlier. What are the strengths and weaknesses of each style of proof? Which format is easier for you to use? Which is easier to read? Title this entry "Two-Column Proofs" and include today's date.

7-83. Suppose you know that $\triangle TAP \cong \triangle DOG$ and that $TA = 14$, $AP = 18$, $TP = 21$, and $DG = 2y + 7$.

    a.   On your paper, draw a reasonable sketch of $\triangle TAP$ and $\triangle DOG$.

    b.   Find y. Show all work.

7-84. $\angle a$, $\angle b$, and $\angle c$ are exterior angles of the triangle at right. Find $m\angle a$, $m\angle b$, and $m\angle c$. Then find $m\angle a + m\angle b + m\angle c$.

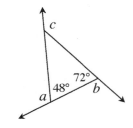

7-85. Prove that if a pair of opposite sides of a quadrilateral are congruent and parallel, then the quadrilateral must be a parallelogram.

For example, for the quadrilateral $ABCD$ at right, given that $\overline{AB} \parallel \overline{CD}$ and $\overline{AB} \cong \overline{CD}$, show that $\overline{BC} \parallel \overline{AD}$. Organize your **reasoning** in a flowchart. Then record your theorem in your Theorem Toolkit (your Lesson 7.2.1A Resource Page).

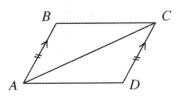

7-86. Find the area and perimeter of the trapezoid at right.

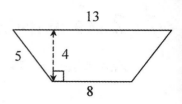

7-87. For each pair of triangles below, determine if the triangles are congruent. If the triangles are congruent,

- complete the correspondence statement,
- state the congruence property,
- and record any other ideas you use that make your conclusion true.

Otherwise, explain why you cannot conclude that the triangles are congruent. Note that the figures are not necessarily drawn to scale.

a. $\triangle ABC \cong \triangle$ _____

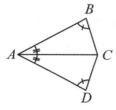

b. $\triangle SQP \cong \triangle$ _____

c. $\triangle PLM \cong \triangle$ _____

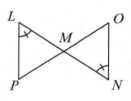

d. $\triangle WXY \cong \triangle$ _____

midpoint of $\overline{WT}$ and $\overline{XZ}$

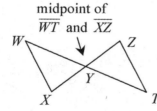

e. $\triangle EDG \cong \triangle$ _____

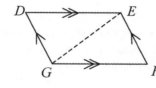

f. $\triangle ABC \cong \triangle$ _____

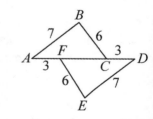

7.2.6 What can I prove?

Explore-Conjecture-Prove

So far, congruent triangles have helped you to discover and prove many new facts about triangles and quadrilaterals. But what else can you discover and prove? Today your work will mirror the real work of professional mathematicians. You will **investigate** relationships, write a conjecture based on your observations, and then prove your conjecture.

7-88.   TRIANGLE MIDSEGMENT THEOREM

As Sergio was drawing shapes on his paper, he drew a line segment that connected the midpoints of two sides of a triangle. (This is called the **midsegment** of a triangle.) "I wonder what we can find out about this midsegment," he said to his team. **Examine** his drawing at right.

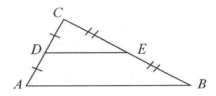

a.   **EXPLORE: Examine** the diagram of $\triangle ABC$, drawn to scale above. How do you think $\overline{DE}$ is related to $\overline{AB}$? How do their lengths seem to be related?

b.   **CONJECTURE:** Write a conjecture about the relationship between segments $\overline{DE}$ and $\overline{AB}$.

c.   **PROVE:** Sergio wants to prove that $AB = 2DE$. However, he does not see any congruent triangles in the diagram. How are the triangles in this diagram related? How do you know? Prove your conclusion with a flowchart.

d.   What is the common ratio between side lengths in the similar triangles? Use this to write a statement relating lengths DE and AB.

e.   Now Sergio wants to prove that $\overline{DE} \parallel \overline{AB}$. Use the similar triangles to find all the pairs of equal angles you can in the diagram. Then use your knowledge of angle relationships to make a statement about parallel segments.

7-89.   The work you did in problem 7-88 mirrors the work of many professional
mathematicians. In the problem, Sergio **examined** a geometric shape and thought
there might be something new to learn. You then helped him by finding possible
relationships and writing a conjecture. Then, to find out if the conjecture was true
for all triangles, you wrote a convincing argument (or proof). This process is
summarized in the diagram below.

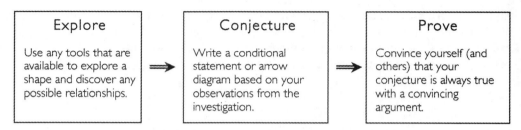

Explore	Conjecture	Prove
Use any tools that are available to explore a shape and discover any possible relationships.	Write a conditional statement or arrow diagram based on your observations from the investigation.	Convince yourself (and others) that your conjecture is always true with a convincing argument.

Discuss this process with the class and describe when you have used this process
before (either in this class or outside of class). Why do mathematicians rely on this
process?

7-90.   RIGHT TRAPEZOIDS

Consecutive angles of a polygon occur at opposite
ends of a side of the polygon. What can you learn
about a quadrilateral with two consecutive right
angles?

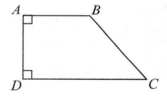

a.   **EXPLORE: Examine** the quadrilateral at right
with two consecutive right angles. What do you
think is true of $\overline{AB}$ and $\overline{DC}$?

b.   **CONJECTURE:** Write a conjecture about what type of quadrilateral has two
consecutive right angles. Write your conjecture in conditional ("If…, then…")
form.

c.   **PROVE:** Prove that your conjecture from part (b) is true for all quadrilaterals
with two consecutive right angles. Write your proof using the two-column
format introduced in Lesson 7.2.4. (Hint: Look for angle relationships.)

d.   The quadrilateral you worked with in this problem is called a **right trapezoid**.
Are all quadrilaterals with two right angles a right trapezoid?

7-91.   ISOSCELES TRAPEZOIDS

An **isosceles trapezoid** is a trapezoid with a pair of
congruent base angles. What can you learn about
the sides of an isosceles trapezoid?

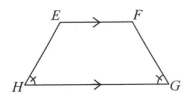

a.   **EXPLORE: Examine** *EFGH* at right. How
do the side lengths appear to be related?

b.   **CONJECTURE:** Write a conjecture about
side lengths in an isosceles trapezoid. Write
your conjecture in conditional ("If…, then…")
form.

c.   **PROVE:** Now prove that your conjecture
from part (b) is true for all isosceles
trapezoids. Write your proof using the two-
column format introduced in Lesson 7.2.5.
To help you get started, the isosceles
trapezoid is shown at right with its sides
extended to form a triangle.

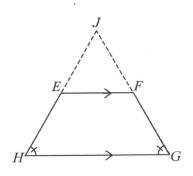

7-92.   Add the theorems you have proved in this lesson to your
Theorem Toolkit (your Lesson 7.2.1A Resource Page). Be
sure that your records include diagrams for each statement.

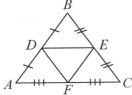

METHODS AND **M**EANINGS

Triangle Midsegment Theorem

MATH NOTES

A **midsegment** of a triangle is a segment that connects the midpoints
of any two sides of a triangle. Every triangle has three midsegments,
as shown below.

A midsegment between two sides of a triangle is
half the length of and parallel to the third side of
the triangle. For example, in $\triangle ABC$ at right, $\overline{DE}$
is a midsegment, $\overline{DE} \parallel \overline{AC}$, and $DE = \frac{1}{2}AC$.

7-93. One way a shape can be special is to have two congruent sides. For example, an isosceles triangle is special because it has a pair of sides that are the same length. Think about all the shapes you know and list the other special properties shapes can have. List as many as you can. Be ready to share your list with the class at the beginning of Lesson 7.3.1.

7-94. Carefully **examine** each diagram below and explain why the geometric figure cannot exist. Support your statements with **reasons**. If a line looks straight, assume that it is.

a.

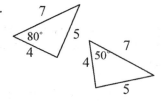

b.

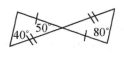

c.

d.

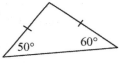

e.

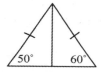

f.

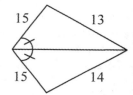

7-95. For each pair of numbers, find the number that is exactly halfway between them.

a.   9 and 15

b.   3 and 27

c.   10 and 21

7-96. Penn started the proof below to show that if $\overline{AD} \parallel \overline{EH}$ and $\overline{BF} \parallel \overline{CG}$, then $a = d$. Unfortunately, he did not provide reasons for his proof. Copy his proof and provide **justification** for each statement.

Statements	Reasons
1. $\overline{AD} \parallel \overline{EH}$ and $\overline{BF} \parallel \overline{CG}$	
2. $a = b$	
3. $b = c$	
4. $a = c$	
5. $c = d$	
6. $a = d$	

7-97. After finding out that her kitchen does not conform to industry standards, Lashayia is back to the drawing board. (See problem 7-73). Where can she locate her sink along her top counter so that its distance from the stove and refrigerator is as small as possible? And will this location keep her perimeter below 26 feet? Show all work.

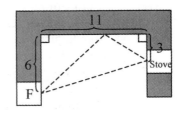

7.3.1 What makes a quadrilateral special?

Studying Quadrilaterals on a Coordinate Grid

In Section 7.2 you **investigated** special types of quadrilaterals, such as parallelograms, kites, and rhombi. Each of these quadrilaterals has special properties you have proved: parallel sides, sides of equal length, equal opposite angles, bisected diagonals, etc.

But not all quadrilaterals have a special name. How can you tell if a quadrilateral belongs to one of these types? And if a quadrilateral doesn't have a special name, can it still have special properties? In Section 7.3 you will use both algebra and geometry to **investigate** quadrilaterals defined on coordinate grids.

7-98. PROPERTIES OF SHAPES

Think about the special quadrilaterals you have studied in this chapter. Each shape has many properties that make it special. For example, a rhombus has two diagonals that are perpendicular. With the class, brainstorm the other types of properties that a shape can have. You may want to refer to your work from problem 7-93. Be ready to share your list with the class.

7-99. Review some of the algebra **tools** you already have. On graph paper, draw $\overline{AB}$ given $A(0, 8)$ and $B(9, 2)$, and $\overline{CD}$ given $C(1, 3)$ and $D(9, 15)$.

    a. Draw these two segments on a coordinate grid. Find the length of each segment.

    b. Find the equation of $\overrightarrow{AB}$ and the equation of $\overrightarrow{CD}$. Write both equations in $y = mx + b$ form.

    c. Is $\overline{AB} \mathbin{/\mkern-5mu/} \overline{CD}$? Is $\overline{AB} \perp \overline{CD}$? **Justify** your answer.

    d. Use algebra to find the coordinates of the point where $\overline{AB}$ and $\overline{CD}$ intersect.

7-100. **AM I SPECIAL?**

Shayla just drew quadrilateral *SHAY*, shown at right. The coordinates of its vertices are:

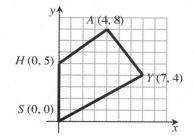

$S(0, 0)$ $H(0, 5)$ $A(4, 8)$ $Y(7, 4)$

a.   Shayla thinks her quadrilateral is a trapezoid. Is she correct? Be prepared to **justify** your answer to the class.

b.   Does Shayla's quadrilateral look like it is one of the other kinds of special quadrilaterals you have studied? If so, which one?

c.   Even if Shayla's quadrilateral doesn't have a special name, it may still have some special properties like the ones you listed in problem 7-98. Use algebra and geometry tools to **investigate** Shayla's quadrilateral and see if it has any special properties. If you find any special properties, be ready to **justify** your claim that this property is present.

7-101. THE MUST BE / COULD BE GAME

Mr. Quincey plays a game with his class. He says, "My quadrilateral has four right angles." His students say, "Then it *must be* a rectangle" and "It *could be* a square." For each description of a quadrilateral below, say what special type the quadrilateral *must be* and/or what special type the quadrilateral *could be*. Look out: Some descriptions may have no "must be"s, and some descriptions may have many "could be"s!

a.   "My quadrilateral has four equal sides."

b.   "My quadrilateral has two pairs of opposite parallel sides."

c.   "My quadrilateral has two consecutive right angles."

d.   "My quadrilateral has two pairs of equal sides."

7-102. The diagram at right shows three bold segments. Find the coordinates of the midpoint of each segment.

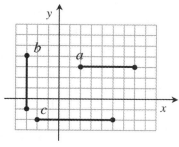

7-103.   **Examine** the diagram at right.

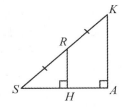

a.   Are the triangles in this diagram similar? **Justify** your answer.

b.   What is the relationship between the lengths of *HR* and *AK*? Between the lengths of *SH* and *SA*? Between the lengths of *SH* and *HA*?

c.   If *SK* = 20 units and *RH* = 8 units, what is *HA*?

7-104.   For each pair of triangles below, determine if the triangles are congruent. If the triangles are congruent, state the congruence property that **justifies** your conclusion. If you cannot conclude that the triangles are congruent, explain why not.

a.   △*CAB* ≅ △_____

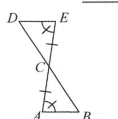

b.   △*CBD* ≅ △_____

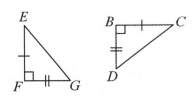

c.   △*LJI* ≅ △_____

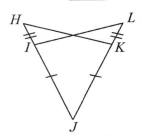

d.   △*PRQ* ≅ △_____

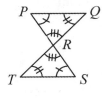

7-105.   Carolina compared her proof to that of Penn in problem 7-96.
Like him, she wanted to prove that if $\overline{AD} \parallel \overline{EH}$ and $\overline{BF} \parallel \overline{CG}$,
then $a = d$. Unfortunately, her statements were in a different
order. **Examine** her proof below and help her decide if her
statements are in a logical order in order to prove that $a = d$.

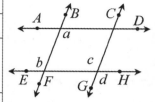

Statements	Reasons
1. $\overline{AD} \parallel \overline{EH}$ and $\overline{BF} \parallel \overline{CG}$	Given
2. $a = b$	If lines are parallel, alternate interior angles are equal.
3. $a = c$	Substitution
4. $b = c$	If lines are parallel, corresponding angles are equal.
5. $c = d$	Vertical angles are equal.
6. $a = d$	Substitution

7-106.   Describe what the minimum information you would need to know about the shapes
below in order to identify it correctly. For example, to know that a shape is a square,
you must know that it has four sides of equal length and at least one right angle. Be
as thorough as possible.

a.   rhombus   b.   trapezoid

7.3.2   How can I find the midpoint?

· ·

Coordinate Geometry and Midpoints

In Lesson 7.3.1, you applied your existing algebraic tools to analyze geometric shapes on a
coordinate grid. What other algebraic processes can help us analyze shapes? And what else can
be learned about geometric shapes?

7-107. Cassie wants to confirm her theorem on midsegments (from Lesson 7.2.6) using a coordinate grid. She started with $\triangle ABC$, with $A(0, 0)$, $B(2, 6)$, and $C(7, 0)$.

a. Graph $\triangle ABC$ on graph paper.

b. With your team, find the coordinates of P, the midpoint of $\overline{AB}$. Likewise, find the coordinates of Q, the midpoint of $\overline{BC}$.

c. Verify that the length of the midsegment, $\overline{PQ}$, is half the length of $\overline{AC}$. Also verify that $\overline{PQ}$ is parallel to $\overline{AC}$.

7-108. As Cassie worked on problem 7-107, her teammate, Esther, had difficulty finding the midpoint of $\overline{BC}$. The study team decided to try to find another way to find the midpoint of a line segment.

a. As part of her team, Cassie wants you to draw $\overline{AM}$, with $A(3, 4)$ and $M(8, 11)$, on graph paper. Then extend the line segment to find a point B so that M is the midpoint of $\overline{AB}$. **Justify** your location of point B by drawing and writing numbers on the graph.

b. Esther thinks she understands how to find the midpoint on a graph. "I always look for the middle of the line segment. But what if the coordinates are not easy to graph?" she asks. With your team, find the midpoint of $\overline{KL}$ if $K(2, 125)$ and $L(98, 15)$. Be ready to share your method with the class.

c. Test your team's method by verifying that the midpoint between $(-5, 7)$ and $(9, 4)$ is $(2, 5.5)$.

7-109. Randy has decided to study the triangle graphed at right.

a. Consider all the special properties this triangle can have. Without using any algebra tools, predict the best name for this triangle.

b. For your answer to part (a) to be correct, what is the minimum amount of information that must be true about $\triangle RND$?

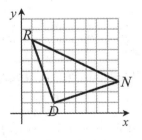

c. Use your algebra tools to verify each of the properties you listed in part (b). If you need, you may change your prediction of the shape of $\triangle RND$.

d. Randy wonders if there is anything special about the midpoint of $\overline{RN}$. Find the midpoint M, and then find the lengths of $\overline{RM}$, $\overline{DM}$, and $\overline{MN}$. What do you notice?

7-110.   Tomika remembers that the diagonals of a rhombus are perpendicular to each other.

a.   Graph on *ABCD* if *A*(1, 4), *B*(6, 6), *C*(4, 1), and *D*(–1, –1). Is *ABCD* a rhombus? Show how you know.

b.   Find the equation of the lines on which the diagonals lie. That is, find the equations of $\overrightarrow{AC}$ and $\overrightarrow{BD}$.

c.   Compare the slopes of $\overrightarrow{AC}$ and $\overrightarrow{BD}$. What do you notice?

7-111.   In your Learning Log, explain what a midpoint is and the method you prefer for finding midpoints of a line segment when given the coordinates of its endpoints. Include any diagram or example that helps explain why this method works. Title this entry "Finding a Midpoint" and include today's date.

METHODS AND MEANINGS

Coordinate Geometry

MATH NOTES

Coordinate geometry is the study of geometry on a coordinate grid. Using common algebraic and geometric tools, you can learn more about a shape such as the if it has a right angle or if two sides are the same length.

One useful tool is the Pythagorean Theorem. For example, the Pythagorean Theorem could be used to determine the length of side $\overline{AB}$ of *ABCD* at right. By drawing the slope triangle between points *A* and *B*, the length of $\overline{AB}$ can be found to be $\sqrt{2^2 + 5^2} = \sqrt{29}$ units.

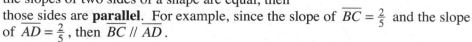

Similarly, slope can help analyze the relationships between the sides of a shape. If the slopes of two sides of a shape are equal, then those sides are **parallel**. For example, since the slope of $\overline{BC} = \frac{2}{5}$ and the slope of $\overline{AD} = \frac{2}{5}$, then $\overline{BC} \parallel \overline{AD}$.

Also, if the slopes of two sides of a shape are opposite reciprocals, then the sides are **perpendicular** (meaning they form a 90° angle). For example, since the slope of $\overline{BC} = \frac{2}{5}$ and the slope of $\overline{AB} = -\frac{5}{2}$, then $\overline{BC} \perp \overline{AB}$.

By using multiple algebraic and geometric tools, you can identify shapes. For example, further analysis of the sides and angles of *ABCD* above shows that $AB = DC$ and $BC = AD$. Furthermore, all four angles measure 90°. These facts together indicate that *ABCD* must be a rectangle.

7-112.   Find another valid, logical order for the statements for Penn's proof from problem 7-96. Explain how you know that changing the order the way you did does not affect the logic.

7-113.   Each of these numberlines shows a segment in bold. Find the midpoint of the segment in bold. (Note that the diagrams are *not* to scale.)

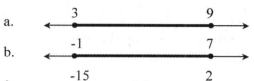

a.

b.

c.

7-114.   **Examine** the diagram at right.

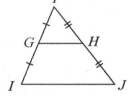

a.   Are the triangles in this diagram similar? Explain.

b.   Name all the pairs of congruent angles in this diagram you can.

c.   Are $\overline{GH}$ and $\overline{IJ}$ parallel? Explain how you know.

d.   If $GH = 4x - 3$ and $IJ = 3x + 14$, find x. Then find the length of $\overline{GH}$.

7-115.   Consider $\triangle ABC$ with vertices $A(2, 3)$, $B(6, 3)$, and $C(6, 10)$.

a.   Draw $\triangle ABC$ on graph paper. What kind of triangle is $\triangle ABC$?

b.   Reflect $\triangle ABC$ across $\overline{AC}$. Where is B'? And what shape is $ABCB'$?

7-116.   MUST BE / COULD BE

Here are some more challenges from Mr. Quincey. For each description of a quadrilateral below, say what special type the quadrilateral *must be* and/or what special type the quadrilateral *could be*. Look out: Some descriptions may have no "must be"s, and some descriptions may have many "could be"s!

a.   "My quadrilateral has a pair of equal sides and a pair of parallel sides."

b.   "The diagonals of my quadrilateral bisect each other."

7.3.3 What kind of quadrilateral is it?

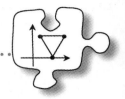

Quadrilaterals on a Coordinate Plane

Today you will use algebra tools to **investigate** the properties of a quadrilateral and then will use those properties to identify the type of quadrilateral it is.

7-117.   MUST BE / COULD BE

Mr. Quincey has some new challenges for you! For each description below, decide what special type the quadrilateral *must be* and/or what special type the quadrilateral *could be*. Look out: Some descriptions may have no "must be"s, and some descriptions may have many "could be"s!

a.   "My quadrilateral has three right angles."

b.   "My quadrilateral has a pair of parallel sides."

c.   "My quadrilateral has two consecutive equal angles."

7-118.   THE SHAPE FACTORY

You just got a job in the Quadrilaterals Division of your uncle's Shape Factory. In the old days, customers called up your uncle and described the quadrilaterals they wanted over the phone: "I'd like a parallelogram with…". "But nowadays," your uncle says, "customers using computers have been emailing orders in lots of different ways." Your uncle needs your team to help analyze his most recent orders listed below to identify the quadrilaterals and help the shape-makers know what to produce.

Your Task: For each of the quadrilateral orders listed below,

- Create a diagram of the quadrilateral on graph paper.

- Decide if the quadrilateral ordered has a special name. To help the shape-makers, your name must be as specific as possible. (Don't just call a shape a rectangle when it's also a square!)

- Record and be ready to present a **justification** that the quadrilateral ordered must be the kind you say it is. It is not enough to say that a quadrilateral *looks* like it is of a certain type or *looks* like it has a certain property. Customers will want to be sure they get the type of quadrilateral they ordered!

Problem continues on next page →

7-118. *Problem continued from previous page.*

Discussion Points

What special properties might a quadrilateral have?

What algebra tools could be useful?

What types of quadrilaterals might be ordered?

The orders:

a. A quadrilateral formed by the intersection of these lines:

$$y = -\frac{3}{2}x + 3 \qquad y = \frac{3}{2}x - 3 \qquad y = -\frac{3}{2}x + 9 \qquad y = \frac{3}{2}x + 3$$

b. A quadrilateral with vertices at these points:

$A(0, 2)$ $B(1, 0)$ $C(7, 3)$ $D(4, 4)$

c. A quadrilateral with vertices at these points:

$W(0, 5)$ $X(2, 7)$ $Y(5, 7)$ $Z(5, 1)$

METHODS AND MEANINGS

MATH NOTES

Finding a Midpoint

A **midpoint** is a point that divides a line segment into two parts of equal length. For example, M is the midpoint of $\overline{AB}$ at right.

There are several ways to find the midpoint of a line segment if the coordinates of the endpoints are known. One way is to average the x-coordinates and to average the y-coordinates. Thus, if $A(2, 3)$ and $B(6, 8)$, then the x-coordinate of M is $\frac{2+6}{2} = 4$ and the y-coordinate is $\frac{3+8}{2} = 5.5$. So M is at $(4, 5.5)$.

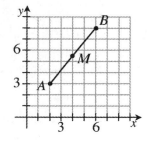

7-119.   Each problem below gives the endpoints of a segment. Find the coordinates of the midpoint of the segment. If you need help, consult the Math Notes box for this lesson.

a.   (5, 2) and (11, 14)   b.   (3, 8) and (10, 4)

c.   (–3, 11) and (5, 6)   d.   (–4, –1) and (8, 9)

7-120.   Below are the equations of two lines and the coordinates of three points. For each line, determine which of the points, if any, lie on that line. (There may be more than one!)

a. $y = \frac{1}{3}x + 15$ X(0, 15)   Y(3, 16)   Z(7, 0)

b. $y - 16 = -4(x - 3)$

7-121.   MUST BE / COULD BE

Here are some more challenges from Mr. Quincey. For each description of a quadrilateral below, say what special type the quadrilateral *must be* and/or what special type the quadrilateral *could be*. Look out: Some descriptions may have no "must be"s, and some descriptions may have many "could be"s!

a.   "My quadrilateral has two right angles."

b.   "The diagonals of my quadrilateral are perpendicular."

7-122.   The angle created by a hinged mirror when forming a regular polygon is called a **central angle**. For example, ∡ABC in the diagram at right is the central angle of the regular hexagon.

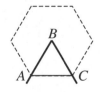

a.   If the central angle of a regular polygon measures 18°, how many sides does the polygon have?

b.   Can a central angle measure 90°? 180°? 13°? For each angle measure, explain how you know.

7-123.   On graph paper, graph lines $\overrightarrow{AB}$ and $\overrightarrow{CD}$ if $\overrightarrow{AB}$ can be represented by $y = -\frac{4}{3}x + 5$ and $\overrightarrow{CD}$ can be represented by $y = \frac{3}{4}x - 1$. Label their intersection E.

a.   What is the relationship between the lines? How do you know?

b.   If E is a midpoint of $\overline{CD}$, what type of quadrilateral could ABCD be? Is there more than one possible type? Explain how you know.

Chapter 7 Closure   What have I learned?

Reflection and Synthesis

The activities below offer you a chance to reflect on what you have learned during this chapter. As you work, look for concepts that you feel very comfortable with, ideas that you would like to learn more about, and topics you need more help with. Look for **connections** between ideas as well as **connections** with material you learned previously.

① TEAM BRAINSTORM

With your team, brainstorm a list for each of the following three topics. Be as detailed as you can. How long can you make your list? Challenge yourselves. Be prepared to share your team's ideas with the class.

Topics: What have you studied in this chapter? What ideas and words were important in what you learned? Remember to be as detailed as you can.

Connections: How are the topics, ideas, and words that you learned in previous courses are **connected** to the new ideas in this chapter? Again, make your list as long as you can.

The following is a list of the vocabulary used in this chapter. The words that appear in bold are new to this chapter. Make sure that you are familiar with all of these words and know what they mean. Refer to the glossary or index for any words that you do not yet understand.

bisect	**central angle**	circle
congruent	conjecture	**coordinate geometry**
diagonal	**diameter**	**exterior angle**
kite	**midpoint**	**midsegment**
opposite	parallel	parallelogram
perpendicular	**proof**	**quadrilateral**
radius	rectangle	**Reflexive Property**
regular polygon	**rhombus**	square
theorem	**three-dimensional**	trapezoid
two-column proof	**two-dimensional**	

Make a concept map showing all of the **connections** you can find among the key words and ideas listed above. To show a **connection** between two words, draw a line between them and explain the **connection**, as shown in the example below. A word can be **connected** to any other word as long as there is a **justified connection**. For each key word or idea, provide a sketch of an example.

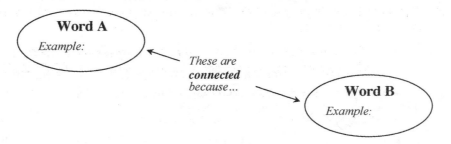

Your teacher may provide you with vocabulary cards to help you get started. If you use the cards to plan your concept map, be sure either to re-draw your concept map on your paper or to glue the vocabulary cards to a poster with all of the **connections** explained for others to see and understand.

While you are making your map, your team may think of related words or ideas that are not listed above. Be sure to include these ideas on your concept map.

③ SUMMARIZING MY UNDERSTANDING

This section gives you an opportunity to show what you know about certain math topics or ideas. Your teacher will give you directions for exactly how to do this. Your teacher may give you a "GO" page to work on.

To use the Quadrilateral "GO" (or Graphic Organizer), complete the diagram to show the relationships between special quadrilaterals. For each type of quadrilateral, draw a diagram and list the special properties (if any) that it has. Use words to explain how one type of quadrilateral is related to the others. The diagram is started below for you. You will need to add: **quadrilateral**, **kite**, **square**, **rectangle**, and **trapezoid**. Each quadrilateral should be connected to at least one other type of quadrilateral, but some can be related to more than one.

④ WHAT HAVE I LEARNED?

This section will help you evaluate which types of problems you have seen with which you feel comfortable and those with which you need more help. This section will appear at the end of every chapter to help you check your understanding. Even if your teacher does not assign this section, it is a good idea to try these problems and find out for yourself what you know and what you need to work on.

Solve each problem as completely as you can. The table at the end of this closure section has answers to these problems. It also tells you where you can find additional help and practice on problems like these.

CL 7-124. **Examine** the triangle pairs below, which are not necessarily drawn to scale. For each pair, determine:

- if they must be congruent, and state the congruence property (such as SAS ≅) and give a correct congruence statement (such as $\triangle PQR \cong \triangle STU$)

- if there is not enough information, and explain why.

- if they cannot be congruent, and explain why.

a. 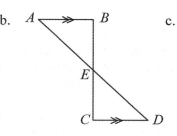   b.

c.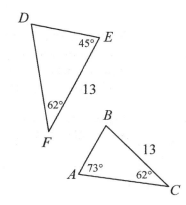

CL 7-125. Complete the following statements.

    a.   If $\triangle YSR \cong \triangle NVD$, then $\overline{DV} \cong$ __?__ and $m\angle RYS =$ __?__

    b.   If $\overrightarrow{AB}$ bisects $\angle DAC$, then __?__ $\cong$ __?__ ?

    c.   In $\triangle WQY$, if $\angle WQY \cong \angle QWY$, then __?__ $\cong$ __?__ .

    d.   If $ABCD$ is a parallelogram, and $m\angle B = 148°$, then $m\angle C =$ __?__ .

CL 7-126. Julius set his hinged mirror so that its angle was 72° and the core region was isosceles, as shown at right.

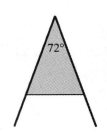

    a.   How many sides did his resulting polygon have? Show how you know.

    b.   What is another name for this polygon?

CL 7-127. Kelly started the proof below to show that if $\overline{TC} \cong \overline{TM}$ and $\overrightarrow{AT}$ bisects $\angle CTM$, then $\overline{CA} \cong \overline{MA}$. Copy and complete her proof.

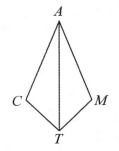

Statements	Reasons
1. $\overline{TC} \cong \overline{TM}$ and $\overrightarrow{AT}$ bisects $\angle CTM$	
2.	Definition of bisect
3. $\overline{AT} \cong \overline{AT}$	
4.	
5.	$\cong \triangle s \rightarrow \cong$ parts

CL 7-128. $ABCD$ is a parallelogram. If $A(3, -4)$, $B(6, 2)$, $C(4, 6)$, then what are the possible locations of point D? Draw a graph and **justify** your answer.

CL 7-129. On graph paper, draw quadrilateral $MNPQ$ if $M(1, 7)$, $N(-2, 2)$, $P(3, -1)$, and $Q(6, 4)$.

    a.   Find the slopes of $\overline{MN}$ and $\overline{NP}$. What can you conclude about $\angle MNP$?

    b.   What is the best name for $MNPQ$? **Justify** your answer.

    c.   Which diagonal is longer? Explain how you know your answer is correct.

    d.   Find the midpoint of $\overline{MN}$.

        Geometry Connections

CL 7-130. **Examine** the geometric relationships in each of the diagrams below. For each one, write and solve an equation to find the value of the variable. Name any geometric property or conjecture that you used.

a.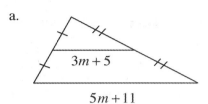

$3m + 5$

$5m + 11$

b. *PQRS* is a rhombus with perimeter = 28 units. *PR* = 8 units.

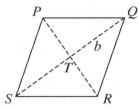

c.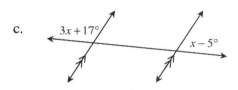

$3x + 17°$

$x - 5°$

d.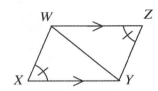

$2x - 5°$

$x + 13°$

CL 7-131. Given the information in the diagram at right, prove that $\triangle WXY \cong \triangle YZW$ using either a flowchart or a two-column proof.

CL 7-132. Check your answers using the table at the end of the closure section. Which problems do you feel confident about? Which problems were hard? Use the table to make a list of topics you need help on and a list of topics you need to practice more.

⑤ HOW AM I THINKING?

This course focuses on five different **Ways of Thinking**: investigating, examining, reasoning & justifying, visualizing, and choosing a strategy/tool. These are some of the ways in which you think while trying to make sense of a concept or to solve a problem (even outside of math class). During this chapter, you have probably used each Way of Thinking multiple times without even realizing it!

Choose three of these Ways of Thinking that you remember using while working in this chapter. For each Way of Thinking that you choose, show and explain where you used it and how you used it. Describe why thinking in this way helped you solve a particular problem or understand something new. Be sure to include examples to demonstrate your thinking.

Answers and Support for Closure Activity #4
What Have I Learned?

Problem	Solution	Need Help?	More Practice
CL 7-124.	a. Congruent (SAS $\cong$), $\triangle ABD \cong \triangle CBD$ b. Not enough information (the triangles are similar (AA $\sim$), but no side lengths are given to know if they are the same size.) c. Congruent (ASA $\cong$ or AAS $\cong$), $\triangle ABC \cong \triangle DEF$	Lessons 2.1.4, 2.2.1, and 6.1.3 Math Notes boxes	Problems 7-6, 7-14, 7-28, 7-42, 7-53, 7-66, 7-87, 7-104
CL 7-125.	a. $\overline{DV} \cong \overline{RS}$, $m\angle RYS = m\angle DNV$ b. $\angle DAB \cong \angle CAB$ c. $\overline{WY} \cong \overline{QY}$ d. $m\angle C = 32°$	Lessons 2.1.4, 3.1.4, and 7.1.3 Math Notes boxes, problems 7-49 and 7-71	Problems 7-26, 7-42, 7-53, 7-87
CL 7-126.	a. $360° \div 72° = 5$ sides b. regular pentagon	Lesson 7.1.4 Math Notes box, problems 7-37 and 7-38	Problems 7-39, 7-50, 7-122
CL 7-127.	<table><tr><th>Statements</th><th>Reasons</th></tr><tr><td>1. $\overline{TC} \cong \overline{TM}$ and $\overline{AT}$ bisects $\angle CTM$</td><td>Given</td></tr><tr><td>2. $\angle CTA \cong \angle MTA$</td><td>Definition of bisect</td></tr><tr><td>3. $\overline{AT} \cong \overline{AT}$</td><td>Reflexive Property</td></tr><tr><td>4. $\triangle CAT \cong \triangle MAT$</td><td>SAS $\cong$</td></tr><tr><td>5. $\overline{CA} \cong \overline{MA}$</td><td>$\cong \triangle s \rightarrow \cong$ parts</td></tr></table>	Lessons 6.1.3, 7.1.3, and 7.2.1 Math Notes boxes, problems 7-45 and 7-79	Problems 7-61, 7-78, 7-85, 7-87, 7-96, 7-104, 7-105
CL 7-128.	Point D is at $(1, 0)$ or at $(5, -8)$.	Lessons 7.2.3 and 7.3.2 Math Notes boxes	Problems 7-29, 7-60, 7-69

Geometry Connections

Problem	Solution	Need Help?	More Practice

CL 7-129.
a. Slope of $\overline{MN} = \frac{5}{3}$ and $\overline{NP} = -\frac{3}{5}$, $\measuredangle MNP$ is a right angle.

b. It is a square because all sides are equal and all angles are right angles.

c. The diagonals have equal length. Each is $\sqrt{68}$ units long.

d. $(-\frac{1}{2}, \frac{9}{2})$

Need Help? Lessons 3.2.4, 7.2.3, 7.3.2, and 7.3.3 Math Notes boxes, problem 7-40

More Practice Problems 7-18, 7-27, 7-29, 7-32, 7-38, 7-40, 7-41, 7-43, 7-69, 7-99, 7-109, 7-110, 7-118, 7-119

CL 7-130.
a. $2(3m+5) = 5m+11$, $m = 1$

b. $b^2 + 4^2 = 7^2$, so $b = \sqrt{33} \approx 5.74$ units

c. $3x + 17° + x - 5° = 180°$, so $x = 42°$

d. $2x - 5° = x + 13°$, so $x = 18°$

Need Help? Lessons 2.1.4, 7.2.4, and 7.2.6 Math Notes boxes, problem 7-49

More Practice Problems 7-16, 7-33, 7-49, 7-52, 7-70

CL 7-131.

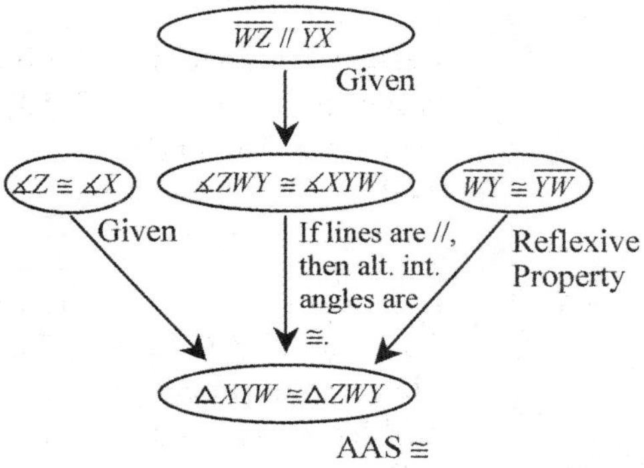

Need Help? Lessons 3.2.4, 6.1.3, and 7.2.1 Math Notes boxes, problems 7-45 and 7-56

More Practice Problems 7-61, 7-78, 7-85, 7-87, 7-96, 7-104, 7-105

CHAPTER 8

Polygons and Circles

In previous chapters, you have extensively studied triangles and quadrilaterals to learn more about their sides and angles. In this chapter, you will broaden your focus to include polygons with 5, 8, 10, and even 100 sides. You will develop a way to find the area and perimeter of a regular polygon and will study how the area and perimeter changes as the number of sides increases.

In Section 8.2, you will re-examine similar shapes to study what happens to the area and perimeter of a shape when the shape is enlarged or reduced.

Finally, in Section 8.3, you will connect your understanding of polygons with your knowledge of the area ratios of similar figures to find the area and circumference of circles of all sizes.

Guiding Questions

Think about these questions throughout this chapter:

How can I measure a polygon?

How does the area change?

Is there another method?

What if the polygon has infinite sides?

What's the connection?

In this chapter, you will learn:

➢ About special types of polygons, such as regular and non-convex polygons.

➢ How the measures of the interior and exterior angles of a regular polygon are related to the number of sides of the polygon.

➢ How the areas of similar figures are related.

➢ How to find the area and circumference of a circle and parts of circles and use this ability to solve problems in various contexts.

Chapter Outline

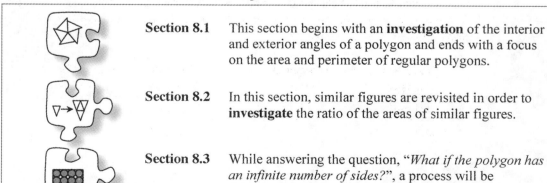

Section 8.1 This section begins with an **investigation** of the interior and exterior angles of a polygon and ends with a focus on the area and perimeter of regular polygons.

Section 8.2 In this section, similar figures are revisited in order to **investigate** the ratio of the areas of similar figures.

Section 8.3 While answering the question, "*What if the polygon has an infinite number of sides?*", a process will be developed to find the area and circumference of a circle.

8.1.1 How can I build it?

· ·

Pinwheels and Polygons

In previous chapters, you have studied triangles and quadrilaterals. In Chapter 8, you will broaden your focus to include all polygons and will study what triangles can tell us about shapes with 5, 8, or even 100 sides.

By the end of this lesson, you should be able to answer these questions:

> *How can you use the number of sides of a regular polygon to find the measure of the central angle?*

> *What type of triangle is needed to form a regular polygon?*

8-1.　PINWHEELS AND POLYGONS

Inez loves pinwheels. One day in class, she noticed that if she put three congruent triangles together so that one set of corresponding angles are adjacent, she could make a shape that looks like a pinwheel.

a.　Can you determine any of the angles of her triangles? Explain how you found your answer.

b.　The overall shape (outline) of Inez's pinwheel is shown at right. How many sides does it have? What is another name for this shape?

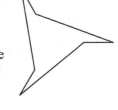

c.　Inez's shape is an example of a **polygon** because it is a closed, two-dimensional figure made of straight line segments connected end-to-end. As you study polygons in this course, it is useful to use the names below because they identify how many sides a particular polygon has. Some of these words may be familiar, while others may be new. On your paper, draw an example of a *heptagon*.

Name of Polygon	Number of Sides	Name of Polygon	Number of Sides
Triangle	3	Octagon	8
Quadrilateral	4	Nonagon	9
Pentagon	5	Decagon	10
Hexagon	6	11-gon	11
Heptagon	7	*n*-gon	*n*

8-2.   Inez is very excited. She wants to know if
you can build a pinwheel using *any* angle of
her triangle. Obtain a Lesson 8.1.1 Resource
Page your teacher and cut out Inez's
triangles. Then work with your team to build
pinwheels and polygons by placing different
corresponding angles together at the center.
You will need to use the triangles from all
four team members together to build one
shape. Be ready to share your results with
the class.

8-3.   Jorge likes Inez's pinwheels but wonders, "Will all triangles build a pinwheel or a
polygon?"

   a.   If you have not already done so, cut out the remaining triangles on the Lesson
8.1.1 Resource Page. Work together to determine which congruent triangles
can build a pinwheel (or polygon) when corresponding angles are placed
together at the center. For each successful pinwheel, answer the questions
below.

   •   How many triangles did it take to build the pinwheel?

   •   Calculate the measure of a **central angle** of the pinwheel. (Remember that
a central angle is an angle of a triangle with a vertex at the center of the
pinwheel.)

   •   Is the shape familiar? Does it have a name? If so, what is it?

   b.   Explain why one triangle may be able to create a pinwheel or polygon while
another triangle cannot.

   c.   Jorge has a triangle with angle measures 32°, 40°, and 108°. Will this triangle
be able to form a pinwheel? Explain.

8-4.   Jasmine wants to create a pinwheel with equilateral triangles.

   a.   How many equilateral triangles will she need? Explain how you know.

   b.   What is the name for the polygon she created?

   c.   Jasmine's shape is an example of a **convex polygon**, while Inez's shape, shown at right, is **non-convex**. Study the examples of convex and non-convex polygons below and then write a definition of a convex polygon on your paper.

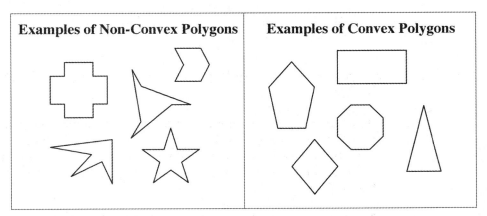

| **Examples of Non-Convex Polygons** | **Examples of Convex Polygons** |

8-5.   When corresponding angles are placed together, why do some triangles form convex polygons while others result in non-convex polygons? Consider this as you answer the following questions.

   a.   Carlisle wants to build a convex polygon using congruent triangles. He wants to select one of the triangles below to use. Which triangle(s) will build a convex polygon if multiple congruent triangles are placed together so that they share a common vertex and do not overlap? Explain how you know.

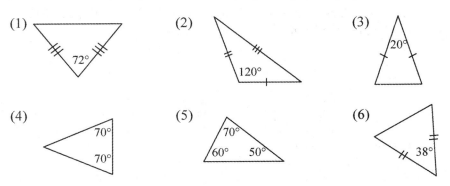

   b.   For each triangle from part (a) that creates a convex polygon, how many sides would the polygon have? What name is most appropriate for the polygon?

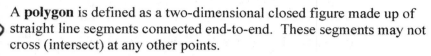

METHODS AND MEANINGS

Convex and Non-Convex Polygons

MATH NOTES

A **polygon** is defined as a two-dimensional closed figure made up of straight line segments connected end-to-end. These segments may not cross (intersect) at any other points.

A polygon is referred to as a **regular polygon** if it is equilateral (all sides have the same length) and equiangular (all interior angles have equal measure). For example, the hexagon shown at right is a regular hexagon because all sides have the same length and each interior angle has the same measure.

A polygon is called **convex** if each pair of interior points can be connected by a segment without leaving the interior of the polygon. See the example of convex and non-convex shapes in problem 8-4.

Review & Preview

8-6. Solve for x in each diagram below.

a.

b.
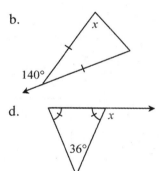

c.

d.

8-7. After solving for x in each of the diagrams in problem 8-6, Jerome thinks he sees a pattern. He notices that the measure of an exterior angle of a triangle is related to two of the angles of a triangle.

a. Do you see a pattern? To help find a pattern, study the results of problem 8-6.

Problem continues on next page →

396 *Geometry Connections*

8-7.   *Problem continued from previous page.*

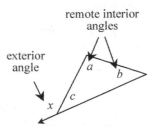
remote interior angles

b.   In the example at right, angles *a* and *b* are called **remote interior angles** of the given exterior angle because they are not adjacent to the exterior angle. Write a conjecture about the relationships between the remote interior and exterior angles of a triangle.

exterior angle

c.   Prove that the conjecture you wrote for part (b) is true for all triangles. Your proof can be written in any form, as long as it is convincing and provides **reasons** for all statements.

8-8.   **Examine** the geometric relationships in the diagram at right. Show all of the steps in your solutions for *x* and *y*.

8-9.   Steven has 100 congruent triangles that each has an angle measuring 15°. How many triangles would he need to use to make a pinwheel? Explain how you found your answer.

8-10.   Find the value of *x* in each diagram below, if possible. If the triangles are congruent, state which triangle congruence property was used. If the triangles are not congruent or if there is not enough information, state, "Cannot be determined."

a.
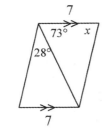

b.
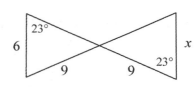

c.
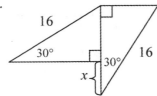

d.
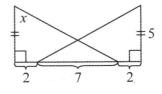

8-11.   Decide if the following statements are true or false. If a statement is false, provide a diagram of a counterexample.

a.   All squares are rectangles.

b.   All quadrilaterals are parallelograms.

c.   All rhombi are parallelograms.

d.   All squares are rhombi.

e.   The diagonals of a parallelogram bisect the angles.

8.1.2 What is its measure?

···

Interior Angles of a Polygon

In an earlier chapter you discovered that the sum of the interior angles of a triangle is always 180°. But what about the sum of the interior angles of other polygons, such as hexagons or decagons? Does it matter if the polygon is convex or not? Consider these questions today as you **investigate** the angles of a polygon.

8-12.   Copy the diagram of the regular pentagon at right onto your paper. Then, with your team, find the <u>sum</u> of the measures of the interior angles *as many ways as you can*. You may want to use the fact that the sum of the angles of a triangle is 180°. Be prepared to share your team's methods with the class.

8-13.   SUM OF THE INTERIOR ANGLES OF A POLYGON

In problem 8-12, you found the sum of the angles of a regular pentagon. But what about other polygons?

a.   Obtain a Lesson 8.1.2 Resource Page from your teacher. Then use one of the methods from problem 8-12 to find the sum of the interior angles of other polygons. Complete the table (also shown below) on the resource page.

Number of Sides of the Polygon	3	4	5	6	7	8	9	10	12
Sum of the Interior Angles of the Polygon	180°								

b.   Does the interior angle sum depend on whether the polygon is convex? Test this idea by drawing a few non-convex polygons (like the one at right) on your paper and determine if it matters whether the polygon is convex. Explain your findings.

c.   Find the sum of the interior angles of a 100-gon. Explain your **reasoning**.

d.   In your Learning Log, write an expression that represents the sum of the interior angles of an *n*-gon. Title this entry "Interior Angles of a Polygon" and include today's date.

8-14. The pentagon at right has been dissected (broken up) into three triangles with the angles labeled as shown. Use the three triangles to prove that the sum of the interior angles of **any** pentagon is always 540°. If you need help, answer the questions below.

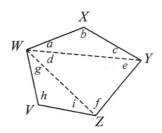

a. What is the sum of the angles of a triangle? Use this fact to write three equations based on the triangles in the diagram.

b. Add the three equations to create one long equation that represents the sum of all nine angles.

c. Substitute the three-letter name for each angle of the pentagon for the lower case letters at each vertex of the pentagon. For example, $m\angle XYZ = c + e$.

8-15. Use the angle relationships in each of the diagrams below to solve for the given variables. Show all work.

a.

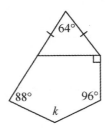

b.

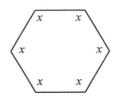

c.

d.

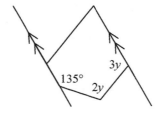

MᴇᴛʜODS AND Mᴇᴀɴɪɴɢꜱ

Special Quadrilateral Properties

In Chapter 7, you examined several special quadrilaterals and proved conjectures regarding many of their special properties. Review what you learned below.

Parallelogram: Opposite sides of a parallelogram are congruent and parallel. Opposite angles are congruent. Also, since the diagonals dissect the parallelogram into four congruent triangles, the diagonals bisect each other.

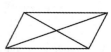

Parallelogram

Rhombus: Since a rhombus is a parallelogram, it has all of the properties of a parallelogram. In addition, its diagonals are perpendicular bisectors and bisect the angles of the rhombus.

Rhombus

Rectangle: Since a rectangle is a parallelogram, it has all of the properties of a parallelogram. In addition, its diagonals must be congruent.

Rectangle

Isosceles Trapezoid: The base angles (angles joined by a base) of an isosceles trapezoid are congruent.

Isosceles Trapezoid

8-16.   On graph paper, graph $\triangle ABC$ if $A(3, 0)$, $B(2, 7)$, and $C(6, 4)$.

 a.   What is the best name for this triangle? **Justify** your answer using slope and/or lengths of sides.

 b.   Find $m\angle A$. Explain how you found your answer.

8-17.   The exterior angles of a quadrilateral are labeled a, b, c, and d in the diagram at right. Find the measures of a, b, c, and d and then find the sum of the exterior angles.

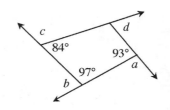

8-18.   Find the area and perimeter of the shape at right. Show all work.

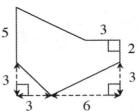

8-19.   Crystal is amazed! She graphed $\triangle ABC$ using the points $A(5, -1)$, $B(3, -7)$, and $C(6, -2)$. Then she rotated $\triangle ABC$ 90° counterclockwise (↺) about the origin to find $\triangle A'B'C'$. Meanwhile, her teammate took a different triangle ($\triangle TUV$) and rotated it 90° clockwise (↻) about the origin to find $\triangle T'U'V'$. Amazingly, $\triangle A'B'C'$ and $\triangle T'U'V'$ ended up using exactly the same points! Name the coordinates of the vertices of $\triangle TUV$.

8-20.   Suzette started to set up a proof to show that if $\overline{BC} \parallel \overline{EF}$, $\overline{AB} \parallel \overline{DE}$, and $AF = DC$, then $\overline{BC} \cong \overline{EF}$. **Examine** her work below. Then complete her missing statements and **reasons**.

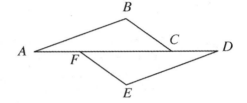

Statements	Reasons
1. $\overline{BC} \parallel \overline{EF}$, $\overline{AB} \parallel \overline{DE}$, and $AF = DC$	1.
2. $m\angle BCF = m\angle EFC$ and $m\angle EDF = m\angle CAB$	2.
3.	3. Reflexive Property
4. $AF + FC = CD + FC$	4. Additive Property of Equality (adding the same amount to both sides of an equation keeps the equation true)
5. $AC = DF$	5. Segment addition
6. $\triangle ABC \cong \triangle DEF$	6.
7.	7. $\cong \triangle s \rightarrow \cong$ parts

8-21.   **Multiple Choice:** Which equation below is **not** a correct statement based on the information in the diagram?

a. $3x + y = 180°$

b. $2x - 1° = 4° - x$

c. $2x - 1° = 5y - 10°$

d. $2x - 1° + 3x = 180°$

e.   None of these is correct

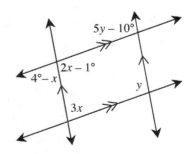

8.1.3 What if it is a regular polygon?

. . . .

Angles of Regular Polygons

In Lesson 8.1.2 you discovered how to determine the sum of the interior angles of a polygon with any number of sides. But what more can you learn about a polygon? Today you will focus on the interior and exterior angles of regular polygons.

As you work today, keep the following focus questions in mind:

Does it matter if the polygon is regular?

Is there another way to find the answer?

What's the connection?

8-22.   Diamonds, the most valuable naturally-occurring gem, have been popular for centuries because of their beauty, durability, and ability to reflect a spectrum of light. In 1919, a diamond cutter from Belgium, Marcel Tolkowsky, used his knowledge of geometry to design a new shape for a diamond, called the "round brilliant cut" (top view shown at right). He discovered that when diamonds are carefully cut with flat surfaces (called "facets" or "faces") in this design, the angles maximize the brilliance and reflective quality of the gem.

Notice that at the center of this design is a **regular octagon** with equal sides and equal interior angles. For a diamond cut in this design to achieve its maximum value, the octagon must be cut carefully and accurately. One miscalculation, and the value of the diamond can be cut in half!

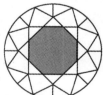

a.   Determine the measure of each interior angle of a regular octagon. Explain how you found your answer.

b.   What about the interior angles of other regular polygons? Find the interior angles of a regular nonagon and a regular 100-gon.

interior angle

c.   Will the process you used for part (a) work for any regular polygon? Write an expression that will calculate the interior angle of an *n*-gon.

8-23.   Fern states, "If a triangle is equilateral, then all angles have equal measure and it must be a regular polygon." Does this logic work for polygons with more than three sides?

   a.   If all of the sides of a polygon (such as a quadrilateral) are equal, does that mean that the angles must be equal? If you can, draw a counterexample.

   b.   What if all the angles are equal? Does that force a polygon to be equilateral? Explain your thinking. Draw a counterexample on your paper if possible.

8-24.   Jeremy asks, "What about exterior angles? What can we learn about them?"

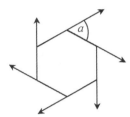

   a.   **Examine** the regular hexagon shown at right. Angle *a* is an example of an **exterior angle** because it is formed on the outside of the hexagon by extending one of its sides. Are all of the exterior angles of a regular polygon equal? Explain how you know.

   b.   Find *a*. Be prepared to share how you found your answer.

   c.   This regular hexagon has six exterior angles, as shown in the diagram above. What is the sum of the exterior angles of a regular hexagon?

   d.   What about the exterior angles of other regular polygons? Explore this with your team. Have each team member choose a different shape from the list below to analyze. For each shape:

      • find the measure of one exterior angle of that shape

      • find the sum of the exterior angles.

      (1) equilateral triangle   (2) regular octagon

      (3) regular decagon   (4) regular dodecagon (12-gon)

   e.   Compare your results from part (d). As a team, write a conjecture about the exterior angles of polygons based on your observations. Be ready to share your conjecture with the rest of the class.

   f.   Is your conjecture from part (e) true for all polygons or for only regular polygons? Does it matter if the polygon is convex? Explore these questions using a dynamic geometric tool or obtain the Lesson 8.1.3 Resource Page and tracing paper from your teacher. Write a statement explaining your findings.

8-25.   Use your understanding of polygons to answer the questions below, if possible. If there is no solution, explain why not.

 a.   Gerardo drew a regular polygon that had exterior angles measuring 40°. How many sides did his polygon have? What is the name for this polygon?

 b.   A polygon has an interior angle sum of 2,520°. How many sides does it have?

 c.   A quadrilateral has four sides. What is the measure of each of its interior angles?

 d.   What is the measure of an interior angle of a regular 360-gon? Is there more than one way to find this answer?

8-26.   How can you find the interior angle of a regular polygon? What is the sum of the exterior angles of a polygon? Write a Learning Log entry about what you learned during this lesson. Title this entry "Interior and Exterior Angles of a Polygon" and include today's date.

8-27.   Find the area and perimeter of each shape below. Show all work.

 a.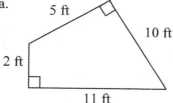

 b.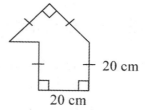

8-28.   In the figure at right, if $PQ = RS$ and $PR = SQ$, prove that $\angle P \cong \angle S$. Write your proof either in a flowchart or in two-column proof form.

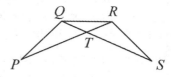

8-29.   Joey used 10 congruent triangles to create a regular decagon.

 a.   What kind of triangles is he using?

 b.   Find the three angle measures of one of the triangles. Explain how you know.

 c.   If the area of each triangle is 14.5 square inches, then what is the area of the regular decagon? Show all work.

8-30.   On graph paper, plot $A(2, 2)$ and $B(14, 10)$. If C is the midpoint of $\overline{AB}$, D is the midpoint of $\overline{AC}$, and E is the midpoint of $\overline{CD}$, find the coordinates of E.

8-31.   The arc at right is called a **quarter circle** because it is one-fourth of a circle.

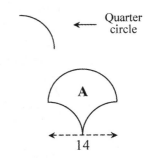

    a.   Copy Region A at right onto your paper. If this region is formed using four quarter circles, can you find another shape that must have the same area as Region A? **Justify** your conclusion.

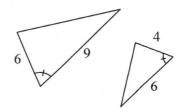

    b.   Find the area of Region A. Show all work.

8-32.   **Multiple Choice:** Which property below can be used to prove that the triangles at right are similar?

    a.   AA ~   b.   SAS ~

    c.   SSS ~   d.   HL ~

    e.   None of these

$8.1.4$ Is there another way?

···

Regular Polygon Angle Connections

During Lessons 8.1.1 through 8.1.3, you have discovered many ways the number of sides of a regular polygon is related to the measures of the interior and exterior angles of the polygon. These relationships can be represented in the diagram at right.

How can these relationships be useful? And what is the most efficient way to go from one measurement to another? This lesson will explore these questions so that you will have a complete set of tools to analyze the angles of a regular polygon.

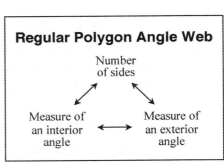

Regular Polygon Angle Web

Number
of sides

Measure of
an interior
angle ⟷ Measure of
an exterior
angle

8-33.   Which connections in the Polygon Angle Web do you
         already have? Which do you still need? Explore this
         as you answer the questions below.

   a.   If you know the number of sides of a regular
         polygon, how can you find the measure of an
         interior angle directly? Find the measurements
         of an interior angle of a 15-gon.

   b.   If you know the number of sides of a regular
         polygon, how can you find the measure of an exterior angle directly? Find the
         measurements of an exterior angle of a 10-gon.

   c.   What if you know that the measure of an interior angle of a regular polygon is
         162°? How many sides must the polygon have? Show all work.

   d.   If the measure of an exterior angle of a regular polygon is 15°, how many sides
         does it have? What is the measure of an interior angle? Show how you know.

8-34.   Suppose a regular polygon has an interior angle measuring 120°. Find the number of
         sides using *two* different **strategies**. Show all work. Which strategy was most
         efficient?

8-35.   Use your knowledge of polygons to answer the questions below, if possible.

   a.   How many sides does a polygon have if the sum of the measures of the interior
         angles is 1980°? 900°?

   b.   If the exterior angle of a regular polygon is 90°, how many sides does it have?
         What is another name for this shape?

   c.   Each interior angle of a regular pentagon has measure $2x + 4°$. What is x?
         Explain how you found your answer.

   d.   The measures of four of the exterior angles of a pentagon are 57°, 74°, 56°,
         and 66°. What is the measure of the remaining angle?

   e.   Find the sum of the interior angles of an 11-gon. Does it matter if it is regular
         or not?

8-36.   In a Learning Log entry, copy the Regular Polygon Angle Web that
         your class created. Explain what it represents and give an example
         of two of the connections. Title this entry "Regular Polygon Angle
         Web" and include today's date.

METHODS AND MEANINGS

Interior and Exterior Angles of a Polygon

MATH NOTES

The properties of interior and exterior angles in polygons, where *n* represents the number of sides in the polygon (*n*-gon), can be summarized as follows:

- The sum of the measures of the interior angles of an *n*-gon is $180(n-2)$.

- The measure of *each* angle in a regular *n*-gon is $\frac{180(n-2)}{n}$.

- The sum of the exterior angles of an *n*-gon is always 360°.

Review & Preview

8-37.   Esteban used a hinged mirror to create an equilateral triangle, as shown in the diagram at right. If the area of the shaded region is 11.42 square inches, what is the area of the entire equilateral triangle? **Justify** your solution

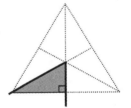

8-38.   Copy each shape below on your paper and state if the shape is convex or non-convex. You may want to compare each figure with the examples provided in problem 8-4.

a.   b.   c.   d.

8-39.   Find the area of each figure below. Show all work.

a. 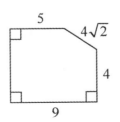   b. 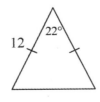   c.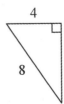

8-40.   Find the number of sides in a regular polygon if each interior angle has the following measures.

   a.   60°   b.   156°   c.   90°   d.   140°

8-41.   At right is a scale drawing of the floor plan for Nzinga's dollhouse. The actual dimensions of the dollhouse are 9 times the measurements provided in the floor plan at right.

a.   Use the measurements provided in the diagram to find the area and perimeter of her floor plan.

b.   Draw a similar figure on your paper. Label the sides with the actual measurements of Nzinga's dollhouse. What is the perimeter and area of the floor of her actual dollhouse? Show all work.

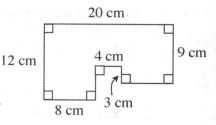

c.   Find the ratio of the perimeters of the two figures. What do you notice?

d.   Find the ratio of the areas of the two figures. How does the ratio of the areas seem to be related to the zoom factor?

8-42.   **Multiple Choice:** A penny, nickel, and dime are all flipped once. What is the probability that at least one coin comes up heads?

a. $\frac{1}{3}$ b. $\frac{3}{8}$ c.   1   d. $\frac{7}{8}$

8.1.5 What's the area?

Finding the Area of Regular Polygons

In Lesson 8.1.4, you found the area of a regular hexagon. But what if you want to find the area of a regular pentagon or a regular decagon? Today you will explore these different polygons and generalize how to find the area of any regular polygon with *n* sides.

8-43.   USING MULTIPLE STRATEGIES

With your team, find the area of each shape below <u>twice</u>, each time using a distinctly different method or **strategy**. Make sure that your results from using different **strategies** are the same. Be sure that each member of your team understands each method.

a.   Square

b.   regular hexagon

8-44.   Create a poster or transparency that shows the two
         different methods that your team used to find the
         area of the regular hexagon in part (b) of problem
         8-43.

         Then, as you listen to other teams present, look for
         strategies that are different than yours. For each
         one, consider the questions below.

         • *Which geometric **tools** does this method use?*

         • *Would this method help find the area of other
           regular polygons (like a pentagon or 100-gon)?*

8-45.   Which method presented by teams in problem 8-44 seemed able to help find the area
         of other regular polygons? Discuss this with your team. Then find the area of the
         two regular polygons below. If your method does not work, switch to a different
         method. Assume *C* is the center of each polygon.

         a.   b.

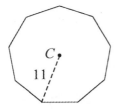   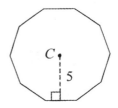

8-46.   So far, you have found the area of a regular hexagon, nonagon, and
         decagon. How can you calculate the area of *any* regular polygon?
         Write a Learning Log entry describing a general process for finding
         the area of a polygon with *n* sides.

8-47.   Beth needs to fertilize her flowerbed, which is in the
         shape of a regular pentagon. A bag of fertilizer states
         that it can fertilize up to 150 square feet, but Beth is
         not sure how many bags of fertilizer she should buy.

         Beth does know that each side of the pentagon is
         15 feet long. Copy the diagram of the regular
         pentagon below onto your paper. Find the area of the
         flowerbed and tell Beth how many bags of fertilizer to
         buy. Explain how you found your answer.

15 ft

8-48.   GO, ROWDY RODENTS!

Recently, your school ordered a stained-glass window
with the design of the school's mascot, the rodent.
Your student body has decided that the shape of the
window will be a regular octagon, shown at right. To
fit in the space, the window must have a **radius** of 2
feet. That is, the distance from the center to each vertex
must be 2 feet.

a.   A major part of the cost of the window is the amount
of glass used to make it. The more glass used, the
more expensive the window. Your principal has
turned to your class to determine how much glass the
window will need. Copy the diagram onto your paper
and find its area. Explain how you found your answer.

b.   The edge of the window will have a polished brass
trim. Each foot of trim will cost $48.99. How much
will the trim cost? Show all work.

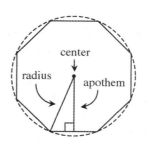

Ⓜ️ETHODS AND MEANINGS

Parts of a Regular Polygon

MATH NOTES

The **center** of a regular polygon is the center
of the smallest circle that completely encloses
the polygon.

A line segment that connects the center of a regular
polygon with a vertex is called a **radius**.

An **apothem** is the perpendicular line segment from
the center of a regular polygon to a side.

8-49.   The exterior angle of a regular polygon is 20°.

a.   What is the measure of an interior angle of this polygon? Show how you
know.

b.   How many sides does this polygon have? Show all work.

8-50.   Without using your calculator, find the exact values of *x* and *y* in each diagram below.

a.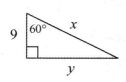

b.

c.

8-51.   Find the coordinates of the point at which the diagonals of parallelogram *ABCD* intersect if *B*(–3, –17) and *D*(15, 59). Explain how you found your answer.

8-52.   Find the area of an equilateral triangle with side length 20 mm. Draw a diagram and show all work.

8-53.   For each equation below, solve for *w*, if possible. Show all work.

a. $5w^2 = 17$ b. $5w^2 - 3w - 17 = 0$ c. $2w^2 = -3$

8-54.   **Multiple Choice:** The triangles at right are congruent because of:

a.   SSA ≅   b.   HL ≅   c.   SAS ≅

d.   SSS ≅   e.   None of these

8-55.   Solve for *x* in each diagram below.

a.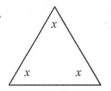

b.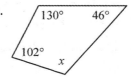

c.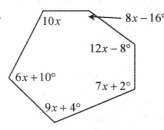

d.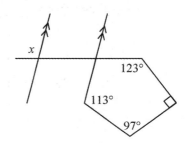

8-56.   What is another (more descriptive) name for each polygon described below?

     a.   A regular polygon with an exterior angle measuring 120°.

     b.   A quadrilateral with four equal angles.

     c.   A polygon with an interior angle sum of 1260°.

     d.   A quadrilateral with perpendicular diagonals.

8-57.   If $\triangle ABC$ is equilateral and if $A(0, 0)$ and $B(12, 0)$, then what do you know about the coordinates of vertex C?

8-58.   In the figure at right, $\overline{AB} \cong \overline{DC}$ and $\angle ABC \cong \angle DCB$.

     a.   Is $\overline{AC} \cong \overline{DB}$? Prove your answer.

     b.   Do the measures of $\angle ABC$ and $\angle DCB$ make any difference in your solution to part (a)? Explain why or why not.

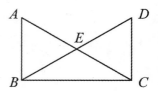

8-59.   On graph paper, graph the parabola $y = 2x^2 - x - 15$.

     a.   What are the roots (*x*-intercepts) of the parabola? Write your points in (x, y) form.

     b.   How would the graph of $y = -(2x^2 - x - 15)$ be the same or different? Can you tell without graphing?

8-60.   **Multiple Choice:** Approximate the length of $\overline{AB}$.

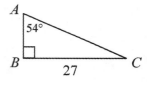

     a.   15.87   b.   21.84   c.   37.16

     d.   19.62   e.   None of these

8.2.1 How does the area change?

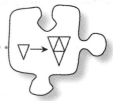

Area Ratios of Similar Figures

Much of this course has focused on similarity. In Chapter 3, you **investigated** how to enlarge and reduce a shape to create a similar figure. You also have studied how to use proportional relationships to find the measures of sides of similar figures. Today you will study how the areas of similar figures are related. That is, as a shape is enlarged or reduced in size, how does the area change?

8-61.   MIGHTY MASCOT

To celebrate the victory of your school's championship girls' ice hockey team, the student body has decided to hang a giant flag with your school's mascot on the gym wall.

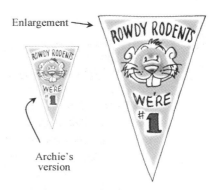

To help design the flag, your friend Archie has created a scale version of the flag measuring 1 foot wide and 1.5 feet tall.

a.   The student body would like the final flag to be 3 feet tall. How wide will the final flag be? **Justify** your solution.

b.   If Archie used $2 worth of cloth to create his scale model, then how much will the cloth cost for the full-sized flag? Discuss this with your team. Explain your **reasoning**.

c.   Obtain the Lesson 8.2.1A Resource Page and scissors from your teacher. Carefully cut enough copies of Archie's scale version to fit into the large flag. How many did it take? Does this confirm your answer to part (b)? If not, what will the cloth cost for the flag?

d.

The student body is reconsidering the size of the flag. It is now considering enlarging the flag so that it is 3 or 4 times the width of Archie's model. How much would the cloth for a similar flag that is 3 times as wide as Archie's model cost? What if the flag is 4 times as wide?

To answer this question, first *estimate* how many of Archie's drawings would fit into each enlarged flag. Then obtain the Lesson 8.2.1B Resource Page (one for you and your team members to share) and confirm each answer by fitting Archie's scale version into the enlarged flags.

8-62.   Write down any observations or patterns you found while working on problem 8-61. For example, if the area of one shape is 100 times larger than the area of a similar shape, then what is the ratio of the corresponding sides (also called the **linear scale factor**)? And if the linear scale factor is r, then how many times larger is the area of the new shape?

8-63.   Use your pattern from problem 8-62 to answer the following questions.

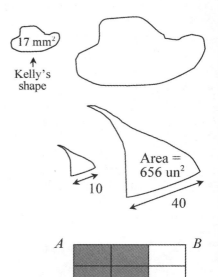

a.   Kelly's shape at right has an area of 17 mm^2. If she enlarges the shape with a linear scale (zoom) factor of 5, what will be the area of the enlargement? Show how you got your answer.

b.   **Examine** the two similar shapes at right. What is the linear scale factor? What is the area of the smaller figure?

c.   Rectangle $ABCD$ at right is divided into nine smaller congruent rectangles. Is the shaded rectangle similar to $ABCD$? If so, what is the linear scale factor? And what is the ratio of the areas? If the shaded rectangle is not similar to $ABCD$, explain how you know.

d.   While ordering carpet for his rectangular office, Trinh was told by the salesperson that a 16'-by-24' piece of carpet costs $200. Trinh then realized that he read his measurements wrong and that his office is actually 8'-by-12'. "Oh, that's no problem," said the salesperson. "That is half the size and will cost $100 instead." Is that fair? Decide what the price should be.

8-64.   If the side length of a hexagon triples, how does the area increase? First make a prediction using your pattern from problem 8-62. Then confirm your prediction by calculating and comparing the areas of the two hexagons shown at right.

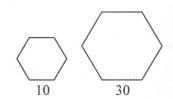

METHODS AND MEANINGS

Ratios of Similarity

Since Chapter 3, you have used the term **zoom factor** to refer to the ratio of corresponding dimensions of two similar figures. However, now that you will be using other ratios of similar figures (such as the ratio of the areas), this ratio needs a more descriptive name. From now on, this text will refer to the ratio of corresponding sides as the **linear scale factor**. The word "linear" is a reference to the fact that the ratio of the side lengths is a comparison of a single dimension of the shapes. Often, this value is represented with the letter r, for ratio.

For example, notice that the two triangles at right are similar because of AA ~. Since the corresponding sides of the new and original shape are 9 and 6, it can be stated that $r = \frac{9}{6} = \frac{3}{2}$.

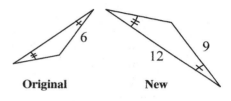

Original   **New**

8-65. **Examine** the shape at right.

    a.   Find the area and perimeter of the shape.

    b.   On graph paper, enlarge the figure so that the linear scale factor is 3. Find the area and perimeter of the new shape.

    c.   What is the ratio of the perimeters of both shapes? What is the ratio of the areas?

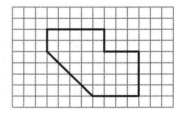

8-66. Sandip noticed that when he looked into a mirror that was lying on the ground 8 feet from him, he could see a clock on the wall. If Sandip's eyes are 64 inches off the ground, and if the mirror is 10 feet from the wall, how high above the floor is the clock? Include a diagram in your solution.

8-67.   Mr. Singer has a dining table in the shape of a regular
         hexagon. While he loves this design, he has trouble finding
         tablecloths to cover it. He has decided to make his own
         tablecloth!

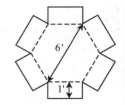

         In order for his tablecloth to drape over each edge, he will add a
         rectangular piece along each side of the regular hexagon as
         shown in the diagram at right. Using the dimensions given in
         the diagram, find the total area of the cloth Mr. Singer will need.

8-68.   Your teacher has offered your class extra credit. She
         has created two spinners, shown at right. Your class
         gets to spin only one of the spinners. The number
         that the spinner lands on is the number of extra credit
         points each member of the class will get. Study both
         spinners carefully.

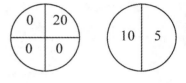

    a.   Assuming that each spinner is divided into equal portions, which spinner do
         you think the class should choose to spin and why?

    b.   What if the spot labeled "20" were changed to "100"? Would that make any
         difference?

8-69.   If the rectangles below have the same area, find x. Is there more than one answer?
         Show all work.

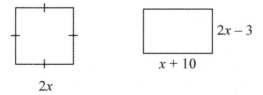

8-70.   **Multiple Choice:** A cable 100 feet long is attached 70 feet up the side of a building.
         If it is pulled taut (i.e., there is no slack) and staked to the ground as far away from
         the building as possible, approximately what angle does the cable make with the
         ground?

    a.   39.99°   b.   44.43°   c.   45.57°   d.   12.22°

8.2.2 How does the area change?

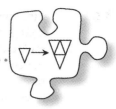

Ratios of Similarity

Today you will continue **investigating** the ratios between similar figures. As you solve today's problems, look for connections between the ratios of similar figures and what you already know about area and perimeter.

8-71. TEAM PHOTO

Alice has a 4"-by-5" photo of your school's championship girls' ice hockey team. To celebrate their recent victory, your principal wants Alice to enlarge her photo for a display case near the main office.

a. When Alice went to the print shop, she was confronted with many choices of sizes: 7"-by-9", 8"-by-10", and 12"-by-16". She's afraid that if she picks the wrong size, part of the photo will be cut off. Which size should Alice pick and why?

b. The cost of the photo paper to print Alice's 4"-by-5" picture is $0.45. Assuming that the cost per square inch of photo paper remains constant, how much should it cost to print the enlarged photo? Explain how you found your answer.

c. Unbeknownst to her, the Vice-Principal also went out and ordered an enlargement of Alice's photo. However, the photo paper for his enlargement cost $7.20! What are the dimensions of his photo?

8-72. So far, you have discovered and used the relationship between the areas of similar figures. How are the perimeters of similar figures related? Confirm your intuition by analyzing the pairs of similar shapes below. For each pair, calculate the areas and perimeters and complete a table like the one shown below. To help see patterns, reduce fractions to lowest terms or find the corresponding decimal values.

	Ratio of Sides	Perimeter	Ratio of Perimeters	Area	Ratio of Areas
small figure					
large figure					

a.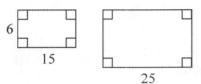

b.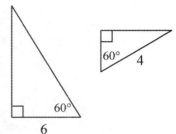

c.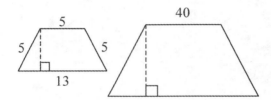

8-73. While Jessie examines the two figures at right, she wonders if they are similar. Decide with your team if there is enough information to determine if the shapes are similar. **Justify** your conclusion.

8-74. Your teacher enlarged the figure at right so that the area of the similar shape is 900 square cm. What is the perimeter of the enlarged figure? Be prepared to explain your method to the class.

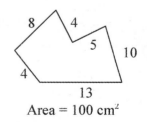

Area = 100 cm^2

8-75. Reflect on what you have learned during Lessons 8.2.1 and 8.2.2. Write a Learning Log entry that explains what you know about the areas and perimeters of similar figures. What connections can you make with other geometric concepts? Be sure to include an example. Title this entry "Area and Perimeter of Similar Figures" and include today's date.

8-76. Assume Figure *A* and Figure *B*, at right, are similar.

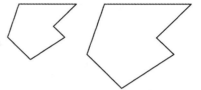

Figure A   Figure B

    a. If the ratio of similarity is $\frac{3}{4}$, then what is the ratio of the perimeters of *A* and *B*?

    b. If the perimeter of Figure A is *p* and the linear scale factor is *r*, what is the perimeter of Figure B?

    c. If the area of Figure A is *a* and the linear scale factor is *r*, what is the area of Figure B?

8-77. Always a romantic, Marris decided to bake his girlfriend a cookie in the shape of a regular dodecagon (12-gon) for Valentine's Day.

    a. If the edge of the dodecagon is 6 cm, what is the area of the top of the cookie?

    b. His girlfriend decides to divide the cookie into 12 separate but congruent pieces. After 9 of the pieces have been eaten, what area of cookie is left?

8-78. As her team was building triangles with linguini, Karen asked for help building a triangle with sides 5, 6, and 1. "I don't think that's possible," said her teammate, Kelly.

    a. Why is this triangle not possible?

    b. Change the lengths of one of the sides so that the triangle is possible.

8-79. Callie started to prove that given the information in the diagram at right, then $\overline{AB} \cong \overline{CD}$. Copy her flowchart below on your paper and help her by **justifying** each statement.

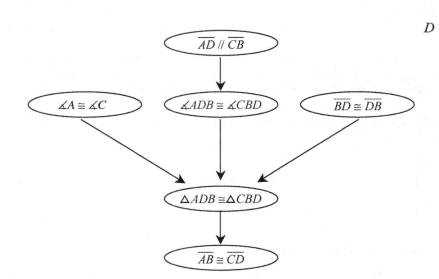

8-80. For each pair of triangles below, decide if the triangles are congruent. If the triangles are congruent:

- State which triangle congruence property proves that the triangles are congruent.

- Write a congruence statement (such as $\triangle ABC \cong \triangle \_\_\_$).

a.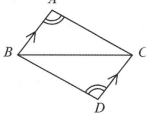

b.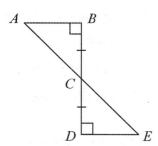

8-81. **Multiple Choice:** What is the solution to the system of equations at right?

$$y = \tfrac{1}{2}x - 4$$
$$x - 4y = 12$$

a. (2, 0)   b. (16, 4)

c. (−2, −5)   d. (4, −2)

e. None of these

8.3.1 What if the polygon has infinite sides?

A Special Ratio

In Section 8.2, you developed a method to find the area and perimeter of a regular polygon with *n* sides. You carefully calculated the area of regular polygons with 5, 6, 8, and even 10 sides. But what if the regular polygon has an infinite number of sides? How can you predict its area?

As you **investigate** this question today, keep the following focus questions in mind:

What's the connection?

Do I see any patterns?

How are the shapes related?

8-82. POLYGONS WITH INFINITE SIDES

In order to predict the area and perimeter of a polygon with infinite sides, your team is going to work with other teams to generate data in order to find a pattern.

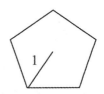

Your teacher will assign your team three of the regular polygons below. For each polygon, find the area and perimeter if the radius is 1 (as shown in the diagram of the regular pentagon at right). Leave your answer accurate to the nearest 0.01. Place your results into a class chart to help predict the area and perimeter of a polygon with an infinite number of sides.

a. equilateral triangle   b. regular octagon   c. regular 30-gon

d. square   e. regular nonagon   f. regular 60-gon

g. regular pentagon   h. regular decagon   i. regular 90-gon

j. regular hexagon   k. regular 15-gon   l. regular 180-gon

8-83. ANALYSIS OF DATA

With your team, analyze the chart created by the class.

a. What do you predict the area will be for a regular polygon with infinite sides? What do you predict its perimeter will be?

b. What is another name for a regular polygon with infinite sides?

c. Does the number 3.14… look familiar? If so, share what you know with your team. Be ready to share your idea with the class.

8-84. Record the area and circumference of a circle with radius you're your Learning Log. Then, include a brief description of how you "discovered" π. Title this entry "Pi" and include today's date.

MⒺTHODS AND MEANINGS

The Area of a Regular Polygon

If a polygon is regular with n sides, it can be subdivided into n congruent isosceles triangles. One way to calculate the area of a regular polygon is to multiply the area of one isosceles triangle by n.

To find the area of the isosceles triangle, it is helpful to first find the measure of the polygon's central angle by dividing 360° by n. The height of the isosceles triangle divides the top vertex angle in half.

For example, suppose you want to find the area of a regular decagon with side length 4 units. The central angle is $\frac{360°}{10} = 36°$. Then the top angle of the shaded right triangle at right would be $36° \div 2 = 18°$.

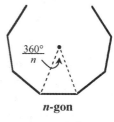

Use right triangle trigonometry to find the measurements of the right triangle, then calculate its area. For the shaded triangle above, $\tan 18° = \frac{4}{h}$ and $h \approx 12.311$. Use the height and the base to find the area of the isosceles triangle: $\frac{1}{2}(8)(12.311) \approx 49.242$ sq. units. Then the area of the regular decagon is approximately $10 \cdot 49.242 \approx 492.42$ sq. units. Use a similar approach if you are given a different length of the triangle.

8-85. Find the area of the shaded region for the regular pentagon at right if the length of each side of the pentagon is 10 units. Assume that point C is the center of the pentagon.

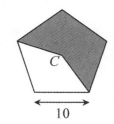

Geometry Connections

8-86.   For each triangle below, find the value of x, if possible. Name which triangle tool you used. If the triangle cannot exist, explain why.

a.

b.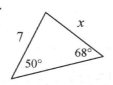

c.

d.   Area of the shaded region is 96 un^2.

8-87.   Find the measure of each interior angle of a regular 30-gon using **two different methods**.

8-88.   **Examine** the diagram at right. Assume that $\overline{BC} \cong \overline{DC}$ and $\angle A \cong \angle E$. Prove that $\overline{AB} \cong \overline{ED}$. Use the form of proof that you prefer (such as the flowchart or two-column proof format). Be sure to copy the diagram onto your paper and add any appropriate markings.

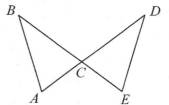

8-89.   On graph paper, plot the points $A(-3, -1)$ and $B(6, 11)$.

a.   Find the midpoint of $\overline{AB}$.

b.   Find the equation of the line that passes through points A and B.

c.   Find the distance between points A and B.

8-90.   **Multiple Choice:** What fraction of the circle at right is shaded?

a. $\frac{60}{360}$

b. $\frac{300}{360}$

c. $\frac{60}{180}$

d. $\frac{120}{180}$

e.   None of these

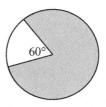

8.3.2 What's the relationship?

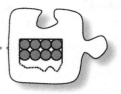

· ·

Area and Circumference of Circles

In Lesson 8.3.1, your class discovered that the area of a circle with radius 1 unit is π un^2 and that the circumference is 2π units. But what if the radius of the circle is 5 units or 13.6 units? Today, you will develop a method to find the area and circumference of circles when the radius is not 1. You will also explore parts of circles (called sectors and arcs) and learn about their measurements.

As you and your team work together, remember to ask each other questions such as:

Is there another way to solve it?

What's the relationship?

What is area? What is circumference?

8-91.   AREA AND CIRCUMFERENCE OF A CIRCLE

Now that you know the area and circumference (perimeter) of a circle with radius 1, how can you find the area and circumference of a circle with any radius?

a.   First **investigate** how the circles are related. **Examine** the circles at right. Since circles always have the same shape, what is the relationship between any two circles?

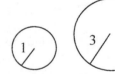

b.   What is the ratio of the circumferences (perimeters)? What is the ratio of the areas? Explain.

c.   If the area of a circle with radius of 1 is π square units, what is the area of a circle with radius 3 units? With radius 10 units? With radius r units?

d.   Likewise, if the circumference (perimeter) of a circle is 2π units, what is the circumference of a circle with radius 3? With radius 7? With radius r?

8-92.   Read the definitions of radius and diameter in the Math Notes box for this lesson. Then answer the questions below.

a.   Find the area of a circle with radius 10 units.

b.   Find the circumference of a circle with diameter 7 units.

c.   If the area of a circle is 121π square units, what is its diameter?

d.   If the circumference of a circle is 20π units, what is its area?

8-93. The giant sequoia trees in California are famous for their immense size and old age. Some of the trees are more than 2500 years old and tourists and naturalists often visit to admire their size and beauty. In some cases, you can even drive a car through the base of a tree!

One of these trees, the General Sherman tree in Sequoia National Park, is the largest living thing on the earth. The tree is so gigantic, in fact, that the base has a circumference of 102.6 feet! Assuming that the base of the tree is circular, how wide is the base of the tree? That is, what is its diameter? How does that diameter compare with the length and width of your classroom?

8-94. To celebrate their victory, the girls' ice-hockey team went out for pizza.

a. The goalie ate half of a pizza that had a diameter of 20 inches! What was the area of pizza that she ate? What was the length of crust that she ate? Leave your answers in exact form. That is, do not convert your answer to decimal form.

b. Sonya chose a slice from another pizza that had a diameter of 16 inches. If her slice had a central angle of 45°, what is the area of this slice? What is the length of its crust? Show how you got your answer.

c. As the evening drew to a close, Sonya noticed that there was only one slice of the goalie's pizza remaining. She measured the central angle and found out that it was 72°. What is the area of the remaining slice? What is the length of its crust? Show how you got your answer.

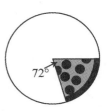

d. A portion of a circle (like the crust of a slice of pizza) is called an **arc**. This is a set of connected points a fixed distance from a central point. The length of an arc is a part of the circle's circumference. If a circle has a radius of 6 cm, find the length of an arc with a central angle of 30°.

arc

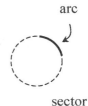

e. A region that resembles a slice of pizza is called a **sector**. It is formed by two radii of a central angle and the arc between their endpoints on the circle. If a circle has radius 10 feet, find the area of a sector with a central angle of 20°.

sector

8-95.   Reflect on what you have learned today. How did you use
         similarity to find the areas and circumferences of circles? How are
         the radius and diameter of a circle related? Write a Learning Log
         entry about what you learned today. Title this entry "Area and
         Circumference of a Circle" and include today's date.

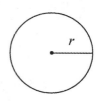 **ETHODS AND MEANINGS**

Circle Facts

The area of a circle with radius $r = 1$ unit is π un^2.
(Remember that $\pi \approx 3.1415926...$)

Since all circles are similar, their areas increase by
a square of the zoom factor. That is, a circle with
radius 6 has an area that is 36 times the area of a
circle with radius 1. Thus, a circle with radius 6
has an area of 36π un^2, and a circle with radius r
has **area** $A = \pi r^2$ un^2.

Area $= \pi r^2$
Circumference $= 2\pi r = \pi d$

The **circumference** of a circle is its perimeter. It is the distance around a
circle. The circumference of a circle with radius $r = 1$ unit is 2π units. Since
the perimeter ratio is equal to the ratio of similarity, a circle with radius r has
circumference $C = 2\pi r$ units. Since the diameter of a circle is twice its radius,
another way to calculate the circumference is $C = \pi d$ units.

A part of a circle is called an **arc**. This is a set of points a
fixed distance from a center and is defined by a central
angle. Since a circle does not include its interior region, an
arc is like the edge of a crust of a slice of pizza.

arc

sector

A region that resembles a slice of pizza is called a **sector**. It is
formed by two radii of a central angle and the arc between their
endpoints on the circle.

Review & Preview

8-96.   The diagram at right shows a circle inscribed in a square.
         Find the area of the shaded region. Show all work.

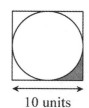

10 units

Geometry Connections

8-97.   Reynaldo has a stack of blocks on his desk, as shown below at right.

   a.   If his stack is 2 blocks wide, 2 blocks long, and 2 blocks tall, how many blocks are in his stack?

   b.   What if his stack instead is 3 blocks wide, 3 blocks long, and 2 blocks tall? How many blocks are in this stack?

8-98.   Find the missing angle(s) in each problem below using the geometric relationships shown in the diagram at right. Be sure to write down the conjecture that **justifies** each calculation. Remember that each part is a separate problem.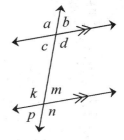

   a.   If $d = 110°$ and $k = 5x - 20°$, write an equation and solve for x.

   b.   If $b = 4x - 11°$ and $n = x + 26°$, write an equation and solve for x. Then find the measure of $\angle n$.

8-99.   An exterior angle of a regular polygon measures 18°.

   a.   How many sides does the polygon have?

   b.   If the length of a side of the polygon is 2, what is the area of the polygon?

8-100.   A regular hexagon with side length 4 has the same area as a square. What is the length of the side of the square? Explain how you know.

8-101.   **Multiple Choice:** Which type of quadrilateral below does not necessarily have diagonals that bisect each other?

   a.   square   b.   rectangle   c.   rhombus   d.   trapezoid

8.3.3 How can I use it?

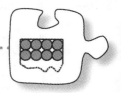

Circles in Context

In Lesson 8.3.1, you developed methods to find the area and circumference of a circle with radius *r*. During this lesson, you will work with your team to solve problems from different contexts involving circles and polygons.

As you and your team work together, remember to ask each other questions such as:

Is there another way to solve it?

What's the connection?

What is area? What is circumference?

8-102. While the earth's orbit (path) about the sun is slightly elliptical, it can be approximated by a circle with a radius of 93,000,000 miles.

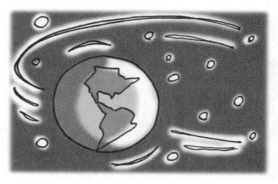

a. How far does the earth travel in one orbit about the sun? That is, what is the approximate circumference of the earth's path?

b. Approximately how fast is the earth traveling in its orbit in space? Calculate your answer in miles per hour.

8-103. A certain car's windshield wiper clears a portion of a sector as shown shaded at right. If the angle the wiper pivots during each swing is 120°, find the area of the windshield that is wiped during each swing.

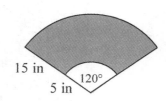

8-104.   THE GRAZING GOAT

Zoe the goat is tied by a rope to one corner of a 15 meter-by-25 meter rectangular barn in the middle of a large, grassy field. Over what area of the field can Zoe graze if the rope is:

a.   10 meters long?

b.   20 meters long?

c.   30 meters long?

d.   Zoe is happiest when she has at least 400 m^2 to graze. What possible lengths of rope could be used?

8-105.   THE COOKIE CUTTER

A cookie baker has an automatic mixer that turns out a sheet of dough in the shape of a square 12" wide. His cookie cutter cuts 3" diameter circular cookies as shown at right. The supervisor complained that too much dough was being wasted and ordered the baker to find out what size cookie would have the least amount of waste.

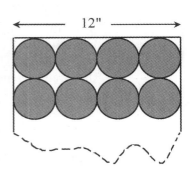

Your Task:

•   Analyze this situation and determine how much cookie dough is "wasted" when 3" cookies are cut. Then have each team member find the amount of dough wasted when a cookie of a different diameter is used. Compare your results.

•   Write a note to the supervisor explaining your results. **Justify** your conclusion.

METHODS AND MEANINGS

Arc Length and Area of a Sector

The ratio of the area of a sector to the area of a circle with the same radius equals the ratio of its central angle to 360°. For example, for the sector in circle C at right, the area of the entire circle is $\pi(8)^2 = 64\pi$ square units. Since the central angle is 50°, then the area of the sector can be found with the proportional equation:

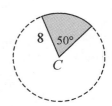

$$\frac{50°}{360°} = \frac{\text{area of sector}}{64\pi}$$

To solve, multiply both sides of the equation by 64π. Thus, the area of the sector is $\frac{50°}{360°}(64\pi) = \frac{80\pi}{9} \approx 27.93$ square units.

The length of an arc can be found using a similar process. The ratio of the length of an arc to the circumference of a circle with the same radius equals the ratio of its central angle to 360°. To find the length of $\overparen{AB}$ at right, first find the circumference of the entire circle, which is $2\pi(5) = 10\pi$ units. Then:

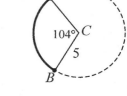

$$\frac{104°}{360°} = \frac{\text{arc length}}{10\pi}$$

Multiplying both sides of the equation by 10π, the arc length is $\frac{104°}{360°}(10\pi) = \frac{26\pi}{9} \approx 9.08$ units.

8-106.   Your teacher has constructed a spinner like the one at right. He has informed you that the class gets one spin. If the spinner lands on the shaded region, you will have a quiz tomorrow. What is the probability that you will have a quiz tomorrow? Explain how you know.

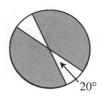

8-107.   Use what you know about the area and circumference of circles to answer the questions below. Show all work. Leave answers in terms of π.

   a.   If the radius of a circle is 14 units, what is its circumference? What is its area?

   b.   If a circle has diameter 10 units, what is its circumference? What is its area?

   c.   If a circle has circumference 100π units, what is its diameter? What is its radius?

8-108.   Larry started to set up a proof to show that if $\overline{AB} \perp \overline{DE}$ and $\overline{DE}$ is a diameter of $\odot C$, then $\overline{AF} \cong \overline{FB}$. **Examine** his work below. Then complete his missing statements and **reasons**.

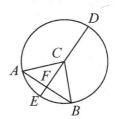

Statements	Reasons
1. $\overline{AB} \perp \overline{DE}$ and $\overline{DE}$ is a diameter of $\odot C$.	1.
2. $\angle AFC$ and $\angle BFC$ are right angles.	2.
3. $FC = FC$	3.
4. $\overline{AC} = \overline{BC}$	4. Definition of a Circle (radii must be equal)
5.	5. HL $\cong$
6. $\overline{AF} \cong \overline{FB}$	6.

8-109.   Match each regular polygon named on the left with a statement about its qualities listed on the right.

   a.   regular hexagon   (1)   Central angle of 36°

   b.   regular decagon   (2)   Exterior angle measure of 90°

   c.   equilateral triangle   (3)   Interior angle measure of 120°

   d.   square   (4)   Exterior angle measure of 120°

8-110.   **Examine** the graph of $f(x)$ at right. Use the graph to find the following values.

   a. $f(1)$ b. $f(0)$

   c. x if $f(x) = 4$ d. x if $f(x) = 0$

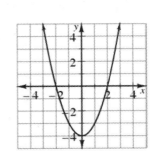

8-111.   **Multiple Choice:** How many cubes with edge
          length 1 unit would fit in a cube with edge length
          3 units?

          a.   3   b.   9

          c.   10   d.   27

          e.   None of these

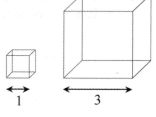

8-112.   The city of Denver wants you to help build a dog park. The
          design of the park is a rectangle with two semicircular ends.
          (Note: A semicircle is half a circle.)

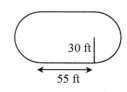

          a.   The entire park needs to be covered with grass. If
                grass is sold by the square foot, how much grass should
                you order?

          b.   The park also needs a fence for its perimeter. A sturdy chain-linked fence
                costs about $8 per foot. How much will a fence for the entire park cost?

          c.   The local design board has rejected the plan because it was too small. "Big
                dogs need lots of room to run," the president of the board said. Therefore, you
                need to increase the size of the park with a zoom factor of 2. What is the area
                of the new design? What is the perimeter?

8-113.   For each diagram below, write and solve an equation to find x.

          a.   b.

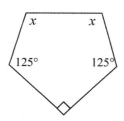

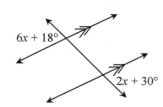

8-114. $\overline{BE}$ is the midsegment of $\triangle ACD$, shown at right.

          a.   Find the perimeter of $\triangle ACD$.

          b.   If the area of $\triangle ABE$ is 54 cm^2, what is the
                area of $\triangle ACD$?

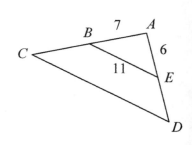

8-115.   Christie has tied a string that is 24 cm long into a closed loop, like the one at right.

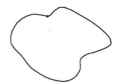

   a.   She decided to form an equilateral triangle with her string. What is the area of the triangle?

   b.   She then forms a square with the same loop of string. What is the area of the square? Is it more or less than the equilateral triangle she created in part (a)?

   c.   If she forms a regular hexagon with her string, what would be its area? Compare this area with the areas of the square and equilateral triangle from parts (a) and (b).

   d.   What shape should Christie form to enclose the greatest area?

8-116.   The **Isoperimetric Theorem** states that of all closed figures on a flat surface with the same perimeter, the circle has the greatest area. Use this fact to answer the questions below.

   a.   What is the greatest area that can be enclosed by a loop of string that is 24 cm long?

   b.   What is the greatest area that can be enclosed by a loop of string that is 18π cm long?

8-117.   **Multiple Choice:** The diagram at right is not drawn to scale. If $\triangle ABC \sim \triangle KLM$, find KM.

   a.   6   b.   12

   c.   15   d.   21

   e.   None of these

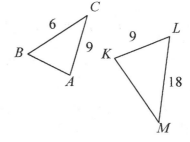

Chapter 8 Closure   What have I learned?

Reflection and Synthesis

The activities below offer you a chance to reflect on what you have learned during this chapter. As you work, look for concepts that you feel very comfortable with, ideas that you would like to learn more about, and topics you need more help with. Look for **connections** between ideas as well as **connections** with material you learned previously.

①   TEAM BRAINSTORM

With your team, brainstorm a list for each of the following three topics. Be as detailed as you can. How long can you make your list? Challenge yourselves. Be prepared to share your team's ideas with the class.

Topics: What have you studied in this chapter? What ideas and words were important in what you learned? Remember to be as detailed as you can.

Problem Solving: What did you do to solve problems? What different strategies did you use?

Connections: How are the topics, ideas, and words that you learned in previous courses are **connected** to the new ideas in this chapter? Again, make your list as long as you can.

② MAKING CONNECTIONS

The following is a list of the vocabulary used in this chapter. The words that appear in bold are new to this chapter. Make sure that you are familiar with all of these words and know what they mean. Refer to the glossary or index for any words that you do not yet understand.

apothem	**arc**	area
central angle	**circumference**	**convex**
diameter	exterior angle	**interior angle**
linear scale factor	**non-convex**	perimeter
pi (π)	polygon	radius
regular polygon	**remote interior angle**	**sector**
similar	zoom factor	

Make a concept map showing all of the **connections** you can find among the key words and ideas listed above. To show a **connection** between two words, draw a line between them and explain the **connection**, as shown in the example below. A word can be **connected** to any other word as long as there is a **justified connection**. For each key word or idea, provide a sketch of an example.

Your teacher may provide you with vocabulary cards to help you get started. If you use the cards to plan your concept map, be sure either to re-draw your concept map on your paper or to glue the vocabulary cards to a poster with all of the **connections** explained for others to see and understand.

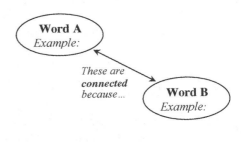

While you are making your map, your team may think of related words or ideas that are not listed above. Be sure to include these ideas on your concept map.

③ SUMMARIZING MY UNDERSTANDING

This section gives you an opportunity to show what you know about certain math topics or ideas. Your teacher will give you directions for exactly how to do this.

This section will help you evaluate which types of problems you have seen with which you feel comfortable and those with which you need more help. This section will appear at the end of every chapter to help you check your understanding. Even if your teacher does not assign this section, it is a good idea to try these problems and find out for yourself what you know and what you need to work on.

Solve each problem as completely as you can. The table at the end of this closure section has answers to these problems. It also tells you where you can find additional help and practice on problems like these.

CL 8-118.

Mrs. Frank loves the clock in her classroom because it has the school colors, green and purple. The shape of the clock is a regular dodecagon with a radius of 14 cm. Centered on the clock's face is a green circle of radius 9 cm. If the region outside the circle is purple, which color has more area?

CL 8-119. Graph the quadrilateral $ABCD$ if $A(-2, 6)$, $B(2, 3)$, $C(2, -2)$, and $D(-2, 1)$.

    a.   What's the best name for this quadrilateral? **Justify** your conclusion.

    b.   Find the area of $ABCD$.

    c.   Find the slope of the diagonals, $\overline{AC}$ and $\overline{BD}$. How are the slopes related?

    d.   Find the point of intersection of the diagonals. What is the relationship between this point and diagonal $\overline{AC}$?

CL 8-120. **Examine** the diagram at right. If M is the midpoint of $\overline{KQ}$ and if $\angle P \cong \angle L$, prove that $\overline{KL} \cong \overline{QP}$.

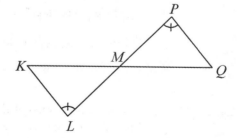

CL 8-121. A running track design is composed of two half circles connected by two straight line segments. Garrett is jogging on the inner lane (with radius r) while Devin is jogging on the outer (with radius R). If $r = 30$ meters and $R = 33$ meters, how much longer does Devin have to run to complete one lap?

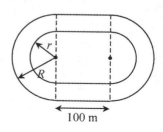

100 m

CL 8-122. Use the relationships in the diagrams below to solve for the given variable. **Justify** your solution with a definition or theorem.

a.

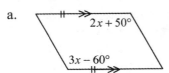

$2x + 50°$

$3x - 60°$

b. The perimeter of the quadrilateral below is 202 units.

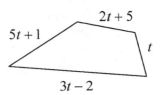

$2t + 5$

$5t + 1$

t

$3t - 2$

c. *CARD* is a rhombus.

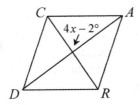

$4x - 2°$

d.

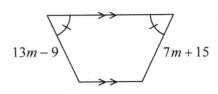

$13m - 9$

$7m + 15$

CL 8-123. Answer the following questions about polygons. If there is not enough information or the problem is impossible, explain why.

a. Find the sum of the interior angles of a dodecagon.

b. Find the number of sides of a regular polygon if its central angle measures 35°.

c. If the sum of the interior angles of a regular polygon is 900°, how many sides does the polygon have?

d. If the exterior angle of a regular polygon is 15°, find its central angle.

e. Find the exterior angle of a polygon with 10 sides.

CL 8-124. Check your answers using the table at the end of the closure section. Which problems do you feel confident about? Which problems were hard? Use the table to make a list of topics you need help on and a list of topics you need to practice more.

⑤ HOW AM I THINKING?

This course focuses on five different **Ways of Thinking**: investigating, examining, reasoning and justifying, visualizing, and choosing a strategy/tool. These are some of the ways in which you think while trying to make sense of a concept or to solve a problem (even outside of math class). During this chapter, you have probably used each Way of Thinking multiple times without even realizing it!

Choose three of these Ways of Thinking that you remember using while working in this chapter. For each Way of Thinking that you choose, show and explain where you used it and how you used it. Describe why thinking in this way helped you solve a particular problem or understand something new. Be sure to include examples to demonstrate your thinking.

Answers and Support for Closure Activity #4
What Have I Learned?

Problem	Solution	Need Help?	More Practice
CL 8-118.	Area of green = $81\pi \approx 254.5$ cm^2; area of purple = $588 - 81\pi \approx 333.5$ cm^2, so the area of purple is greater.	Lessons 5.1.2, 8.1.4, 8.1.5, 8.3.1, and 8.3.2 Math Notes boxes	Problems 8-45, 8-47, 8-48, 8-64, 8-67, 8-77, 8-82, 8-85, 8-92, 8-112
CL 8-119.	a. Rhombus. It is a quadrilateral with four equal sides. b. 20 square units c. The slopes are -2 and $\frac{1}{2}$. They are opposite reciprocals. d. The point of intersection is (0, 2). It is the midpoint of the diagonal.	Lessons 2.2.4, 7.2.3, 7.3.2, and 7.3.3 Math Notes boxes	Problems 7-29, 7-32, 7-69, 7-99, 7-107, 7-109, 7-110, 8-51, 8-89

Problem	Solution	Need Help?	More Practice

CL 8-120.

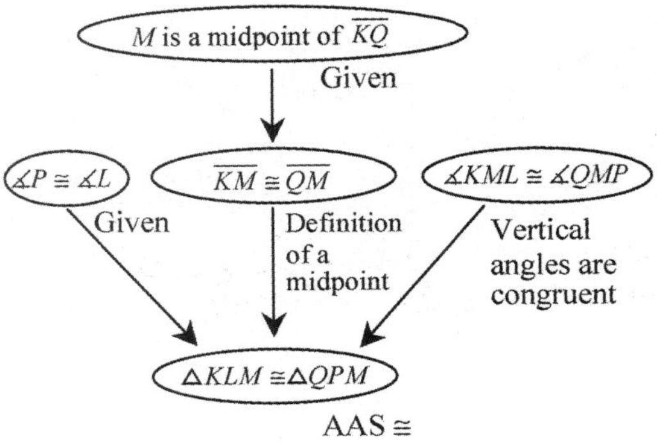

| | | Lessons 3.2.4, 6.1.3, and 7.1.3 Math Notes boxes, problems 7-56 and 7-79 | Problems 7-61, 7-78, 7-85, 7-87, 7-96, 7-104, 7-105, 8-20, 8-28, 8-58, 8-79, 8-88 |

CL 8-121. Devin must run 6π meters farther than Garrett on each lap.

Lessons 8.3.1 and 8.3.2 Math Notes boxes

Problems 8-92, 8-93, 8-102, 8-107, 8-112

CL 8-122.
a. $x = 110°$ (Opposite angles in a parallelogram are equal.)

b. $t = 18$

c. $x = 23°$ (Diagonals of a rhombus are perpendicular.)

d. $m = 4$ (Nonparallel sides of an isosceles trapezoid are congruent.)

Lessons 1.1.3, 2.1.4, 7.2.4, and 8.1.2 Math Notes boxes

Problems 7-16, 7-33, 7-40, 7-49, 7-52, 7-70, 8-6, 8-15, 8-21, 8-55, 8-113

CL 8-123.
a. 1800°

b. Impossible. In a regular polygon, the central angle must be a factor of 360°.

c. 7 sides

d. 15°

e. 36°

Lessons 7.1.4, 8.1.1, and 8.1.4 Math Notes boxes, problems 8-1, 8-13, and 8-14

Problems 8-15, 8-25, 8-29, 8-33, 8-34, 8-35, 8-40, 8-49, 8-55, 8-56, 8-87, 8-99, 8-109

SOLIDS AND CONSTRUCTIONS

9

CHAPTER 9   Solids and Constructions

In your study of geometry so far, you have focused your attention on two-dimensional shapes. You have **investigated** the special properties of triangles, parallelograms, regular polygons and circles, and have developed tools to help you describe and analyze those shapes. For example, you have tools to find an interior angle of a regular hexagon, to calculate the length of the hypotenuse of a right triangle, and to measure the perimeter of a triangle or the area of a circle.

In Section 9.1, you will turn your focus to three-dimensional shapes (called **solids**), such as cubes and cylinders. You will learn several ways to represent three-dimensional solids and develop methods to measure their volume and surface area.

Then, in Section 9.2, you will learn how to use special tools to construct accurate diagrams of two-dimensional shapes and geometric relationships. During this **investigation**, you will revisit many of the geometric conjectures and theorems that you have developed so far.

In this chapter, you will learn:

> How to find the surface area and volume of three-dimensional solids, such as prisms and cylinders.

> How to represent a three-dimensional solid with a mat plan, a net, and side and top views.

> How the volume changes when a three-dimensional solid is enlarged proportionally.

> How to construct familiar geometric shapes (such as a rhombus and a regular hexagon) using construction tools such as tracing paper, a compass and straightedge, and a dynamic geometry tool.

Guiding Questions

Think about these questions throughout this chapter:

How does it change?

How can I represent it?

How can I construct it?

What's the connection?

Is there another way?

Chapter Outline

Section 9.1   This section is devoted to the study of three-dimensional solids and their measurement. You will also learn to use a variety of methods to represent the shapes of solids.

Section 9.2   This section will introduce you to the study of constructing geometric shapes and relationships. For example, you will learn how to construct a perpendicular bisector using only a compass and a straightedge.

9.1.1 How can I build it?

Three-Dimensional Solids

With your knowledge of polygons and circles, you are able to create and explore new, interesting shapes and make elaborate designs such as the one shown in the stained glass window at right. However, in the physical world, the objects we encounter every day are three-dimensional. In other words, physical objects cannot exist entirely on a flat surface, such as a tabletop.

To understand the shapes that you encounter daily, you will need to learn more about how three-dimensional shapes (called **solids**) can be created, described, and measured.

As you work with your team today, be especially careful to explain to your teammates how you "see" each solid. Remember that spatial **visualization** takes time and effort, so be patient with your teammates and help everyone understand how each solid is built.

Reprinted with permission by Rob Mielke, Blue Feather Stained Glass Designs.

9-1.   Using blocks provided by your teacher, work with your team to build the three-dimensional solid at right. Assume that blocks cannot hover in midair. That is, if a block is on the second level, assume that it has a block below it to prop it up.

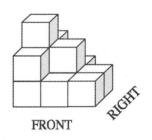

a.   Is there more than one arrangement of blocks that could look like the solid drawn at right? Why or why not?

b.   To avoid confusion, a **mat plan** can be used to show how the blocks are arranged in the solid. The number in each square represents the number of the blocks stacked in that location if you are looking from above. For example, in the lower right-hand corner, the solid is only 1 block tall, so there is a "1" in the corresponding corner of its mat plan. .

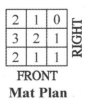

Mat Plan

Verify that the solid your team built matches the solid represented in the mat plan above.

c.   What is the **volume** of the solid? That is, if each block represents a "cubic unit," how many blocks (cubic units) make up this solid?

9-2.   Another way to represent a three-
        dimensional solid is by its **side**
        and **top views**.

        For example, the solid from
        problem 9-1 can also be represented
        by a top, front, and right-hand view,
        as shown at right. Each view shows
        all of the blocks that are visible
        when looking directly at the solid
        from that direction.

        Examine the diagram of
        blocks below. On graph
        paper, draw the front, right,
        and top views of this solid.
        Assume that there are no
        hidden blocks.

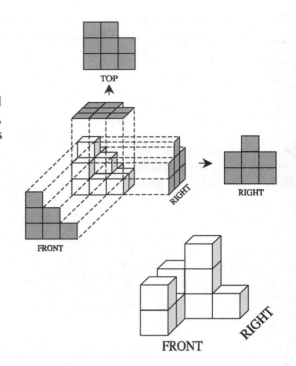

9-3.   For each of the mat plans below:

        • Build the three-dimensional solid with the blocks provided by your teacher.

        • Find the volume of the solid in cubic units.

        • Draw the front, right, and top views of the solid on a piece of graph paper.

a.

0	3	0
2	3	1
0	2	0

RIGHT

FRONT

b.

0	2	1
0	3	0
3	2	1

RIGHT

FRONT

c.

1	1	3
2	1	2
0	0	1

RIGHT

FRONT

9-4.   Meagan built a shape with blocks and then drew
        the views shown at right.

        a.   Build Meagan's shape using blocks
             provided by your teacher. Use as few
             blocks as possible.

        b.   What is the volume of Meagan's shape?

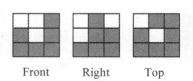

Front   Right   Top

9-5. Draw a mat plan for each of the following solids. There may be more than one possible answer! Then find the possible volumes of each.

a.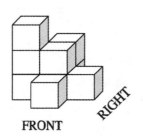

FRONT   RIGHT

b.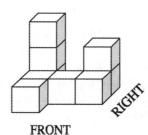

FRONT   RIGHT

9-6. During this lesson, you have found the volume of several three-dimensional solids. However, what *is* volume? What does it measure? Write a Learning Log entry describing volume. Add at least one example. Title this entry "Volume of a Three-Dimensional Shape" and include today's date.

Review & Preview

9-7. **Examine** the solid at right.

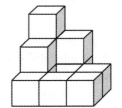

a. On your paper, draw a possible mat plan for this solid.

b. Find the volume of this solid.

9-8. Assume that two figures, *A* and *B*, are similar.

a. If the linear scale factor is $\frac{2}{5}$, then what is the ratio of the areas of *A* and *B*?

b. If the ratio of the perimeters of *A* and *B* is 14:1, what is the ratio of the areas?

c. If the area of *A* is 81 times that of *B*, what is the ratio of the perimeters?

9-9. Find the area of a regular decagon with perimeter 100 units. Show all work.

9-10. The diagram at right shows a circle inscribed in a square. Find the area of the shaded region if the side length of the square is 6 meters.

9-11.   Solve each system of equations below. Write your solution in the form (x, y). Check
         your solution.

   a. $3x - y = 14$

         $x = 2y + 8$

   b. $x = 2y + 2$

         $x = -y - 10$

   c. $16x - y = -4$

         $2x + y = 13$

9-12.   **Multiple Choice:** What information would you need to know
         about the diagram at right in order to prove that
         $\triangle ABD \cong \triangle CBD$ by SAS $\cong$?

   a. $\overline{AD} \cong \overline{CD}$

   b. $\overline{AB} \cong \overline{CB}$

   c. $\angle A \cong \angle C$

   d. $\angle ABD \cong \angle CBD$

   e.   None of these

9.1.2 How can I measure it?

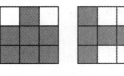

Volume and Surface Area of Prisms

Today you will continue to study three-dimensional solids and will practice representing a solid
using a mat plan and its side and top views. You will also learn a new way to represent a three-
dimensional object, called a **net**. As you work today, you will learn about a special set of solids
called **prisms** and will study how to find the surface area and volume of a prism.

9-13.   The front, top, and right-hand views
         of Heidi's solid are shown at right.

Front   Top   Right

   a.   Build Heidi's solid using blocks
         provided by your teacher. Use the
         smallest number of blocks possible.
         What is the volume of her solid?

   b.   Draw a mat plan for Heidi's solid. Be sure to indicate where the front and right
         sides are located.

   c.   Oh no! Heidi accidentally dropped her entire solid into a bucket of paint!
         What is the **surface area** of her solid? That is, what is the area that is now
         covered in paint?

9-14. So far, you have studied three ways to represent a solid: a three-dimensional drawing, a mat plan, and its side and top views.

Another way to represent a three-dimensional solid is with a **net**, such as the one shown at right. When folded, a net will form the three-dimensional solid it represents.

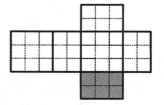

a. With your team, predict what the three-dimensional solid formed by this net will look like. Assume the shaded squares make up the base (or bottom) of the solid.

b. Obtain a Lesson 9.1.2 Resource Page and scissors from your teacher and cut out the net. Fold along the solid lines to create the three-dimensional solid. Did the result confirm your prediction from part (a)?

c. Now build the shape with blocks and complete the mat plan at right for this solid.

d. What is the volume of this solid? How did you get your answer?

e. What is the surface area of the solid? How did you find your answer? Be prepared to share any shortcuts with the class.

9-15. Paul built a tower by stacking six identical layers of the shape at right on top of each other.

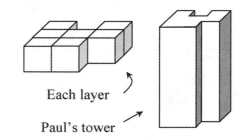

Each layer

Paul's tower

a. What is the volume of his tower? How can you tell without building the shape?

b. What is the surface area of his tower?

c. Paul's tower is an example of a **prism** because it is a solid and two of its faces (called **bases**) are congruent and parallel. A prism must also have sides that connect the bases (called **lateral faces**). Each lateral face must be a parallelogram.

For each of the prisms below, find the volume and surface area.

(1) 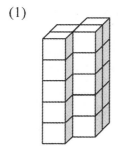 (2) 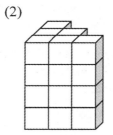 (3)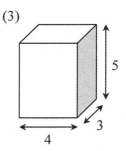

9-16.   Heidi created several more solids, represented below. Find the volume of each one.

a.

0	3	5
22	10	25
18	15	8
16	12	0

RIGHT

FRONT

b.

c.

9-17.   Pilar built a tower by stacking identical layers on top of each other. If her tower used a total of 312 blocks and if the bottom layer has 13 blocks, how tall is her tower? Explain how you know.

9-18.   What is the relationship between the area of the base of a prism, its height, and its volume? In a Learning Log entry, summarize how to find the volume of a solid. Be sure to include an example. Title this entry "Finding Volume" and include today's date.

METHODS AND MEANINGS

Polyhedra and Prisms

MATH NOTES

A closed three-dimensional solid that has flat, polygonal faces is called a **polyhedron**. The plural of polyhedron is **polyhedra**. "Poly" is the Greek root for "many," and "hedra" is the Greek root for "faces."

A **prism** is a special type of polyhedron. It must have two congruent, parallel **bases** that are polygons. Also, its **lateral faces** (the faces connecting the bases) are parallelograms formed by connecting the corresponding vertices of the two bases. Note that lateral faces may be any type of parallelogram, such as rectangles, rhombi, or squares.

height

Two congruent and parallel bases

9-19. Mr. Wallis is designing a home. He found the plan for his dream house on the Internet and printed it out on paper.

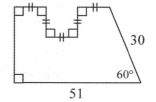

a. The design of the home is shown at right. If all measurements are in millimeters, find the area of the diagram.

b. Mr. Wallis took his home design to the copier and enlarged it 400%. What is the area of the diagram now? Show how you know.

9-20. At right is the solid from problem 9-7.

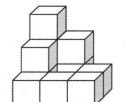

a. On graph paper, draw the front, right, and top views.

b. Find the total surface area of the solid.

9-21. Review what you know about the angles of polygons below.

a. If the exterior angle of a polygon is 29°, what is the interior angle?

b. If the interior angle of a polygon is 170°, can it be a regular polygon? Why or why not?

c. Find the sum of the interior angles of a regular 29-gon.

9-22. For each geometric relationship represented below, write and solve an equation for x. Show all work.

a.

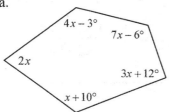

b.

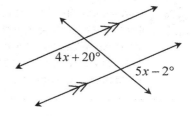

9-23. On graph paper, graph $\triangle ABC$ if $A(-3, -4)$, $B(-1, -6)$, and $C(-5, -8)$.

    a.   What is AB (the length of $\overline{AB}$)?

    b.   Reflect $\triangle ABC$ across the x-axis to form $\triangle A'B'C'$. What are the coordinates of B'?

    c.   Rotate $\triangle A'B'C'$ 90° clockwise (↻) about the origin to form $\triangle A''B''C''$. What are the coordinates of C''?

    d.   Translate $\triangle ABC$ so that $(x,y) \rightarrow (x+5, y+1)$. What are the new coordinates of point A?

9-24.   **Multiple Choice:** Find the perimeter of the sector at right.

    a. 12π units   b. 3π units   c. $6 + 3\pi$ units

    d. $12 + \pi$ units   e.   None of these

9.1.3 What if the bases are not rectangles?

Prisms and Cylinders

In Lessons 9.1.1 and 9.1.2, you **investigated** volume, surface area, and special three-dimensional solids called prisms. Today you will explore different ways to find the volume and surface area of a prism and a related solid called a cylinder. You will also consider what happens to the volume of a prism or cylinder if it slants to one side or if it is enlarged proportionally.

9-25.   **Examine** the three-dimensional solid at right.

    a.   On graph paper, draw a net that, when folded, will create this solid.

    b.   Compare your net with those of your teammates. Is there more than one possible net? Why or why not?

    c.   Find the surface area and volume of this solid.

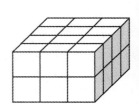

9-26. **SPECIAL PRISMS**

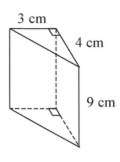

3 cm

4 cm

9 cm

The prism in problem 9-25 is an example of a **rectangular prism**, because its bases are rectangular. Similarly, the prism at right is called a **triangular prism** because the two congruent bases are triangular.

a. Carefully draw the prism at right onto your paper. One way to do this is to draw the two triangular bases first and then to connect the corresponding vertices of the bases. Notice that hidden edges are represented with dashed lines.

b. Find the surface area of the triangular prism. Remember that the surface area includes the areas of <u>all</u> surfaces – the sides and the bases. Carefully organize your work and verify your solution with your teammates.

c. Find the volume of the triangular prism. Be prepared to share your team's method with the class.

d. Does your method for finding surface area and volume work on other prisms? For example, what if the bases are hexagonal, like the one shown at right? Work with your team to find the surface area and volume of this hexagonal prism. Assume that the bases are regular hexagons with side length 4 inches.

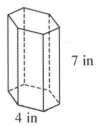

7 in

4 in

9-27. **CYLINDERS**

Carter wonders, "*What if the bases are circular?*"

a. Copy the **cylinder** at right onto your paper. Discuss with your team how to find its surface area and volume if the radius of the base is 5 units and the height of the cylinder is 8 units.

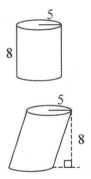

5

8

5

8

b. Now Carter wants to figure out what happens to the volume of a cylinder when it slants as shown in the diagram at right. When the lateral faces of a prism or cylinder are not perpendicular to its base, the solid is referred to as an **oblique** cylinder or prism.

With your team, discuss whether the volume of the cylinder will increase, decrease or stay the same when the prism or cylinder is slanted. Assume that the radius and height of the cylinder do not change. When you agree, explain your answer on your paper. Be sure to provide **reasons** for your statements.

9-28. Hernando needs to replace the hot water tank at his house. He estimates that his family needs a tank that can heat at least 75 gallons of water. His local water tank supplier has a cylindrical model that has a diameter of 2 feet and a height of 3 feet. If 1 gallon of water is approximately 0.1337 cubic feet, determine if the supplier's tank will provide enough water.

METHODS AND MEANINGS

Volume and Total Surface Area of a Solid

Volume measures the size of a three-dimensional space enclosed within an object. It is expressed as the number of 1x1x1 cubes (or parts of cubes) that fit inside a solid.

For example, the solid shown at right has a volume of 6 cubic units.

Since volume reflects the number of cubes that fit within a solid, it is measured in **cubic units**. For example, if the dimensions of a solid are measured in feet, then the volume would be measured in cubic feet (a cube with dimensions 1' x 1' x 1').

1 ft.
1 ft.
1 ft.

On the other hand, the **total surface area** of a solid is the area of all of the external faces of the solid. For example, the total surface area of the solid above is 24 square units.

Review & Preview

9-29. In the diagram at right, $\overline{DE}$ is a midsegment of $\triangle ABC$. If the area of $\triangle ABC$ is 96 square units, what is the area of $\triangle ADE$?

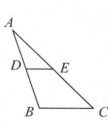

9-30. Draw a rectangular prism as neatly as possible on your paper. If the width is 9 cm, the height is 14 cm, and the depth is 7 cm, find the surface area and volume.

9-31. Are $\triangle EHF$ and $\triangle FGE$ congruent? If so, explain how you know. If not, explain why not.

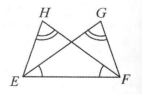

9-32. Remember that the absolute value of a number is its positive value. For example, $|-5|=5$ and $|5|=5$. Use this understanding to solve the equations below, if possible. If there is no solution, explain how you know.

    a. $|x|=6$ b. $|x|=-2$ c. $|x+7|=10$

9-33. Cindy's cylindrical paint bucket has a diameter of 12 inches and a height of 14.5 inches. If 1 gallon ≈ 231 in^3, how many gallons does her paint bucket hold?

9-34. **Multiple Choice:** Which ratio below is the best approximation of the ratio between the circumference of a circle and its diameter?

    a.   2   b.   3

    c.   4   d.   6

9.1.4 How does the volume change?

Volumes of Similar Solids

As you continue your study of three-dimensional solids, you will explore how the volume of a solid changes as the solid is enlarged proportionally.

9-35. HOW DOES THE VOLUME CHANGE?

    In Lesson 9.1.3, you began a study of the surface area and volume of similar solids. Today, you will continue that **investigation** in order to generalize about the ratios of similar solids.

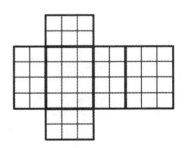

    a.   Describe the solid formed by the net at right. What are its dimensions (its length, width, and height)?

    b.   Have each team member select a different enlargement ratio from the list below. On graph paper, carefully draw the net of a similar solid using your enlargement ratio. Then cut out your net and build the solid (so that the gridlines end up on the outside the solid) using scissors and tape.

        (1) 1   (2) 2   (3) 3   (4) 4

Problem continues on next page →

9-35.   *Problem continued from previous page.*

c.   Find the volume of your solid and compare it to the volume of the original solid. What is the ratio of these volumes? Share the results with your teammates so that each person can complete a table like the one below.

Linear Scale Factor	Original Volume	New Volume	Ratio of Volumes
1			
2			
3			
4			
r			

d.   How does the volume change when a three-dimensional solid is enlarged or reduced to create a similar solid? For example, if a solid's length, width, and depth are enlarged by a zoom factor of 10, then how many times bigger does the volume get? What if the solid is enlarged by a zoom factor of *r*? Explain.

9-36.   **Examine** the 1x1x3 solid at right.

a.   Build this solid with blocks provided by your teacher.

b.   If this shape is enlarged by a linear scale factor of 2, how wide will the new shape be? How tall? How deep?

c.   How many of the 1x1x3 solids would you need to build the enlargement described in part (b) above? Use blocks to prove your answer.

d.   What if the 1x1x3 solid is enlarged with a linear scale factor of 3? How many times larger would the volume of the new solid be? Explain how you found your answer.

9-37.      At the movies, Maurice counted the number of kernels of popcorn that filled his tub and found that it had 316 kernels. He decided that next time, he will get an enlarged tub that is similar, but has a linear scale factor of 1.5. How many kernels of popcorn should the enlarged tub hold?

9-38.   In your Learning Log, explain how the volume changes when a solid is enlarged proportionally. That is, if a three-dimensional object is enlarged by a zoom factor of 2, by what factor does the volume increase? Title this entry "Volumes of Similar Solids" and include today's date.

9-39. Koy is inflating a spherical balloon for her brother's birthday party. She has used three full breaths so far and her balloon is only half the width she needs. Assuming that she puts the same amount of air into the balloon with each breath, how many more breaths does she need to finish the task? Explain how you know.

9-40. Draw a cylinder on your paper. Assume the radius of the cylinder is 6 inches and the height is 9 inches.

   a. What is the surface area of the cylinder? What is the volume?

   b. If the cylinder is enlarged with a linear scale factor of 3, what is the volume of the enlarged cylinder? How do you know?

9-41. While Katarina was practicing her figure skating, she wondered how far she had traveled. She was skating a "figure 8," which means she starts between two circles and then travels on the boundary of each circle, completing the shape of an "8." If both circles have a radius of 5 feet, how far does she travel when skating one "figure 8"?

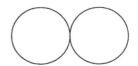

9-42. For each triangle below, solve for x, if possible. If no solution is possible, explain why.

   a.
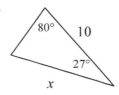

   b.
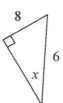

   c.
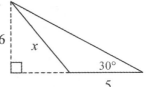

9-43. The graph of the inequality $y > 2x - 3$ is shown at right. On graph paper, graph the inequality $y \le 2x - 3$. Explain what you changed about the graph.

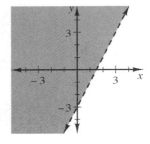

9-44. **Multiple Choice:** The point $A(-2, 5)$ is rotated 90° counter-clockwise (↺). What are the new coordinates of point A?

   a. (2, 5)   b. (5, −2)   c. (2, −5)   d. (−5, −2)

9.1.5 How does the volume change?

Ratios of Similarity

Today, work with your team to analyze the following problems. As you work, think about whether the problem involves volume or area. Also think carefully about how similar solids are related to each other.

9-45. A statue to honor Benjamin Franklin will be placed outside the entry to the Liberty Bell exhibit hall. The designers decide that a smaller, similar version will be placed on a table inside the building. The dimensions of the life-size statue will be four times those of the smaller statue. Planners expect to need 1.5 pints of paint to coat the small statue. They also know that the small statue will weigh 14 pounds.

a. How many pints of paint will be needed to paint the life-size statue?

b. If the small statue is made of the same material as the enlarged statue, then its weight will change just as the volume changes as the statue is enlarged. How much will the life-size statue weigh?

9-46.

The Blackbird Oil Company is considering the purchase of 20 new jumbo oil storage tanks. The standard model holds 12,000 gallons. Its dimensions are $\frac{4}{5}$ the size of the similarly shaped jumbo model, that is, the ratio of the dimensions is 4:5.

a. How much more storage capacity would the purchase of the twenty jumbo models give Blackbird Oil?

b. If jumbo tanks cost 50% more than standard tanks, which tank is a better buy?

9-47. In problem 7-13, your class constructed a large tetrahedron like the one at right. Assume the dimensions of the shaded tetrahedron at right are half of the dimensions of the similar enlarged tetrahedron.

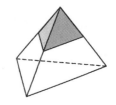

a. If the volume of the large tetrahedron is 138 in³, find the volume of the small shaded tetrahedron.

b. Each face of a tetrahedron is an equilateral triangle. If the small shaded tetrahedron has an edge length of 16 cm, find the total surface area of the both tetrahedra.

c. Your class tried to construct a tetrahedron using four smaller congruent tetrahedra. However, the result left a gap in the center, as shown in the diagram at right. If the volume of each small shaded tetrahedron is 50 in³, what is the volume of the gap? Explain how you know.

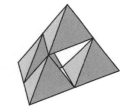

Methods and Meanings

MATH NOTES

The $r : r^2 : r^3$ Ratios of Similarity

When a two-dimensional figure is enlarged proportionally, its perimeter and area also grow. If the linear scale factor is r, then the perimeter of the figure is enlarged by a factor of r while the area of the figure is enlarged by a factor of r^2. Examine what happens when the square at right is enlarged by a linear scale factor of 3.

$P = 4$ un $P = 4 \cdot 3 = 12$ un
$A = 1$ un² $A = 1 \cdot 3^2 = 9$ un²

When a solid is enlarged proportionally, its surface area and volume also grow. If it is enlarged by a linear scale factor of r, then the surface area grows by a factor of r^2 and the volume grows by a factor of r^3. The example at right shows what happens to a solid when it is enlarged by a linear scale factor of 2.

Original solid   Width, height,   **Result:**
SA = 14 un²   and depth are   SA = 56 un²
V = 3 un³   doubled   V = 24 un³

Thus, if a solid is enlarged proportionally by a linear scale factor of r, then:

New edge length = $r \cdot$ (corresponding edge length of original solid)

New surface area = $r^2 \cdot$ (original surface area)

New volume = $r^3 \cdot$ (original volume)

9-48. Consider the two similar solids at right.

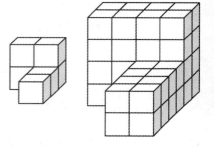

a. What is the linear scale factor?

b. Find the surface area of each solid. What is the ratio of the surface areas? How is this ratio related to the linear scale factor?

c. Now find the volumes of each solid. How are the volumes related? Compare this to the linear scale factor and record your observations.

9-49. Elliot has a modern fish tank that is in the shape of an oblique prism, shown at right. If the slant of the prism makes a 60° angle, find the volume of water the tank can hold. Assume all measurements are in inches.

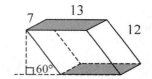

9-50. Decide if the following statements are true or false. If they are true, explain how you know. If they are false, provide a counterexample.

a. If a quadrilateral has two sides that are parallel and two sides that are congruent, then the quadrilateral must be a parallelogram.

b. If the interior angles of a polygon add up to 360°, then the polygon must be a quadrilateral.

c. If a quadrilateral has 3 right angles, then the quadrilateral must be a rectangle.

d. If the diagonals of a quadrilateral bisect each other, then the quadrilateral must be a rhombus.

9-51. Write and solve an equation based on the geometric relationship shown at right.

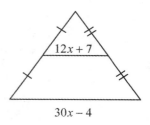

9-52. Solve each equation below. Check your solution.

a. $20 - 6(5 + 2x) = 10 - 2x$

b. $2x^2 - 9x - 5 = 0$

c. $\frac{3}{5x-1} = \frac{1}{x+1}$

d. $|2x - 1| = 5$

9-53. **Multiple Choice:** For $\angle ABE \cong \angle BEF$ in the diagram at right, what must be true?

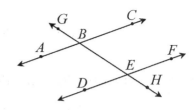

a. $\angle ABE \cong \angle BED$

b. $\angle ABE \cong \angle GBC$

c. $\overline{AC} \parallel \overline{GH}$

d. $\overline{AC} \parallel \overline{DF}$

e. None of these.

9.2.1 How can I construct it?

Introduction to Construction

So far in this course, you have used tools such as rulers, tracing paper, templates, protractors, and even computers to draw geometric relationships and shapes. But how did ancient mathematicians accurately construct shapes such as squares or equilateral triangles without these types of tools?

Today you will start by exploring how to construct several geometric relationships and figures with tracing paper. You will then **investigate** how to construct geometric shapes with tools called a compass and a straightedge, much like the ancient Greeks did over 2000 years ago. As you study these forms of **construction**, you will not only learn about new geometric tools, but also gain a deeper understanding of some of the special geometric relationships and shapes you have studied so far in this course.

9-54. CONSTRUCTING WITH TRACING PAPER

To start this focus on construction, you will begin with a familiar tool: tracing paper. Obtain several sheets of tracing paper and a straightedge from your teacher. Note: A straightedge is *not* a ruler. It does not have any markings or measurements on it. A 3x5 index card makes a good straightedge.

a. Starting with a smooth, square piece of tracing paper, find a way to create parallel lines (or creases). Make sure the lines are *exactly* parallel. Be ready to share with the class how you accomplished this.

b. On a new piece of tracing paper, trace line segment $\overline{AB}$ at right. Use your straightedge for accuracy. Can you fold the tracing paper so that the resulting crease not only finds the midpoint of $\overline{AB}$ but also is perpendicular to $\overline{AB}$? (This is called a **perpendicular bisector**.) Again, be ready to share your method.

Problem continues on next page →

9-54.   *Problem continued from previous page.*

   c.   On the perpendicular bisector from part (b) above, choose a point C and then connect $\overline{AC}$ and $\overline{BC}$ to form $\triangle ABC$. What type of triangle did you construct? Use your geometry knowledge to **justify** your answer.

   d.   In part (b), you figured out how to use tracing paper and a straightedge to construct a line that bisects another line. How can you construct an angle bisector?

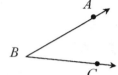

On a piece of tracing paper, trace $\angle ABC$ at right. Construct an angle bisector. That is, find $\overline{BD}$ so that $\angle ABD \cong \angle CBD$.

9-55.   CONSTRUCTING WITH A COMPASS AND A STRAIGHTEDGE

Producing a geometric shape with a compass and a straightedge is another form of **construction**. Obtain a Lesson 9.2.1 Resource Page from your teacher (or download from www.cpm.org) and explore what types of shapes you can construct using these tools.

   a.   Find point C on the resource page. Use your compass to construct two circles with different radii that have a center at point C. (Note: Circles that have the same center are called **concentric** circles.)

   b.   With tracing paper, copying a line segment means just putting the tracing paper over the line and tracing it. But how can you copy a line using only a compass and a straightedge?

On the resource page, find $\overline{AB}$. Next to $\overline{AB}$, use your straightedge to draw a new line. With your team, decide how to use the compass to mark off two points (C and D) so that $\overline{AB} \cong \overline{CD}$. Be ready to share your method with the class.

   c.   Now construct a new line segment, labeled $\overline{EF}$, that is twice as long as $\overline{AB}$. How can you be sure that $\overline{EF}$ is twice as long as $\overline{AB}$?

9-56.   In problem 9-55, you learned how to use a compass and a straightedge to copy a line segment. But how can you use these tools to copy an angle? On your Lesson 9.2.1 Resource Page, find $\angle X$. With your team, discuss how you can construct a new angle ($\angle Y$) that is congruent to $\angle X$. If you need help, use parts (a) through (c) below to guide you.

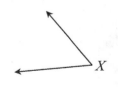

   a.   On the resource page, draw a ray with endpoint Y.

   b.   With your compass point at X, draw an arc that intersects both sides of $\angle X$. Now draw an arc with the same radius and with center Y.

Problem continues on next page →

9-56.   *Problem continued from previous page.*

    c.   How can you use your compass to measure the "width" of ∡*X*? Discuss this with your teammates and then determine how to complete ∡*Y*. Be ready to share your method with the class.

9-57.   REGULAR HEXAGON

As Shui was completing her homework, she noticed that a regular hexagon has a special quality: when dissected into congruent triangles, the hexagon contains triangles that are all equilateral! "I bet I can use this fact to help me construct a regular hexagon," she told her team.

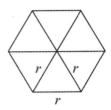

    a.   On the Lesson 9.2.1 Resource Page, construct a circle with radius *r* and center *H*.

    b.   Mark one point on the circle to be a starting vertex. Since each side of the hexagon has length *r*, the radius of the circle, carefully use the compass to mark off the other vertices of the hexagon on the circle. Then connect the vertices to create the regular hexagon.

    c.   When all vertices of a polygon lie on the same circle, the polygon is called **inscribed**. For example, the hexagon you constructed in part (b) is inscribed in ⊙*H*. After consulting with your teammates, construct an equilateral triangle that is also inscribed in ⊙*H*. You may want to use colored markers or pencils to help distinguish between the hexagon and the triangle.

Review & Preview

9-58.   **Examine** the diagram of *ABCD* at right.

    a.   If opposite sides of the quadrilateral are parallel and all sides are congruent, what type of quadrilateral is *ABCD*?

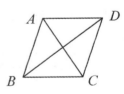

    b.   List what you know about the diagonals of *ABCD*.

    c.   Find the area of *ABCD* if *BC* = 8 and *m*∡*ABC* = 60°.

9-59.   For a rectangular prism with base dimensions 3 cm and 5 cm and height 8 cm:

   a.   Sketch the prism on your paper.

   b.   Find the volume of the prism.

   c.   Find the surface area of the prism.

9-60.   Use the relationships given in the diagram at
         right to write and solve an equation for x.
         Show all work.

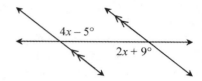

9-61.   For each pair of triangles below, determine if the triangles are congruent. If they are
         congruent, state the congruence property that assures their congruence and write a
         congruence statement (such as $\triangle ABC \cong \triangle$ _____).

   a.   b.   c.

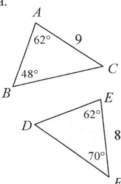

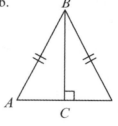

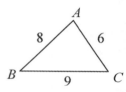

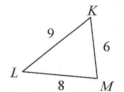

9-62.   Write the equation represented by the table below.

IN (x)	−4	−3	−2	−1	0	1	2	3	4
OUT (y)	−26	−20	−14	−8	−2	4	10	16	22

9-63.   **Multiple Choice:** Which net below will not produce a closed cube?

   a.   b.   c.   d.

9.2.2 How can I construct it?

Constructing Bisectors

During Lesson 9.2.1, you studied how to construct geometric relationships such as congruent line segments using tools that include a compass and tracing paper. But what other geometric relationships and shapes can we construct using these tools? Today, as you **investigate** new ways to construct familiar geometric figures, look for connections to previous course material.

9-64.   INTERSECTING CIRCLES

As Ventura was doodling with his compass, he drew the diagram at right.

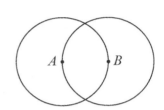

a.   Explain why ⊙A and ⊙B must have the same radius.

b.   On the Lesson 9.2.2 Resource Page provided by your teacher, construct two intersecting circles so that each passes through the other's center. Label the centers A and B.

c.   On your construction, locate the two points where the circles intersect each other. Label these points C and D. Then construct quadrilateral ACBD. What type of quadrilateral is ACBD? **Justify** your answer.

d.   Use what you know about the diagonals of ACBD to describe the relationship of $\overline{AB}$ and $\overline{CD}$. Make as many statements as you can.

9-65.   In problem 9-64, you constructed a rhombus and a perpendicular bisector.

a.   In your own words, describe how this process works. That is, given any line segment, how can you find its midpoint? How can you find a line perpendicular to it? Be sure to **justify** your statements.

b.   Test that your directions in part (a) work for line $\overline{KM}$ on the Lesson 9.2.2 Resource Page. In other words, construct a perpendicular bisector of $\overline{KM}$. Label the midpoint of $\overline{KM}$ point N.

c.   Return to your work from part (b) and use it to construct a 45°- 45°- 90° triangle. Prove that your triangle must be isosceles.

9-66.   In problem 9-64, you used the fact that the diagonals of a rhombus are perpendicular bisectors of each other to develop a construction. In fact, most constructions are rooted in the properties of many of the geometric shapes you have studied so far. A rhombus can help us with another important construction.

a.   **Examine** the rhombus *ABCD* at right. What is the relationship between $\angle ABC$ and $\overline{BD}$?

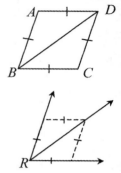

b.   Since the diagonals of a rhombus bisect the angles, use this relationship to construct an angle bisector of $\angle R$ on the resource page. That is, construct a rhombus so that *R* is one of its vertices. Use only a compass, a straightedge, and a pencil.

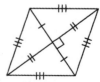

9-67.   CONSTRUCTION CHALLENGE

On the Lesson 9.2.2 Resource Page, locate $\overline{PQ}$, $\overline{ST}$, and $\angle V$. In the space provided, use the construction **strategies** you have developed so far to construct a triangle with legs congruent to $\overline{PQ}$ and $\overline{ST}$, with an angle congruent to $\angle V$ in between. Be sure you know how to do this two ways: with a compass and a straightedge and with tracing paper.

METHODS AND MEANINGS

Rhombus Facts

Review what you have previously learned about a rhombus below.

A **rhombus** is a quadrilateral with four equal sides. All rhombi (the plural of rhombus) are parallelograms.

The diagonals of a rhombus are perpendicular bisectors of each other. That is, they intersect each other at their midpoints and form right angles at that point. Examine these relationships in the diagram at right.

9-68.   Unlike a straightedge, a ruler has measurement markings. With a ruler, it is fairly simple to construct a line segment of length 6 cm or a line segment with length 3 inches. But how can we construct a line segment of $\sqrt{2} \approx 1.414213562...$ centimeters? Consider this as you answer the questions below.

   a.   With a ruler, construct a line segment of 1 cm.

   b.   What about 1.4 cm? Adjust your line segment from part (a) so that its length is 1.4 cm. Did your line get longer or shorter?

   c.   Now change the line segment so that its length is 1.41 cm. How did it change?

   d.   Karen wants to continue this process until her line segment is exactly $\sqrt{2} \approx 1.414213562...$ centimeters long. What do you think will happen?

9-69.   The floor plan of Marina's local drug store is shown at right. While shopping one day, Marina tied her dog, Mutt, to the building at point F. If Mutt's leash is 4 meters long and all measurements in the diagram are in meters, what is the area that Mutt can roam? Draw a diagram and show all work.

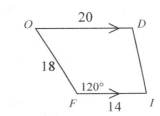

9-70.   Find the area of the Marina's drugstore (*FIDO*) in problem 9-69. Show all work.

9-71.   Given the information in the diagram at right, prove that $\angle C \cong \angle D$. Write your proof using any format studied so far.

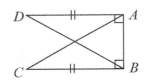

9-72.   Which has greater measure: an exterior angle of an equilateral triangle or an interior angle of a regular heptagon (7-gon)? Show all work.

9-73.   **Multiple Choice:** A solid with a volume of 26 in³ was enlarged to create a similar solid with a volume of 702 in³. What is the linear scale factor between the two solids?

   a.   1   b.   2   c.   3   d.   4

9.2.3 How do I construct it?

More Exploration with Constructions

So far, several geometric relationships and properties have helped you develop constructions using a compass and a straightedge. For example, constructing a rhombus helped you construct an angle bisector. Constructing intersecting circles helped you construct a perpendicular bisector. What other relationships can help you develop constructions?

Today you will review some of your triangle knowledge to **investigate** how to construct congruent triangles and special triangles, such as 30°- 60°- 90° triangles. You'll also find a way to construct a line segment with a seemingly impossible length!

In Lesson 9.2.2, you developed a method to construct a rhombus within a given angle. This not only allowed you to construct an angle bisector, but it also helped you construct parallel lines, since the opposite sides of a rhombus are parallel. Today you will explore how to use your parallel line conjectures to construct a line parallel to a given line through a point not on the line.

9-74. Find △*ABC* on the Lesson 9.2.3 Resource Page provided by your teacher.

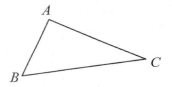

a. Using a compass and a straightedge, construct △*DEF* so that △*DEF* ≅ △*ABC*. Share construction ideas with your teammates.

b. Are there other ways to copy a triangle with a compass and a straightedge? Brainstorm as many ways as you can with your team. Be ready to share your ideas with the class.

9-75. Consider what you know about all 30°- 60°- 90° triangles.

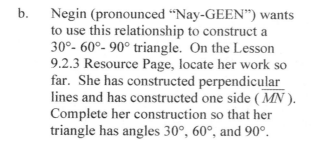

a. Using the information in the triangle at right, how long is the hypotenuse? Explain how you know.

b. Negin (pronounced "Nay-GEEN") wants to use this relationship to construct a 30°- 60°- 90° triangle. On the Lesson 9.2.3 Resource Page, locate her work so far. She has constructed perpendicular lines and has constructed one side ($\overline{MN}$). Complete her construction so that her triangle has angles 30°, 60°, and 90°.

9-76.   CONSTRUCTING AN IRRATIONAL LENGTH

Revisit your work from problem 9-68 from homework.

a.   Explain why you cannot construct a line segment of exactly length $\sqrt{2} \approx 1.414213562...$ with a ruler.

b.   The number $\sqrt{2}$ is known as an **irrational number** because it cannot be represented as a fraction of two integers. One way to spot an irrational number is by looking at its decimal form. Irrational numbers have decimal numbers that never repeat and "go on forever" (meaning they never terminate, like $\frac{1}{2} = 0.5$ or $\frac{3}{8} = 0.375$ do).

Negin thinks that a right triangle may be able to help her construct a line segment of length $\sqrt{2}$ units. First find two lengths of the legs of a right triangle that will have a hypotenuse of $\sqrt{2}$ units. Then, on your Lesson 9.2.3 Resource Page, construct a right triangle with these dimensions.

9-77.   CONSTRUCTING PARALLEL LINES

So far, you have used geometric concepts such as triangle congruence and the special properties of a rhombus to create constructions. How can angle relationships formed by parallel lines help with construction? Consider this as you answer the questions below.

a.   **Examine** the diagram at right. If $l \parallel m$, what do you know about $\angle a$ and $\angle b$? $\angle a$ and $\angle c$? **Justify** your answer.

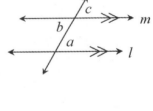

b.   Negin thinks that angle relationships can help her construct a line parallel to another line through a given point not on the line. On the Lesson 9.2.3 Resource Page, find line l and point P. Help Negin construct a line parallel to l through point P by first constructing a transversal through point P that intersects line l.

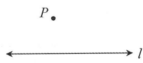

c.   If you have not already done so, complete Negin's construction by copying an angle formed by the transversal and line l. Explain how you used alternate interior angles or corresponding angles.

9-78.   Negin started to construct a parallel line with tracing paper
         but got off-task. She started by tracing line *l* and point *P*
         on her tracing paper, as shown in the diagram at right.
         While experimenting, she folded the tracing paper so that
         line *l* passed through point *P*. After creating a crease, she
         unfolded the tracing paper and then folded it again at a
         different place so that line *l* still passed through point *P*.
         She continued this process until she had over 20 creases
         on her tracing paper!

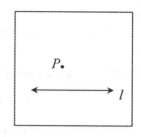

   a.   With your team, predict what shape the creases created.

   b.   With your own tracing paper, recreate Negin's experiment. First draw a line *l*
         and a point *P* that is not on the line, as shown above. Then fold the tracing
         paper as described above so that each fold causes line *l* to pass through point *P*
         at a different point on line *l*. What shape emerged?

METHODS AND MEANINGS

MATH NOTES

Constructing a Perpendicular Bisector

A perpendicular bisector of a given segment can be constructed using
tracing paper or using a compass and a straightedge.

With tracing paper: To construct a perpendicular bisector with tracing
paper, first copy the line segment onto the tracing paper. Then fold the
tracing paper so that the endpoints coincide (so that they lie on top of each
other). When the paper is unfolded, the resulting crease is the perpendicular
bisector of the line segment.

With a compass and a straightedge: One
way to construct a perpendicular bisector with
a compass and a straightedge is to construct a
circle at each endpoint of the line segment
with a radius equal to the length of the line
segment. Then use the straightedge to draw a
line through the two points where the circles
intersect. This line will be the perpendicular
bisector of the line segment.

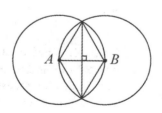

9-79.   **Examine** the mat plan of a three-dimensional solid at right.

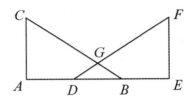

6	0	0
3	0	1
2	6	6

FRONT

Mat Plan

   a.   On your paper, draw the front, right, and top views of this solid.

   b.   Find the volume of the solid.

   c.   If the length of each edge of the solid is divided by 2, what will the new volume be? Show how you got your answer.

9-80.   **Examine** the diagram at right. Given that $\triangle ABC \cong \triangle EDF$, prove that $\triangle DBG$ is isosceles. Use any format of proof that you prefer.

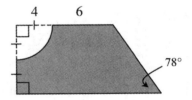

9-81.   The Portland Zoo is building a new children's petting zoo. One of the designs being considered is shown at right (the shaded portion). If the measurements are in meters, find:

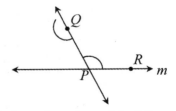

   a.   The area of the petting zoo.

   b.   The length of fence needed to enclose the petting zoo area.

9-82.   Sylvia has 14 coins, all nickels and quarters. If the value of the coins is $2.90, how many of each type of coin does she have? Explain your method.

9-83.   West High School has a math building in the shape of a regular polygon. When Mrs. Woods measured an interior angle of the polygon (which was in her classroom), she got 135°. How many sides does the math building have? Show how you got your answer.

9-84.   **Multiple Choice:** Jamila has started to construct a line parallel to line m through point Q at right. Which of the possible **strategies** below make the most sense to help her find the line parallel to m through point Q?

   a.   Measure $\angle QPR$ with a protractor.

   b.   Use the compass to measure the arc centered at P, then place the point of the compass where the arc centered at Q meets $\overline{QP}$, and mark that measure off on the arc.

   c.   Construct $\overline{QR}$.

   d.   Measure PR with a ruler.

9.2.4 What more can I construct?

· ·

Finding a Centroid

So far in this section, you have developed a basic library of constructions that can help create many of the geometric shapes and relationships you have studied in Chapters 1 through 8. For example, you can construct a rhombus, an isosceles triangle, a right triangle, a regular hexagon, and an equilateral triangle.

As you continue your **investigation** of geometric constructions today, keep in mind the following focus questions:

What geometric principles or properties can I use?

Why does it work?

Is there another way?

9-85.   TEAM CHALLENGE

Albert has a neat trick. Given any triangle, he can place it on the tip of his pencil and it balances on his first try! The whole class wonders, "How does he do it?"

Your Task: Construct a triangle and find its point of balance. This point, called a **centroid**, is special not only because it is the center of balance, but also because it is where the **medians** of the triangle meet. Read more about medians of a triangle in the Math Notes box for this lesson and then follow the directions below.

a.   After reading about medians and centroids in the Math Notes box for this lesson, draw a large triangle on a piece of unlined paper provided by your teacher. (Note: Your team will work together on one triangle.)

b.   Working together, carefully construct the three medians and locate the centroid of the triangle.

c.   Once your team is convinced that your centroid is accurate, glue the paper to a piece of cardstock or cardboard provided by your teacher. Carefully cut out the triangle and demonstrate that your centroid is, in fact, the center of balance of your triangle! Good luck!

9-86. CONSTRUCTING OTHER GEOMETRIC SHAPES

On a plain, unlined piece of paper, use a compass and a straightedge to construct a kite. Remember that a kite is defined as a quadrilateral with two pairs of adjacent, congruent sides. Be prepared to explain to the class how you constructed your kite.

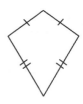

9-87. In Lesson 9.2.3, you figured out how to construct a triangle congruent to a given triangle. However, what if you are not given the triangle and are instead given only its side lengths?

1 unit

a. On a plain, unlined piece of paper, use a compass and a straightedge to construct a triangle that has side lengths 3, 4, and 5 units. Note that the length of 1 unit is provided above.

b. What kind of triangle did you construct? **Justify** your conclusion.

9-88. Albert wants to construct a triangle with side lengths 2, 3, and 6 units. On a plain, unlined piece of paper, use a compass and a straightedge to construct Albert's triangle. Use the unit length provided below. Explain to him what happened.

1 unit

METHODS AND MEANINGS

Centroid and Medians of a Triangle

A line segment connecting a vertex of a triangle to the midpoint of the side opposite the vertex is called a **median**.

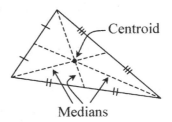

Medians

Since a triangle has three vertices, it has three medians. An example of a triangle with its three medians is provided at right.

The point at which the three medians intersect is called a **centroid**. The centroid is also the center of balance of a triangle.

Since the three medians intersect at a single point, this point is called a **point of concurrency.** You will learn about other points of concurrency in a later chapter.

9-89.   Find the volumes of the solids below.

    a.   cylinder

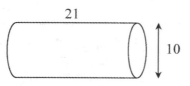
21
10

    b.   regular octagonal prism

2
7

9-90.   Jillian is trying to construct a square. She
         has started by constructing two
         perpendicular lines, as shown at right. If
         she wants each side of the square to have
         length k, as defined at right, describe how
         she should finish her construction.

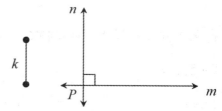
n
k
P
m

9-91.   Without using a calculator, find the sum of the interior angles of a 1,002-gon. Show
         all work.

9-92.   York County, Maine, is roughly triangular in
         shape. To help calculate its area, Sergio has
         decided to use a triangle, as shown at right.
         According to his map, the border with New
         Hampshire is 165 miles long, while the
         coastline along the Atlantic Ocean is
         approximately 100 miles long. If the angle at
         the tip of Maine is 43°, as shown in the diagram, what is the area of York County?

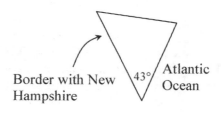
Border with New
Hampshire
43°
Atlantic
Ocean

9-93.   Copy the following words and their lines of reflection onto your paper. Then use
         your **visualization** skills to help draw the reflected images.

    a.   **REFLECT**

    b.   **PRISM**

9-94.   **Multiple Choice:** Solve this problem without a
calculator:

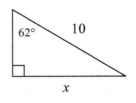

Examine the triangle at right. Find the approximate
value of *x*. Use the values in the trigonometric table
below as needed.

a.   4.69   b.   5.32

c.   8.83   d.   18.81

e.   None of these

θ	$\cos\theta$	$\sin\theta$	$\tan\theta$
28°	0.883	0.469	0.532
62°	0.469	0.883	1.881

Chapter 9 Closure   What have I learned?

Reflection and Synthesis

The activities below offer you a chance to reflect on what you have learned during this chapter.
As you work, look for concepts that you feel very comfortable with, ideas that you would like to
learn more about, and topics you need more help with. Look for **connections** between ideas as
well as **connections** with material you learned previously.

① TEAM BRAINSTORM

With your team, brainstorm a list
for each of the following three
topics. Be as detailed as you can.
How long can you make your
list? Challenge yourselves. Be
prepared to share your team's
ideas with the class.

Topics: What have you studied in this chapter? What ideas and
words were important in what you learned? Remember to
be as detailed as you can.

Problem Solving: What did you do to solve problems? What different
strategies did you use?

Connections: How are the topics, ideas, and words that you learned in
previous courses are **connected** to the new ideas in this
chapter? Again, make your list as long as you can.

The following is a list of the vocabulary used in this chapter. The words that appear in bold are new to this chapter. Make sure that you are familiar with all of these words and know what they mean. Refer to the glossary or index for any words that you do not yet understand.

base	bisect	**centroid**
circle	**compass**	**concentric circles**
construction	cylinder	**inscribed**
irrational number	**lateral face**	line segment
linear scale factor	**mat plan**	**median**
net	**oblique**	perimeter
perpendicular bisector	polygon	**polyhedra**
prism	ratio	rhombus
similar	**solid**	**straightedge**
surface area	three-dimensional	**volume**

Make a concept map showing all of the **connections** you can find among the key words and ideas listed above. To show a **connection** between two words, draw a line between them and explain the **connection**, as shown in the example below. A word can be **connected** to any other word as long as there is a **justified connection**. For each key word or idea, provide a sketch of an example.

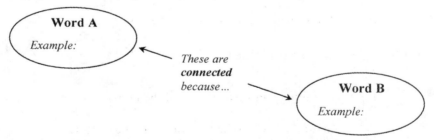

Your teacher may provide you with vocabulary cards to help you get started. If you use the cards to plan your concept map, be sure either to re-draw your concept map on your paper or to glue the vocabulary cards to a poster with all of the **connections** explained for others to see and understand.

While you are making your map, your team may think of related words or ideas that are not listed above. Be sure to include these ideas on your concept map.

③   SUMMARIZING MY UNDERSTANDING

This section gives you an opportunity to show what you know about certain math topics or ideas. Your teacher will give you directions for exactly how to do this. Your teacher may give you a "GO" page to work on. "GO" stands for "Graphic Organizer," a tool you can use to organize your thoughts and communicate your ideas clearly.

④   WHAT HAVE I LEARNED?

This section will help you evaluate which types of problems you have seen with which you feel comfortable and those with which you need more help. This section will appear at the end of every chapter to help you check your understanding. Even if your teacher does not assign this section, it is a good idea to try these problems and find out for yourself what you know and what you need to work on.

Solve each problem as completely as you can. The table at the end of this closure section has answers to these problems. It also tells you where you can find additional help and practice on problems like these.

CL 9-95.   On her paper, Kaye has a line with points A and B on it. Explain how she can use a compass to find a point C so that B is a midpoint of $\overline{AC}$. If you have access to a compass, try this yourself.

CL 9-96.   Assume that the solid at right has no hidden cubes.

a.   On graph paper, draw the front, right, and top views of this solid.

b.   Find the volume and surface area of the cube.

c.   Which net(s) below would have the same volume as the solid at right when it is folded to create a box?

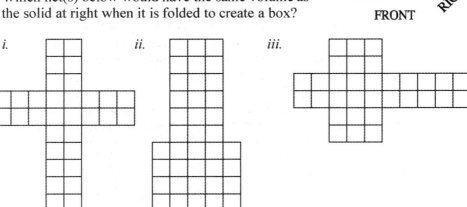

FRONT   RIGHT

i.   *ii.*   *iii.*

CL 9-97. The solid from problem CL 9-96 is redrawn at right.

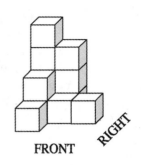

a. If this solid were enlarged by a linear scale factor of 4, what would the volume and surface area of the new solid be?

b. Enrique enlarged the solid at right so that its volume was 1500 cubic units. What was his linear scale factor? **Justify** your answer.

CL 9-98. After constructing a $\triangle ABC$, Pricilla decided to try a little experiment. She chose a point V outside of $\triangle ABC$ and then constructed rays $\overrightarrow{VA}$, $\overrightarrow{VB}$, and $\overrightarrow{VC}$. Her result is shown at right. Copy this diagram onto your paper.

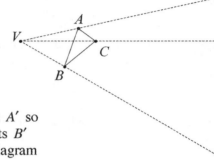

a. Pricilla then used a compass to mark point A' so that $VA = AA'$. She also constructed points B' and C' using the same method. For the diagram on your paper, locate A', B', and C'.

b. Now connect $\triangle A'B'C'$. What do you notice? What appears to be the relationship between $\triangle ABC$ and $\triangle A'B'C'$? Explain what happened.

c. If the area of $\triangle ABC$ is 19 cm^2 and its perimeter is 15 cm, find the area and perimeter of $\triangle A'B'C'$.

CL 9-99. Find the volume and surface area of the prism at right if the base is a regular octagon with side length 14 mm and the height of the prism is 28 mm.

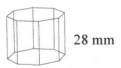

28 mm

CL 9-100. Answer the questions about the angles of polygons below, if possible. If it is not possible, explain how you know it is not possible.

a. Find the sum of the interior angles of a 28-gon.

b. If the exterior angle of a regular polygon is 42°, how many sides does the polygon have?

c. Find the measure of each interior angle of a pentagon.

d. Find the measure of each interior angle of a regular decagon.

Geometry Connections

CL 9-101. Fill in the blanks in each statement below with one of the quadrilaterals listed at right so that the statement is <u>true</u>. Use each quadrilateral name only once.

List:

Kite

Rectangle

Rhombus

Trapezoid

a.   If a shape is a square, then it must also be a _____ .

b.   The diagonals of a _____ must be perpendicular to each other.

c.   If the quadrilateral has only one line of symmetry, then it could be a _____ .

d.   If a quadrilateral has only two sides that are congruent, then the shape could be a _____ .

CL 9-102. Copy quadrilateral *DART*, shown at right, onto your paper. If $\overline{DR}$ bisects $\angle ADT$ and if $\angle A \cong \angle T$, prove that $\overline{DA} \cong \overline{DT}$.

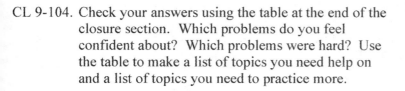

CL 9-103. After Myong's cylindrical birthday cake was sliced, she received the slice at right. If her birthday cake originally had a diameter of 14 inches and a height of 6 inches, find the volume of her slice of cake.

CL 9-104. Check your answers using the table at the end of the closure section. Which problems do you feel confident about? Which problems were hard? Use the table to make a list of topics you need help on and a list of topics you need to practice more.

⑤   HOW AM I THINKING?

This course focuses on five different **Ways of Thinking**: investigating, examining, reasoning and justifying, visualizing, and choosing a strategy/tool. These are some of the ways in which you think while trying to make sense of a concept or to solve a problem (even outside of math class). During this chapter, you have probably used each Way of Thinking multiple times without even realizing it!

Choose three of these Ways of Thinking that you remember using while working in this chapter. For each Way of Thinking that you choose, show and explain where you used it and how you used it. Describe why thinking in this way helped you solve a particular problem or understand something new. Be sure to include examples to demonstrate your thinking.

Answers and Support for Closure Activity #4
What Have I Learned?

Problem	Solution	Need Help?	More Practice
CL 9-95.	She should match the length of $\overline{AB}$ with her compass. Then, with the point of the compass at B, she should mark a point on the line on the side of point B opposite point A. Then she should label that point C.	Lesson 7.3.3 Math Notes box, problem 9-55	Problems 7-108, 8-30, 9-64, 9-65, 9-67, 9-74, 9-75, 9-76, 9-86, 9-87, 9-90
CL 9-96.	a. Front Right Top b. $V = 12$ un^3, $SA = 42$ un^2 c. All three nets will form a box with volume 12 un^3.	Lesson 9.1.3 Math Notes box, problems 9-1, 9-2, and 9-14	Problems 9-3, 9-4, 9-5, 9-7, 9-13, 9-15, 9-16, 9-20, 9-25, 9-35, 9-63, 9-79
CL 9-97.	a. $V = 12(4)^3 = 768$ un^3, $SA = 42(4)^2 = 672$ un^2 b. Linear scale factor $= 5$	Lesson 9.1.5 Math Notes box, problems 9-1, 9-35 and 9-36	Problems 9-37, 9-39, 9-40, 9-45, 9-46, 9-47, 9-48, 9-73, 9-79
CL 9-98.	a. b. $\triangle ABC$ was enlarged (or dilated) to create a similar triangle with a linear scale factor of 2. c. $A = 19(2)^2 = 76$ un^2; $P = 15(2) = 30$ un	Lessons 3.1.1, 7.2.6, and 9.1.5 Math Notes boxes	Problems 7-114, 7-103, 8-63, 8-65, 8-74, 8-76, 8-114, 9-8, 9-19, 9-29
CL 9-99.	Area of base ≈ 946.37 un^2 Volume $\approx 26,498.41$ un^3 Surface Area ≈ 5028.74 un^2	Lessons 8.3.1, 9.1.2, and 9.1.3 Math Notes boxes, problem 9-15	Problems 9- 16, 9-17, 9-26, 9-27, 9-28, 9-33, 9-40, 9-59, 9-89

Problem	Solution	Need Help?	More Practice
CL 9-100.	a. 4680° b. Not possible because 42° does not divide evenly into 360°. c. Not possible because it is not stated that the pentagon is regular. d. 144°	Lessons 7.1.4, 8.1.1, and 8.1.4 Math Notes boxes, problem 8-1	Problems 8-15, 8-25, 8-29, 8-33, 8-34, 8-35, 8-40, 8-49, 8-55, 8-56, 8-87, 8-99, 8-109, 9-21, 9-50, 9-72, 9-83, 9-91
CL 9-101.	a. Rectangle b. Rhombus c. Kite d. Trapezoid	Lessons 7.2.3, 8.1.2, and 9.2.2 Math Notes boxes	Problems 7-101, 7-106, 7-116, 7-117, 7-121, 8-11, 8-56, 9-50
CL 9-102.		Lessons 3.2.4, 6.1.3, 7.1.3, and 7.2.1 Math Notes boxes, problems 7-56 and 7-79	Problems 7-61, 7-78, 7-85, 7-87, 7-96, 7-104, 7-105, 8-20, 8-28, 8-58, 8-79, 8-88, 9-12, 9-31, 9-71, 9-80
CL 9-103.	$V \approx 97.49$ cubic inches	Lessons 8.3.2, 8.3.3, 9.1.2, and 9.1.3 Math Notes boxes	Problems 8-94, 8-96, 8-103, 8-104, 8-106, 9-16, 9-17, 9-26, 9-27, 9-28, 9-33, 9-40, 9-59, 9-89

CIRCLES AND EXPECTED VALUE

10

CHAPTER 10   Circles and Expected Value

In Chapter 8, you developed a method for finding the area and circumference of a circle, while in Chapter 9 you constructed many shapes and relationships using circles. In Section 10.1, you will explore the relationships between angles, arcs, and chords in a circle.

The focus turns to probability and games of chance in Section 10.2. As you analyze the probabilities of different outcomes on spinners, you will develop an understanding of expected value, which is a method to predict the outcome of a random event.

Circles will be revisited in Section 10.3 when you find the equation of a circle using the Pythagorean Theorem.

Guiding Questions

Think about these questions throughout this chapter:

What's the relationship?

How can I solve it?

What's the connection?

Is there another method?

How can I predict it?

In this chapter, you will learn:

➤ How to use the relationships between angles, arcs, and line segments within a circle to solve problems.

➤ How to find a circle inscribed in (and circumscribed about) a triangle.

➤ How to find the expected outcome of a game of chance.

➤ How to find the equation of a circle.

Chapter Outline

Section 10.1 The relationships between angles, arcs, and line segments in a circle will be **investigated** to develop "circle tools" that can help solve problems involving circles.

Section 10.2 After data is collected, the design of a spinner will be revealed and analyzed. Then the concept of expected value will be developed as a tool to predict the outcome of a random generator.

Section 10.3 The Pythagorean Theorem will help to find the equation of a circle when it is graphed on coordinate axes.

10.1.1 What's the diameter?

Introduction to Chords

In Chapter 8, you learned that the diameter of a circle is the distance across the center of the circle. This length can be easily measured if the entire circle is in front of you and the center is marked, or if you know the radius of the circle. However, what if you only have part of a circle (called an **arc**)? Or what if the circle is so large that it is not practical to measure its diameter using standard measurement tools (such as finding the diameter of the Earth's equator)?

Today you will consider a situation that demonstrates the need to learn more about the parts of a circle and the relationships between them.

10-1.   THE WORLD'S WIDEST TREE

The baobab tree is a species of tree found in Africa and Australia. It is often referred to as the "world's widest tree" because it has been known to be up to 45 feet in diameter!

While digging at an archeological site, Rafi found a fragment of a fossilized baobab tree that appears to be wider than any tree on record! However, since he does not have the remains of the entire tree, he cannot simply measure across the tree to find its diameter. He needs your help to determine the radius of this ancient tree. Assume that the shape of the tree's cross-section is a circle.

Tree fragment

a.   Obtain the Lesson 10.1.1 Resource Page from your teacher. On it, locate $\overset{\frown}{AB}$, which represents the curvature of the tree fragment. Trace this arc as neatly as possible on tracing paper. Then decide with your team how to fold the tracing paper to find the center of the tree. (Note: This will take more than one fold.) Be ready to share with the class how you found the center.

b.   In part (a), you located the center of a circle. Use a ruler to measure the radius of that circle. If 1 cm represents 10 feet of tree, find the approximate radius and diameter of the tree. Does the tree appear to be larger than 45 feet in diameter?

10-2.   PARTS OF A CIRCLE, Part One

A line segment that connects the endpoints of an arc is
called a **chord**. Thus, $\overline{AB}$ in the diagram at right is an
example of a chord.

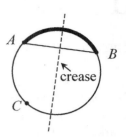

a.   One way to find the center of a circle when given an
arc is to fold it so that the two parts of the arc
coincide (lie on top of each other).

If you fold $\overparen{AB}$ so that A lies on B, what is the
relationship between the resulting crease and the
chord $\overline{AB}$? Explain how you know.

b.   The tree fragment in problem 10-1 was an arc between points A and B.
However, the missing part of the tree formed another larger arc of the tree.
With your team, find the larger arc formed by the circle and points A and B
above. Then propose a way to name the larger arc to distinguish it from $\overparen{AB}$.

c.   In problem 10-1, the tree fragment formed the shorter arc between two
endpoints. The shorter arc between points A and B is called the **minor arc** and
is written $\overparen{AB}$. The larger arc is called a **major arc** and is usually written
using three points, such as $\overparen{ACB}$. What do you know about $\overparen{AB}$ if the minor
and major arcs are the same length? Explain how you know.

10-3.   In problem 10-1, folding the arc several times resulted in a point that seemed to be
the center of the circle. But how can we prove that the line bisecting an arc (or
chord) will pass through the center? To consider this, first assume that the
perpendicular bisector does *not* pass through the center. (This is an example of a
proof by contradiction.)

a.   According to our assumption, if the perpendicular
bisector does not pass through the center, then the
center, C, will be off the line in the circle, as shown at
right. Copy this diagram onto your paper.

b.   Now consider $\triangle ACD$ and $\triangle BCD$. Are these two
triangles congruent? Why or why not?

c.   Explain why your result from part (b) contradicts the original assumption.
That is, explain why the center must lie on the perpendicular bisector of $\overline{AB}$.

10-4.   What if you know the lengths of two chords in a circle? How can you use the chords to find the center of the circle?

a.   On the Lesson 10.1.1 Resource Page, locate the chords provided for ⊙*P* and ⊙*Q*. Work with your team to determine how to find the center of each circle. Then use a compass to draw the circles that contain the given chords. Tracing paper may be helpful.

b.   Describe how to find the center of a circle without tracing paper. That is, how would you find the center of ⊙*P* with only a compass and a straightedge? Be prepared to share your description with the rest of the class.

10-5.   **Examine** the chord $\overline{WX}$ in ⊙*Z* at right. If *WX* = 8 and the radius of ⊙*Z* is 5, how far from the center is the chord? Draw the diagram on your paper and show all work.

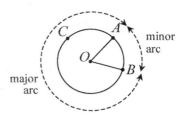

ETHODS AND MEANINGS

Circle Vocabulary

MATH NOTES

An **arc** is a part of a circle. Remember that a circle does not contain its interior. A bicycle tire is an example of a circle. The piece of tire between any two spokes of the bicycle wheel is an example of an arc.

Any two points on a circle create two arcs. When these arcs are not the same length, the larger arc is referred to as the **major arc**, while the smaller arc is referred to as the **minor arc**.

To name an arc, an arc symbol is drawn over the endpoints, such as $\overarc{AB}$. To refer to a major arc, a third point on the arc should be used to identify the arc clearly, such as $\overarc{ACB}$.

A **chord** is a line segment that has both endpoints on a circle. $\overline{AB}$ in the diagram at right is an example of a chord. When a chord passes through the center of the circle, it is called a **diameter.**

10-6. A rectangular prism has a cylindrical hole removed, as shown at right. If the radius of the cylindrical hole is 2 inches, find the volume and total surface area of the solid.

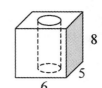

10-7. In the diagram below, $\overline{AD}$ is a diameter of $\odot B$.

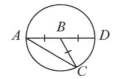

a. If $m\angle A = 35°$, what is $m\angle CBD$?

b. If $m\angle CBD = 100°$, what is $m\angle A$?

c. If $m\angle A = x$, what is $m\angle CBD$?

10-8. Lavinia started a construction at right. Explain what she is constructing. Then copy her diagram and finish her construction.

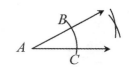

10-9. A sector is attached to the side of a parallelogram, as shown in the diagram at right. Find the area and perimeter of the figure.

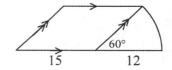

10-10. On the same set of axes, graph both equations listed below. Then name all points of intersection in the form (x, y). How many times do the graphs intersect?

$$y = 4x - 7$$
$$y = x^2 - 2x + 2$$

10-11. **Multiple Choice:** Dillon starts to randomly select cards out of a normal deck of 52 playing cards. After selecting a card, he does not return it to the deck. So far, he has selected a 3 of clubs, an ace of spades, a 4 of clubs, and a 10 of diamonds. Find the probability that his fifth card is an ace.

a. $\frac{1}{16}$ b. $\frac{3}{52}$ c. $\frac{1}{13}$ d. $\frac{1}{52}$

10.1.2 What's the relationship?

Angles and Arcs

In order to learn more about circles, we need to **investigate** the different types of angles and chords that are found in circles. In Lesson 10.1.1, you studied an application with a tree to learn about the chords of a circle. Today you will study a different application that will demonstrate the importance of knowing how to measure the angles and arcs within a circle.

10-12.

ERATOSTHENES' REMARKABLE DISCOVERY

Eratosthenes (who lived in the 3rd century B.C.) was able to determine the circumference of the Earth at a time when most people thought the world was flat! Since he knew that the Earth was round, he discovered that he could use a shadow to help calculate the Earth's radius.

Eratosthenes knew that Alexandria was located about 500 miles north of a town near the equator, called Syene. When the sun was directly overhead at Syene, a meter stick had no shadow. However, at the same time in Alexandria, a meter stick had a shadow due to the curvature of the Earth. Since the sun is so far away from the Earth, Eratosthenes assumed that the sun's rays were essentially parallel once they entered the Earth's atmosphere and realized that he could therefore use the stick's shadow to help calculate the Earth's radius.

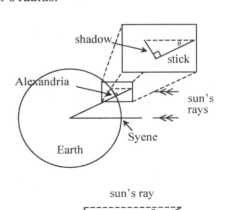

a. Unfortunately, the precise data used by Eratosthenes was lost long ago. However, if Eratosthenes used a meter stick for his experiment today, then the stick's shadow in Alexandria would be 127 mm long. Determine the angle θ that the sunrays made with the meter stick. Remember that a meter stick is 1000 millimeters long.

b. Assuming that the sun's rays are essentially parallel, determine the central angle of the circle if the angle passes through Alexandria and Syene. How did you find your answer?

Problem continues on next page →

10-12. *Problem continued from previous page.*

c.

Alexandria

Since the distance along the Earth's surface from Alexandria to Syene is about 500 miles, that is the length of the arc between Alexandria and Syene. Use this information to approximate the circumference of the Earth.

d. Use your result from part (c) to approximate the radius of the Earth.

10-13. PARTS OF A CIRCLE, Part Two

In order to find the circumference of the Earth, Eratosthenes used an angle that had its vertex at the center of the circle. Like the angles in polygons that you studied in Chapter 8, this angle is called a **central angle**.

a. An **arc** is a part of a circle. Every central angle has a corresponding arc. For example, in $\odot T$ at right, $\angle STU$ is a central angle and corresponds to $\overset{\frown}{SU}$. Since the measure of an angle helps us know what part of 360° the angle is, an arc can also be measured in degrees, representing what fraction of an entire circle it is. Thus, an **arc's measure** is equal to the measure of its corresponding central angle.

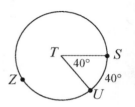

Examine the circle above. What is the measure of $\overset{\frown}{SU}$ (written $m\overset{\frown}{SU}$)? What is $m\overset{\frown}{SZU}$? Show how you got your answer.

b. When Eratosthenes measured the distance from Syene to Alexandria, he measured the length of an arc. This distance is called **arc length** and is measured with units like centimeters or feet. One way to find arc length is to wrap a string about a part of a circle and then to straighten it out and measure its length. Calculate the arc length of $\overset{\frown}{SU}$ above if the radius of $\odot T$ is 12 inches.

10-14. **INSCRIBED ANGLES**

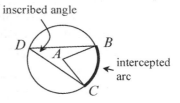
inscribed angle

In the diagram at right, $\angle BDC$ is an example of an **inscribed angle**, because it lies in $\odot A$ and its vertex lies on the circle. It corresponds to central angle $\angle BAC$ because they both intercept the same arc, $\overarc{BC}$. (An **intercepted arc** is an arc with endpoints on each side of the angle.)

intercepted arc

Investigate the measure of inscribed angles as you answer the questions below.

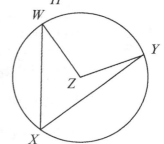

a.   In the circle at right, $\angle F$, $\angle G$, and $\angle H$ are examples of inscribed angles. Notice that all three angles intercept the same arc ($\overarc{JK}$). Use tracing paper to compare their measures. What do you notice?

b.   Now compare the measurements of the central angle (such as $\angle WZY$ in $\odot Z$ at right) and an inscribed angle (such as $\angle WXY$). What is the relationship of an inscribed angle and its corresponding central angle? Use tracing paper to test your idea.

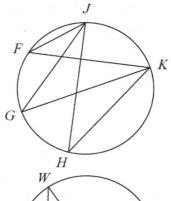

10-15. In problem 10-14, you found that the measure of an inscribed angle is always half of the measure of its corresponding central angle. Since the measure of the central angle always equals the measure of its intercepted arc, then the measure of the inscribed angle must be half of the measure of its intercepted arc.

Examine the diagrams below. Find the measures of the indicated angles. If a point is labeled C, assume it is the center of the circle.

a.

b.

c.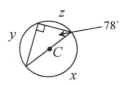

d.

e.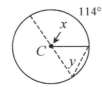

f.

10-16. Reflect on what you have learned during this lesson. Write a Learning Log entry describing the relationships between inscribed angles and their intercepted arcs. Be sure to include an example. Title this entry "Inscribed Angles" and include today's date.

MᴇᴛʜODS AND MᴇᴀNINGS

More Circle Vocabulary

The vertex of a **central angle** is at the center of a circle. An **inscribed angle** has its vertex on the circle with each side intersecting the circle at a different point.

One way to discuss an arc is to consider it as a fraction of 360°, that is, as a part of a full circle. When speaking about an arc using degrees, we call this the **arc measure**. The arc between the endpoints of the sides of a central angle has the same measure (in degrees) as its corresponding central angle.

When we want to know how *far* it is from one point to another as we travel along an arc, we call this the **arc length** and measure it in feet, miles, etc.

For example, point O is the **center** of $\odot O$ at right, and $\angle AOB$ is a **central angle**. The sides of the angle intersect the circle at points A and B, so $\angle AOB$ **intercepts** $\overset{\frown}{AB}$. In this case, the **measure** of $\overset{\frown}{AB}$ is 60°, while the measure of the major arc, $m\overset{\frown}{ACB}$, is 300° because the sum of the major and minor arcs is 360°. The **length** of $\overset{\frown}{AB}$ is $\frac{60}{360} = \frac{1}{6}$ of the circumference.

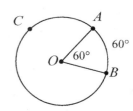

10-17. In $\odot A$ at right, $\overline{CF}$ is a diameter and $m\angle C = 64°$. Find:

a. $m\angle D$ b. $m\overset{\frown}{BF}$ c. $m\angle E$

d. $m\overset{\frown}{CBF}$ e. $m\angle BAF$ f. $m\angle BAC$

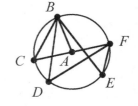

10-18. Find the area of a regular polygon with 100 sides and with a perimeter of 100 units.

10-19. For each of the geometric relationships represented below, write and solve an equation for the given variable. For parts (a) and (b), assume that C is the center of the circle. Show all work.

a.

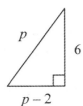

$5m + 1$

C

$3m + 9$

b.

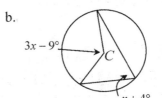

$3x - 9°$

C

$x + 4°$

c.

p

6

$p - 2$

d.

$2t + 9°$

$3t + 1°$

$5t$ $8t - 10°$

10-20. On graph paper, plot $\triangle ABC$ if $A(-1, -1)$, $B(1, 9)$ and $C(7, 5)$.

a. Find the midpoint of $\overline{AB}$ and label it D. Also find the midpoint of $\overline{BC}$ and label it E.

b. Find the length of the midsegment, $\overline{DE}$. Use it to predict the length of $\overline{AC}$.

c. Now find the length of $\overline{AC}$ and compare it to your prediction from (b).

10-21. $ABCDE$ is a regular pentagon inscribed in $\odot O$.

a. Draw a diagram of $ABCDE$ and $\odot O$ on your paper.

b. Find $m\angle EDC$. How did you find your answer?

c. Find $m\angle BOC$. What relationship did you use?

d. Find $m\widehat{EBC}$. Is there more than one way to do this?

10-22. **Multiple Choice:** Jill's car tires are spinning at a rate of 120 revolutions per minute. If her car tires' radii are each 14 inches, how far does she travel in 5 minutes?

a. 140π b. 8400π in   c. 3360π in   d. 16800π in

10.1.3 What more can I learn about circles?

Chords and Angles

As you **investigate** more about the parts of a circle, look for connections you can make to other shapes and relationships you have studied so far.

10-23.   WHAT IF IT'S A SEMICIRCLE?

What is the measure of an angle when it is inscribed in a **semicircle** (an arc with measure 180°)? Consider this as you answer the questions below.

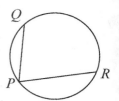

a.   Assume that the diagram at right is not drawn to scale. If $m\widehat{QR} = 180°$, then what is $m\angle P$? Why?

b.   Since you have several tools to use with right triangles, the special relationship you found in part (a) can be useful. For example, $\overline{UV}$ is a diameter of the circle at right. If $TU = 6$ and $TV = 8$, what is the radius of the circle? What is its area?

10-24.   In Lesson 10.1.1, you learned that a chord is a line segment that has its endpoints on a circle. What geometric tools do you have that can help find the length of a chord?

a.   **Examine** the diagram of chord $\overline{LM}$ in $\odot P$ at right. If the radius of $\odot P$ is 6 units and if $m\widehat{LM} = 150°$, find LM. Be ready to share your method with the class.

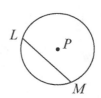

b.   What if you know the length of a chord? How can you use it to reverse the process? Draw a diagram of a circle with radius 5 units and chord $\overline{AB}$ with length 6 units. Find $m\widehat{AB}$.

10-25.   Timothy asks, "What if two chords intersect inside a circle? Can triangles help me learn something about these chords?" Copy his diagram at right in which chords $\overline{AB}$ and $\overline{CD}$ intersect at point E.

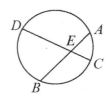

a.   Timothy decided to create two triangles ($\triangle BED$ and $\triangle ACE$). Add line segments $\overline{BD}$ and $\overline{AC}$ to your diagram.

b.   Compare $\angle B$ and $\angle C$. Which is bigger? How can you tell? Likewise, compare $\angle D$ and $\angle A$. Write down your observations.

c.   How are $\triangle BED$ and $\triangle ACE$ related? **Justify** your answer.

d.   If $DE = 8$, $AE = 4$, and $EB = 6$, then what is EC? Show your work.

10-26.   Use the relationships in the diagrams below to solve for the variable. **Justify** your solution.

a.

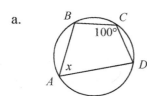

b. $\overline{KL}$ and $\overline{MP}$ intersect at Q and $KL = 8$ units

c. $\overline{RT}$ is a diameter

d.

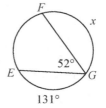

10-27.   Look over your work from today. Consider all the geometric tools you applied to learn more about angles and chords of circles. In a Learning Log entry, describe which connections you made today. Title this entry "Connections with Circles" and include today's date.

METHODS AND **M**EANINGS

MATH NOTES

Inscribed Angle Theorem

The measure of any inscribed angle is half of the measure of its intercepted arc. Likewise, any intercepted arc is twice the measure of any inscribed angles whose sides pass through the endpoints of the arc.

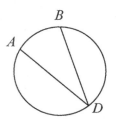

For example, in the diagram at right:

$$m\angle ADB = \tfrac{1}{2}m\overset{\frown}{AB} \text{ and } m\overset{\frown}{AB} = 2m\angle ADB.$$

Proof:

To prove this relationship, consider the relationship between an inscribed angle and its corresponding central angle. In problem 10-7, you used the isosceles triangle $\triangle ABC$ to demonstrate that if one of the sides of the inscribed angle is a diameter of the circle, then the inscribed angle must be half of the measure of the corresponding central angle. Therefore, in the diagram at right, $m\angle DAC = \tfrac{1}{2}m\overset{\frown}{DC}$.

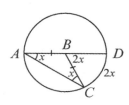

But what if the center of the circle instead lies in the interior of an inscribed angle, such as $\angle EAC$ shown at right? By constructing the diameter $\overline{AD}$, the work above shows that if $m\angle EAD = k$ then $m\overset{\frown}{ED} = 2k$ and if $m\angle DAC = p$, then $m\overset{\frown}{DC} = 2p$. Since $m\angle EAC = k + p$, then $m\overset{\frown}{EC} = 2k + 2p = 2(k + p) = 2m\angle EAC$.

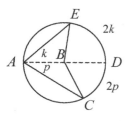

The last possible case to consider is when the center lies outside of the inscribed angle, as shown at right. Again, constructing a diameter $\overline{AD}$ helps show that if $m\angle CAD = k$ then $m\overset{\frown}{CD} = 2k$ and if $m\angle EAD = p$, then $m\overset{\frown}{ED} = 2p$. Since $m\angle EAC = p - k$, then $m\overset{\frown}{EC} = 2p - 2k = 2(p - k) = 2m\angle EAC$.

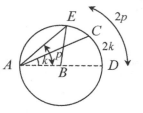

Therefore, an arc is always twice the measure of any inscribed angle that intercepts it.

10-28.   Assume point B is the center of the circle below. Match each item in the left column with the best description for it in the right column.

a. $\overline{AB}$ 1.   inscribed angle

b. $\overline{CD}$ 2.   semicircle

c. $\overparen{AD}$ 3.   radius

d. $\angle CDA$ 4.   minor arc

e. $\overparen{AC}$ 5.   central angle

f. $\angle ABC$ 6.   chord

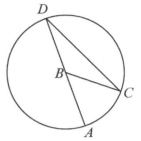

10-29.   The figure at right shows two concentric circles.

a.   Which arc has greater **measure**: $\overparen{AB}$ or $\overparen{CD}$? Explain.

b.   Which arc has greater **length**? Explain how you know.

c.   If $m\angle P = 60°$ and $PD = 14$, find the length of $\overparen{CD}$. Show all work.

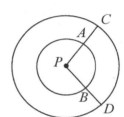

10-30.   In $\odot Y$ at right, assume that $m\overparen{PO} = m\overparen{EK}$. Prove that $\overline{PO} \cong \overline{EK}$. Use the format of your choice.

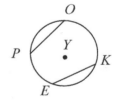

10-31.   While working on the quadrilateral hotline, Jo Beth got this call: "I need help identifying the shape of the quadrilateral flowerbed in front of my apartment. Because a shrub covers one side, I can only see three sides of the flowerbed. However, of the three sides I can see, two are parallel and all three are congruent. What are the possible shapes of my flowerbed?" Help Jo Beth answer the caller's question.

10-32.   For each pair of triangles below, decide if the triangles are similar or not and explain how you know. If the triangles are similar, complete the similarity statement $\triangle ABC \sim \triangle$_____ .

a.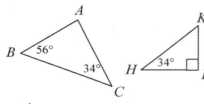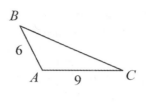

b.

c.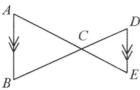

10-33.   **Multiple Choice:** Which equation below is perpendicular to $y = \frac{-2}{5}x - 7$ and passes through the point $(4, -1)$?

a. $2x - 5y = 13$ b. $2x + 5y = 3$ c. $5x - 2y = 22$

d. $5x + 2y = 18$ e.   None of these

10.1.4 What's the relationship?

Tangents and Chords

So far, you have studied about the relationships that exist between angles and chords (line segments) in a circle. Today you will extend these ideas to include the study of lines and circles.

10-34.   Consider all the ways a circle and a line can intersect. Can you **visualize** a line and a circle that intersect at exactly one point? What about a line that intersects a circle twice? On your paper, draw a diagram for each of the situations below, if possible. If it is not possible, explain why.

a.   Draw a line and a circle that do not intersect.

b.   Draw a line and a circle that intersect at exactly one point. When this happens, the line is called a **tangent**.

c.   Draw a line and a circle that intersect at exactly two points. A line that intersects a circle twice is called a **secant**.

d.   Draw a line and a circle that intersect three times.

10-35. A line that intersects a circle exactly once is called a **tangent**. What is the relationship of a tangent to a circle?

To **investigate**, carefully copy the diagram showing line *l* tangent to ⊙*A* at right onto tracing paper. Fold the tracing paper so that the crease is perpendicular to line *l* through point *P*. Your crease should pass through point *A*. What does this tell you about the tangent line?

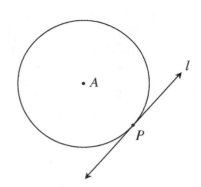

10-36. In the figure at right, $\overleftrightarrow{PA}$ is tangent to ⊙*R* at *E* and $PE = EA$. Is $\triangle PER \cong \triangle AER$? If so, prove it. If not, show why not.

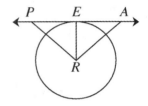

10-37. Use the relationships in the diagrams below to answer the following questions. Be sure to name what relationship(s) you used.

a. $\overleftrightarrow{PQ}$ is tangent to ⊙*C* at *P*. If $PQ = 5$ and $CQ = 6$, find CP and $m\angle C$.

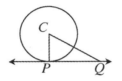

b. In ⊙*H*, $m\widehat{DR} = 40°$ and $m\widehat{GOR} = 210°$. Find $m\widehat{GD}$, $m\widehat{OR}$, and $m\angle RGO$.

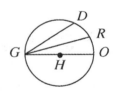

c. $\overline{AC}$ is a diameter of ⊙*E* and $\overline{BC} \parallel \overline{ED}$. Find the measure of $\widehat{CD}$.

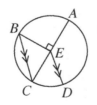

d. $\overline{HJ}$ and $\overline{IK}$ intersect at *G*. If $HG = 9$, $GJ = 8$, and $GK = 6$, find IG.

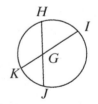

e. $\overline{AC}$ is a diameter of ⊙*E*, the area of the circle is 289π un², and $AB = 16$ units. Find BC and $m\widehat{BC}$.

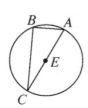

f. $\triangle ABC$ is inscribed in the circle at right. Using the measurements provided in the diagram, find $m\widehat{AB}$.

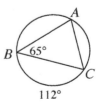

METHODS AND MEANINGS

Intersecting Chords

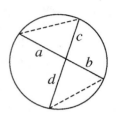

When two chords in a circle intersect, an interesting relationship between the lengths of the resulting segments occurs. If the ends of the chords are connected as shown in the diagram, similar triangles are formed (see problem 10-25). Then, since corresponding sides of similar triangles have a common ratio, $\frac{a}{d} = \frac{c}{b}$, and

$$ab = cd$$

MATH NOTES

Review & Preview

10-38. If $\overline{QS}$ is a diameter and $\overline{PO}$ is a chord of the circle at right, find the measure of the geometric parts listed below.

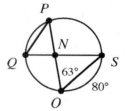

    a. $m\angle QSO$ b. $m\angle QPO$ c. $m\angle ONS$

    d. $m\overarc{PS}$ e. $m\overarc{PQ}$ f. $m\angle PQN$

10-39. For each triangle below, solve for the given variables.

    a. 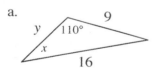   b.   c.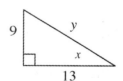

10-40. The spinner at right is designed so that if you randomly spin the spinner and land in the shaded sector, you win $1,000,000. Unfortunately, if you land in the unshaded sector, you win nothing. Assume point C is the center of the spinner.

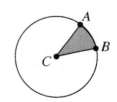

    a.   If $m\angle ACB = 90°$, how many times would you have to spin to reasonably expect to land in the shaded sector at least once? How did you get your answer?

    b.   What if $m\angle ACB = 1°$? How many times would you have to spin to reasonably expect to land in the shaded sector at least once?

    c.   Suppose $P(\text{winning } \$1,000,000) = \frac{1}{5}$ for each spin. What must $m\angle ACB$ equal? Show how you got your answer.

Geometry Connections

10-41.   Calculate the total surface area and volume of the prism at right. Assume that the base is a regular pentagon.

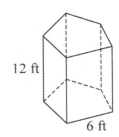

12 ft

6 ft

10-42.   Quadrilateral *ABCD* is graphed so that $A(3, 2)$, $B(1, 6)$, $C(5, 8)$, and $D(7, 4)$.

   a.   Graph *ABCD* on graph paper. What shape is *ABCD*? **Justify** your answer.

   b.   *ABCD* is rotated 180° about the origin to create $A'B'C'D'$. Then $A'B'C'D'$ is reflected across the *x*-axis to form $A''B''C''D''$. Name the coordinates of C' and D''.

10-43.   **Multiple Choice:** Which graph below represents $y > -\frac{1}{2}x + 1$?

   a.   b.   c.   d.

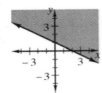   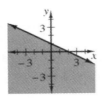   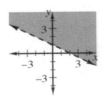   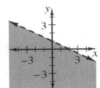

10.1.5 How can I solve it?
. . . .

Problem Solving with Circles

Your work today is focused on consolidating your understanding of the relationships between angles, arcs, chords, and tangents in circles. As you work today, ask yourself the following focus questions:

Is there another way?

What's the relationship?

10-44. On a map, the coordinates of towns A, B, and C are $A(-3, 3)$, $B(5, 7)$, and $C(6, 0)$. City planners have decided to connect the towns with a circular freeway.

a. Graph the map of the towns on graph paper. Once the freeway is built, $\overline{AB}$, $\overline{BC}$, and $\overline{AC}$ will be chords of the circle. Use this information to find the center of the circle (called the **circumcenter** of the triangle because it is the center of the circle that circumscribes the triangle).

b. Use a compass to draw the circle connecting all three towns on your graph paper. Then find the radius of the circular freeway.

c. The city planners also intend to locate a new restaurant at the point that is an equal distance from all three towns. Where on the map should that restaurant be located? **Justify** your conclusion.

10-45. An 8-inch dinner knife is sitting on a circular plate so that its ends are on the edge of the plate. If the minor arc that is intercepted by the knife measures 120°, find the diameter of the plate. Show all work.

10-46. A cylindrical block of cheese has a 6-inch diameter and is 2 inches thick. After a party, only a sector remains that has a central angle of 45°. Find the volume of the cheese that remains. Show all work.

10-47. Dennis plans to place a circular hot tub in the corner of his backyard so that it is tangent to a fence on two sides, as shown in the diagram at right.

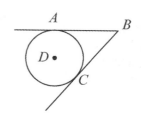

a. Prove that $\overline{AB} \cong \overline{CB}$.

b. The switch to turn on the air jets is located at point B. If the diameter of the hot tub is 6 feet and $AB = 4$ feet, how long does his arm need to be for him to reach the switch from the edge of the tub? (Assume that Dennis will be in the tub when he turns the air jets on and that the switch is level with the edge of the hot tub.)

METHODS AND MEANINGS

Points of Concurrency

MATH NOTES

In Chapter 9, you learned that the **centroid** of a triangle is the intersection of the three medians of the triangle, as shown at right. When three lines intersect at a single point, that point is called a **point of concurrency**.

Another point of concurrency, located where the perpendicular bisectors of each side of a triangle meet, is called the **circumcenter**. This point is the center of the circle that circumscribes the triangle. See the example at right. Note that the point that represents the location of the restaurant in problem 10-44 is a circumcenter.

The point where the three angle bisectors of a triangle meet is called the **incenter**. It is the center of the circle that is inscribed in a triangle. See the example at right.

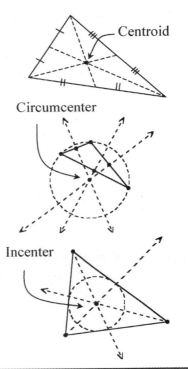

Centroid

Circumcenter

Incenter

Review & Preview

10-48.   In the diagram at right, $\odot M$ has radius 14 feet and $\odot A$ has radius 8 feet. $\overleftrightarrow{ER}$ is tangent to both $\odot M$ and $\odot A$. If $NC = 17$ feet, find ER.

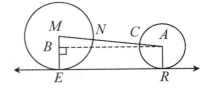

10-49.   Phinneus is going to spin both spinners at right once each. If he lands on the same color twice, he will go to tonight's dance. Otherwise, he will stay home. What is the probability that Phinneus will attend the dance?

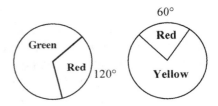

10-50. In the figure at left, find the interior height (h) of the obtuse triangle. Show all work.

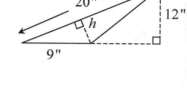

10-51. A cylinder with volume 500π cm^3 is similar to a smaller cylinder. If the scale factor is $\frac{1}{5}$, what is the volume of the smaller cylinder? Explain your **reasoning**.

10-52. In the figure at right, $\overrightarrow{EX}$ is tangent to $\odot O$ at point X. $OE = 20$ cm and $XE = 15$ cm.

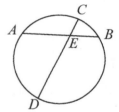

a. What is the area of the circle?

b. What is the area of the sector bounded by $\overline{OX}$ and $\overline{ON}$?

c. Find the area of the region bounded by $\overline{XE}$, $\overline{NE}$, and $\overarc{NX}$.

10-53. **Multiple Choice:** In the circle at right, $\overline{CD}$ is a diameter. If $AE = 10$, $CE = 4$, and $AB = 16$, what is the radius of the circle?

a.   15   b.   16   c.   18

d.   19   e.   None of these

10.2.1 What's the probability?

Designing Spinners

In Chapter 4, you played several games and learned how to determine if a game is fair. You also used several models, such as tree diagrams and area models, to represent the probabilities of the various outcomes.

Today you will look at probability from a new perspective. What if you want to design a game that has particular, predictable outcomes? How can you design a spinner so that the result of many spins matches a desired outcome?

10-54. To review your understanding of probability, play the
game as described below 50 times to determine a winner.
You will need a paperclip and a Lesson 10.2.1 Resource
Page. Then answer the questions that follow.

- Choose a different member of your
  team to be responsible for the
  following tasks:
    o Keeping track of time
    o Spinning a paperclip
    o Recording the result of each spin
    o Tallying the number of spins

- Assign each team member a region
  (or pair of regions) alphabetically by
  first name. That is, the team member
  whose name is first alphabetically
  will be assigned region A, the next
  person region B, and so on. You
  may want to color the spinner so that
  the four regions are different colors.

- Place the resource page on a flat, level surface. Then place a paperclip at
  the center of the spinner, hold it in place with the point of a pen or pencil,
  and spin it 50 times. Each time the spinner lands on a player's letter, that
  player gets a point. The person with the most points wins.

a. Which player (A, B, C, or D) won the game? Is the result what you expected?
   Why or why not?

b. Use a protractor to measure the central angles for each region. What is the
   probability that the spinner will land in each region?

c. Calculate the percentage of the points scored for each region based on your
   results from playing the game and compare them to the probabilities you
   calculated in part (b). How closely did the results from spinning match the
   actual probabilities? Explain any large differences.

10-55.   Do you have to collect data to predict the outcomes? For each spinner below, predict how many times a spinner would land in each region if you spun it 60 times randomly. Show all work.

a.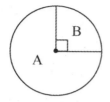

b.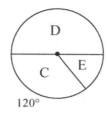

120°

c.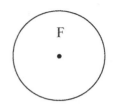

10-56.   Your teacher will now spin a hidden spinner. Your team's task is to use the results to predict what the spinner looks like. Then, using the blank spinner on the resource page, use a protractor to design the spinner. As your teacher gives you the result of each spin, take careful notes! Your accuracy depends on it.

10-57.   For a school fair, Donny is going to design a spinner with red, white, and blue regions. Since he has a certain proportion of three types of prizes, he wants the P(red) = 40% and P(white) = 10%.

a.   If the spinner only has red, white, and blue regions, then what is P(blue)? Explain how you know.

b.   Find the central angles of this spinner if it has only three sections. Then draw a sketch of the spinner. Be sure to label the regions accurately.

c.   Is there a different spinner that has the same probabilities? If so, sketch another spinner that has the same probabilities. If not, explain why there is no other spinner with the same probabilities.

METHODS AND MEANINGS

Probability

While the information below was provided in Chapter 1, it is reprinted here for your reference during this section.

Probability is a measure of the likelihood that an event will occur at random. It is expressed using numbers with values that range from 0 to 1, or from 0% to 100%. For example, an event that has no chance of happening is said to have a probability of 0 or 0%. An event that is certain to happen is said to have a probability of 1 or 100%. Events that "might happen" have values somewhere between 0 and 1 or between 0% and 100%.

The probability of an event happening is written as the ratio of the number of ways that the desired outcome can occur to the total number of possible outcomes (assuming that each possible outcome is equally likely).

$$P(\text{event}) = \frac{\text{Number of Desired Outcomes}}{\text{Total Possible Outcomes}}$$

For example, on a standard die, P(5) means the probability of rolling a 5. To calculate the probability, first determine how many possible outcomes exist. Since a die has six different numbered sides, the number of possible outcomes is 6. Of the six sides, only one of the sides has a 5 on it. Since the die has an equal chance of landing on any of its six sides, the probability is written:

$$P(5) = \frac{1 \text{ side with the number five}}{6 \text{ total sides}} = \frac{1}{6} \text{ or } 0.1\overline{6} \text{ or approximately } 16.7\%$$

10-58. When the net at right is folded, it creates a die with values as shown.

	3		
1	5	2	1
	1		

a.   If the die is rolled randomly, what is P(even)? P(1)?

b.   If the die is rolled randomly 60 times, how many times would you expect an odd number to surface? Explain how you know.

c.   Now create your own net so that the resulting die has P(even) = $\frac{1}{3}$, P(3) = 0, and P(a number less than 5) = 1.

10-59.   In the diagram at right, $\overline{AB}$ is a diameter of $\odot L$. If $BC = 5$
          and $AC = 12$, use the relationships shown in the diagram to
          solve for the quantities listed below.

          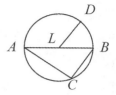

          a. AB b.   radius of $\odot L$

          c. $m\angle ABC$ d. $m\overset{\frown}{AC}$

10-60.   When Erica and Ken explored a cave, they
          each found a gold nugget. Erica's nugget
          is similar to Ken's nugget. They measured
          the length of two matching parts of the
          nuggets and found that Erica's nugget is
          five times longer than Ken's. When they
          took their nuggets to the metallurgist to be
          analyzed, they learned that it would cost
          $30 to have the surface area and weight of
          the smaller nugget calculated, and $150 to
          have the same analysis done on the larger
          nugget.

          "I won't have that kind of money until I
          sell my nugget, and then I won't need it
          analyzed!" Erica says.

          "Wait, Erica. Don't worry. I'm pretty sure we can get all the information we need
          for only $30."

          a.   Explain how they can get all the information they need for $30.

          b.   If Ken's nugget has a surface area of 110 cm^2, what is the surface area of
                Erica's nugget?

          c.   If Ken's nugget weighs 56 g (about 1.8 oz), what is the weight of Erica's
                nugget?

10-61.   Find x if the angles of a quadrilateral are $2x$, $3x$, $4x$, and $5x$.

10-62.   A graph of an inequality is shown at right. Decide if
          each of the points (x, y) listed below would make the
          inequality true or not. For each point, explain how
          you know.

          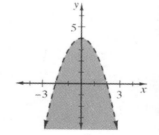

          a. $(1, 1)$ b. $(-3, 2)$

          c. $(-2, 0)$ d. $(0, -2)$

10-63.   **Multiple Choice:** Which expression below represents the
           length of the hypotenuse of the triangle at right?

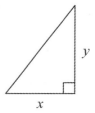

a. $\frac{y}{x}$ b. $\sqrt{x^2 + y^2}$ c. $x + y$

d. $\sqrt{y^2 - x^2}$ e. None of these

10.2.2 What should I expect?

Expected Value

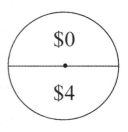

Around the world, different cultures have developed creative forms of games of chance. For
example, native Hawaiians play a game called Konane, which uses markers and a board and is
similar to checkers. Native Americans play a game called To-pe-di, in which tossed sticks
determine how many points a player receives.

When designing a game of chance, much attention must
be given to make sure the game is fair. If the game is
not fair, or if there is not a reasonable chance that
someone can win, no one will play the game. In
addition, if the game has prizes involved, care needs to
be taken so that prizes will be distributed based on
availability. In other words, if you only want to give
away one grand prize, you want to make sure the game
is not set up so that 10 people win the grand prize!

Today your team will analyze different games to learn
about **expected value**, which helps to predict the result
of a game of chance.

10-64.   TAKE A SPIN

           Consider the following game: After you spin the wheel at
           right, you win the amount spun.

           a.   If you play the game 10 times, how much money would
                you expect to win? What if you played the game 30
                times? 100 times? Explain your process.

           b.   What if you played the game *n* times? Write a rule that governs how much
                money one can expect to win after playing the game *n* times.

           c.   If you were to play only once, what should you expect to earn according to
                your rule in part (b)? It is actually possible to win that amount? Explain why
                or why not.

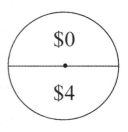

10-65.   What if the spinner looks like the one at right instead?

a.   If you win the amount that comes up on each spin, how much would you expect to win after 4 spins? What about after 100 spins?

b.   Find this spinner's **expected value**. That is, what is the expected amount you will win for each spin? Be ready to **justify** your answer.

c.   Gustavo describes his thinking this way: "Half the time, I'll earn nothing. One-fourth the time, I'll earn $4 and the other one-fourth of the time I'll earn $100. So, for one spin, I can calculate $\frac{1}{2}(0) + \frac{1}{4}(\$4) + \frac{1}{4}(\$100)$. Calculate Gustavo's expression. Does his result match your result from part (b)?

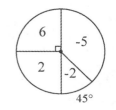

10-66.   Jesse has created the spinner at right. This time, if you land on a positive number, you win that amount of money. However, if you land on a negative number, you lose that amount of money! Want to try it?

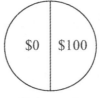

a.   Before analyzing the spinner, predict whether a person would win money or lose money after many spins.

b.   Now calculate the actual expected value. How does the result compare to your estimate from part (a)?

10-67.   Finding an expected value is similar to finding a **weighted average** because it takes into account the different probabilities for each possible outcome. For example, in problem 10-66, –5 is expected to result three times as often as –2. Therefore, in averaging these values, –5 must be weighted three times for every –2. However, the 2 and the 6 have equal probabilities, so they must be averaged using the same weighting.

To understand the effect of weighted averaging, consider the two spinners at right. Each has two sections, labeled $100 and $0. Which spinner has the greater expected value? How can you tell?

Spinner A   Spinner B

10-68.   In your Learning Log, explain what "expected value" means. What does it find? When is it useful? Be sure to include an example. Title this entry "Expected Value" and include today's date.

10-69.   The spinner at right has three regions: A, B, and C. If it is spun 80 times, how many times would you expect each region to result? Show your work.

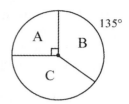

10-70.   Review what you know about the angles and arc of circles below.

   a.   A circle is divided into nine congruent sectors. What is the measure of each central angle?

   b.   In the diagram at right, find $m\widehat{AD}$ and $m\angle C$ if $m\angle B = 97°$.

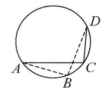

   c.   In $\odot C$ at right, $m\angle ACB = 125°$ and $r = 8$ inches. Find $m\widehat{AB}$ and the length of $\widehat{AB}$. Then find the area of the smaller sector.

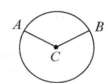

10-71.   **Examine** the diagram at right. Use the given geometric relationships to solve for x, y, and z. Be sure to **justify** your work by stating the geometric relationship and applicable theorem.

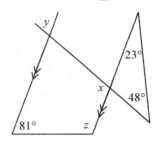

10-72.   Solve each equation below for x. Check your work.

   a. $\frac{x}{2} = 17$

   b. $\frac{x}{4} = \frac{1}{3}$

   c. $\frac{x+6}{2} + 2 = \frac{5}{2}$

   d. $\frac{4}{x} = \frac{5}{8}$

10-73.   Mrs. Cassidy solved the problem $(w - 3)(w + 5) = 9$ and got $w = 3$ and $w = -5$. Is she correct? If so, show how you know. If not, show how you know and find the correct solution.

10-74.   **Multiple Choice:** Which expression represents the area of the trapezoid at right?

   a. $\frac{c(a+b)}{4}$

   b. $\frac{c(a+b)}{2}$

   c. $\frac{bc}{2}$

   d. $\frac{a+b+c}{2}$

   e.   None of these

10.2.3 What can I expect?

. . . .

More Expected Value

Today you will continue to focus on mathematical expectation to look for new ways to find the expected value of a game of chance.

10-75. Janine's teacher has presented her with this opportunity to raise her grade: She can roll a die and possibly gain points. If a positive number is rolled, Janine gains the number of points indicated on the die. However, if a negative roll occurs, then Janine loses that many points.

Janine does not know what to do! The die, formed when the net at right is folded, offers four sides that will increase her number of points and only two sides that will decrease her grade. She needs your help to determine if this die is **fair**.

a. What are the qualities of a fair game? How can you tell if a game is fair? Discuss this with your team and be ready to share your ideas with the class.

b. What is the expected value of one roll of this die? Show how you got your answer. Is this die fair?

c. Change only one side of the die in order to make the expected value 0.

d. What does it mean if a die or spinner has an expected value of 0? Elaborate.

10-76. **Examine** the spinner at right. If the central angle of Region A is 7°, find the expected value of one spin **two different ways**. Be ready to share your methods with the class.

10-77. Now reverse the process. For each spinner below, find x so that the expected value of the spinner is 3. Be prepared to explain your method to the class.

a.

b.

c.

510   *Geometry Connections*

10-78.   Revisit your work from part (c) of problem 10-77.

    a.   To solve for x, Julia wrote the equation:

$$\tfrac{140}{360}(9) + \tfrac{40}{360}(18) + \tfrac{90}{360}(-3) + \tfrac{90}{360}x = 3$$

        Explain how her equation works.

    b.   She's not sure how to solve her equation. She'd like to rewrite the equation so that it does not have any fractions. What could she do to both sides of the equation to eliminate the fractions? Rewrite her expression and solve for x.

    c.   Review the equation-rewriting techniques you learned in algebra by solving the equations below. You may benefit by reading the Math Notes box for this lesson.

        (1) $\tfrac{4}{3} + \tfrac{x}{7} = 5$
                                               (2) $\tfrac{1}{2}(5x - 3) + \tfrac{7}{4} = \tfrac{x}{2}$

10-79.   If you have not done so already, write an equation and solve for x for parts (a) and (b) of problem 10-75. Did your answers match those you found in problem 10-75?

10-80.   During this lesson, you examined two ways to find the expected value of a game of chance. What do these methods have in common? How are they different? Explain any connections you can find. Title this entry "Method for Finding Expected Value" and include today's date.

METHODS AND MEANINGS

Solving Equations by Rewriting (Fraction Busters)

Two equations are **equivalent** if they have the same solution(s). There are many ways to change one equation into a different, equivalent equation. If an equation contains a fraction, it may be easier to solve if it is first rewritten so that it has no fractions. This process is sometimes referred to as **fraction busters.**

Example: Solve for x: $\frac{x}{3} + \frac{x}{5} = 2$

$$\frac{x}{3} + \frac{x}{5} = 2$$

The complicating issue in this problem is dealing with the fractions. We could add them by first writing them in terms of a common denominator, but there is an easier way.

The lowest common denominator of $\frac{x}{3}$ and $\frac{x}{5}$ is 15.

There is no need to use the time-consuming process of adding the fractions if we can "eliminate" the denominators. To do this, we will need to find a common denominator of all fractions and multiply both sides of the equation by that common denominator. In this case, the lowest common denominator is 15, so we multiply both sides of the equation by 15. Be sure to multiply every term on each side of the equation!

$$15 \cdot \left(\frac{x}{3} + \frac{x}{5}\right) = 15 \cdot 2$$

$$15 \cdot \frac{x}{3} + 15 \cdot \frac{x}{5} = 15 \cdot 2$$

$$5x + 3x = 30$$

$$8x = 30$$

$$x = \frac{30}{8} = \frac{15}{4} = 3.75$$

The result is an equivalent equation without fractions! Now the equation looks like many you have seen before, and it can be solved using standard methods, as shown above. Note: If you cannot determine the common denominator, then multiply both sides by the product of the denominators.

10-81.   For each spinner below, find the expected value of one spin.

a.

b.

c.
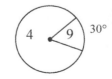

10-82.   For each equation below, write an equivalent equation that contains no fractions.
          Then solve your equation for x and check your answer.

          a. $\frac{2}{3}x - \frac{1}{4} = \frac{x}{2}$

          b. $\frac{7x}{1000} + \frac{2}{500} = \frac{11}{100}$

10-83.   The mat plan for a three-dimensional solid is shown at right.

          a.   On graph paper, draw all of views of this solid. (There
                are six views.) Compare the views. Are any the same?

          b.   Find the volume and surface area of the solid. Explain
                your method.

          c.   Do the views you drew in part (a) help calculate volume or surface area?
                Explain.

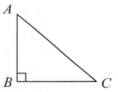

10-84.   For the triangle at right, find each trigonometric ratio
          below. The first one is done for you.

          a. $\tan C = \frac{AB}{BC}$ b. $\sin C$ c. $\tan A$

          d. $\cos C$ e. $\cos A$ f. $\sin A$

10-85.   Review circle relationships as you answer the questions below.

          a.   On your paper, draw a diagram of $\odot B$ with arc $\overset{\frown}{AC}$. If $m\overset{\frown}{AC} = 80°$ and the
                radius of $\odot B$ is 10, find the length of chord $\overline{AC}$.

          b.   Now draw a diagram of a circle with two chords, $\overline{EF}$ and $\overline{GH}$, that intersect at
                point K. If $EF = 15$, $EK = 6$, and $HK = 3$, what is GK?

10-86.   **Multiple Choice: Examine $\odot L$ at right.** Which of the
          mathematical statements below is not necessarily true?

          a. $LD = AL$ b. $m\angle DLB = m\overset{\frown}{DB}$

          c. $\overline{LD} \parallel \overline{CB}$ d. $m\overset{\frown}{BC} = 2m\angle BAC$

          e. $2AL = AB$

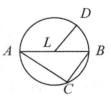

10.3.1 What's the equation?

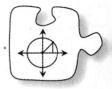

The Equation of a Circle

During Chapters 7 through 10, you studied circles *geometrically*, that is, based on the geometric shape of a circle. For example, the relationship of circles and polygons helped you develop a method to find the area and circumference of a circle, while geometric relationships of intersecting circles helped you develop constructions of shapes such as a rhombus and a kite.

However, how can circles be represented *algebraically* or *graphically*? And how can you use these representations to learn more about circles? Today your team will develop the equation of a circle.

10-87.   EQUATION OF A CIRCLE

We have equations for lines and parabolas, but what type of equation could represent a circle? On a piece of graph paper, draw a set of $x \rightarrow y$ axes. Then use a compass to construct a circle with radius 10 units centered at the origin (0, 0).

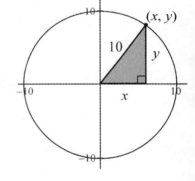

a.   What do all of the points on this circle have in common? That is, what is true about each point on the circle?

b.   Find all of the points on the circle where $x = 6$. For each point, what is the y-value? Use a right triangle (like the one shown at right) to **justify** your answer.

c.   What if $x = 3$? For each point on the circle where $x = 3$, find the corresponding y-value. Use a right triangle to **justify** your answer.

d.   Mia picked a random point on the circle and labeled it (x, y). Unfortunately, she does not know the value of x or y! Help her write an equation that relates x, y, and 10 based on her diagram above.

e.   Does your equation from part (d) work for the points (10, 0) and (0, 10)? What about (–8, –6)? Explain.

Geometry Connections

10-88. In problem 10-87, you wrote an equation of a circle with radius 10 and center at (0, 0).

    a.   What if the radius were instead 4 units long? Discuss this with your team and write an equation of a circle with center (0, 0) and radius 4.

    b.   Write the equation of a circle centered at (0, 0) with radius r.

    c.   On graph paper, sketch the graph of $x^2 + y^2 = 36$. Can you graph it without a table? Explain your method.

    d.   Describe the graph of the circle $x^2 + y^2 = 0$.

10-89. What if the center of the circle is not at (0, 0)? On graph paper, construct a circle with a center $A(3, 1)$ and radius 5 units.

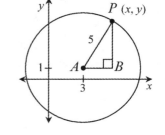

    a.   On the diagram at right, point P represents a point on the circle with no special characteristics. Add a point P to your diagram and then draw a right triangle like $\triangle ABC$ in the circle at right.

    b.   What is the length of $\overline{PB}$? Write an expression to represent this length. Likewise, what is the length of $\overline{AB}$?

    c.   Use your expressions for AB and BP, along with the fact that the radius of the circle is 5, to write an equation for this circle. (Note: You do not need to worry about multiplying any binomials.)

    d.   Find the equation of each circle represented below.

        (1)   The circle with center (2, 7) and radius 1.

        (2)

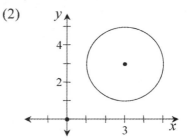

        (3)   The circle for which (6, 0) and (–6, 0) are the endpoints of a diameter.

10-90. On graph paper, graph and shade the solutions for the inequalities below. Then find the area of each shaded region.

    a. $x^2 + y^2 \leq 49$

    b. $(x - 3)^2 + (y - 2)^2 \leq 4$

10-91. In a Learning Log entry, describe what you learned in this lesson about the equation of a circle. What connections did you make to other areas of algebra or geometry? Be sure to include an example of how to find the equation of a circle given its center and radius. Title this entry "Equation of a Circle" and include today's date.

METHODS AND MEANINGS

MATH NOTES

Expected Value

The amount you would expect to win (or lose) per game after playing a game of chance many times is called the **expected value.** This value does not need to be a possible outcome of a single game, but instead reflects an average amount that will be won or lost per game.

For example, the "$9" portion of the spinner at right makes up $\frac{30°}{360°} = \frac{1}{12}$ of the spinner, while the "$4" portion is the rest, or $\frac{11}{12}$, of the spinner. If the spinner was spun 12 times, probability predicts that it would land on "$9" once and "$4" eleven times. Therefore, someone spinning 12 times would expect to receive $1(\$9) + 11(\$4) = \$53$. On average, each spin would earn an expected value of $\frac{\$53}{12 \text{ spins}} \approx \$4.42 \text{ per spin}$. You could use this value to predict the result for any number of spins. For example, if you play 30 times, you would expect to win $30(\$4.42) = \$132.50$.

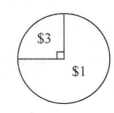

Another way to calculate expected value involves the probability of each possible outcome. Since "$9" is expected $\frac{1}{12}$ of the time, and "$4" is expected $\frac{11}{12}$ of the time, then the expected value can be calculated with the expression $(\$9)(\frac{1}{12}) + (\$4)(\frac{11}{12}) = \frac{\$53}{12} \approx \$4.42$.

10-92. Jamika designed a game that allows some people to win money and others to lose money, but overall Jamika will neither win nor lose money. Each player will spin the spinner at right and will win the amount of money shown in the result. How much should each player pay to spin the spinner? Explain your **reasoning**.

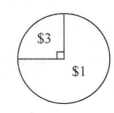

Geometry Connections

10-93.   For each diagram below, write an equation to represent the relationship between x and y.

a.

b.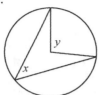

c.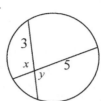

d.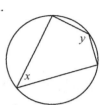

10-94.   For each triangle below, use the information in the diagram to decide if it is a right triangle. **Justify** each conclusion. Assume the diagrams are not drawn to scale.

a.

b.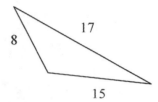

10-95.   A cube (a rectangular prism in which the length, width, and depth are equal) has an edge length of 16 units. Draw a diagram of the cube and find its volume and surface area.

10-96.   For each pair of triangles below, decide if the pair is similar, congruent or neither. **Justify** your conclusion (such as with a similarity or congruence property like AA ~ or SAS ~ or the reasons why the triangles cannot be similar or congruent). Assume that the diagrams are not drawn to scale.

a.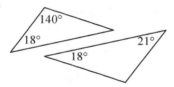

b.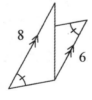

c.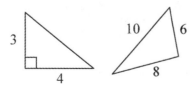

d.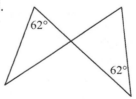

10-97.   **Multiple Choice:** $\triangle ABC$ is a right triangle and is graphed on coordinate axes. If $m\angle B = 90°$ and if the slope of $\overline{AB}$ is $-\frac{4}{5}$, what is the slope of $\overline{BC}$?

a. $\frac{4}{5}$ b. $\frac{5}{4}$ c. $-\frac{5}{4}$ d. $-\frac{4}{5}$

e.   Cannot be determined

Chapter 10 Closure   What have I learned?

Reflection and Synthesis

The activities below offer you a chance to reflect on what you have learned during this chapter. As you work, look for concepts that you feel very comfortable with, ideas that you would like to learn more about, and topics you need more help with. Look for **connections** between ideas as well as **connections** with material you learned previously.

①   TEAM BRAINSTORM

With your team, brainstorm a list for each of the following three topics. Be as detailed as you can. How long can you make your list? Challenge yourselves. Be prepared to share your team's ideas with the class.

Topics: What have you studied in this chapter? What ideas and words were important in what you learned? Remember to be as detailed as you can.

Problem Solving: What did you do to solve problems? What different **strategies** did you use?

Connections: How are the topics, ideas, and words that you learned in previous courses are **connected** to the new ideas in this chapter? Again, make your list as long as you can.

② MAKING CONNECTIONS

The following is a list of the vocabulary used in this chapter. The words that appear in bold are new to this chapter. Make sure that you are familiar with all of these words and know what they mean. Refer to the glossary or index for any words that you do not yet understand.

arc length	**arc measure**	center
central angle	**chord**	circle
circumference	**circumscribed**	diameter
expected value	**fair**	inscribed
major arc	measure	**minor arc**
perpendicular	probability	radius
secant	**semicircle**	similar
tangent	$x^2 + y^2 = r^2$	**weighted average**

Make a concept map showing all of the **connections** you can find among the key words and ideas listed above. To show a **connection** between two words, draw a line between them and explain the **connection**, as shown in the example below. A word can be **connected** to any other word as long as there is a **justified connection**. For each key word or idea, provide a sketch of an example.

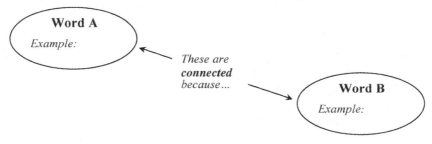

Your teacher may provide you with vocabulary cards to help you get started. If you use the cards to plan your concept map, be sure either to re-draw your concept map on your paper or to glue the vocabulary cards to a poster with all of the **connections** explained for others to see and understand.

While you are making your map, your team may think of related words or ideas that are not listed above. Be sure to include these ideas on your concept map.

③ SUMMARIZING MY UNDERSTANDING

This section gives you an opportunity to show what you know about certain math topics or ideas. Your teacher will give you directions for exactly how to do this.

④ WHAT HAVE I LEARNED?

This section will help you evaluate which types of problems you have seen with which you feel comfortable and those with which you need more help. This section will appear at the end of every chapter to help you check your understanding. Even if your teacher does not assign this section, it is a good idea to try these problems and find out for yourself what you know and what you need to work on.

Solve each problem as completely as you can. The table at the end of this closure section has answers to these problems. It also tells you where you can find additional help and practice on problems like these.

CL 10-98. Copy the diagram at right onto your paper. Assume $\overrightarrow{AD}$ is tangent to $\odot C$ at D.

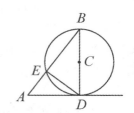

a. If $AD = 9$ and $AB = 15$, what is the area of $\odot C$?

b. If the radius of $\odot C$ is 10 and the $m\overset{\frown}{ED} = 30°$, what is $m\overset{\frown}{EB}$? AD?

c. If $m\overset{\frown}{EB} = 86°$ and if $BC = 7$, find EB.

CL 10-99. A game is set up so that a person randomly selects a shape from the shape bucket shown at right. If the person selects a triangle, he or she wins $5. If the person selects a circle, he or she loses $3. If any other shape is selected, the person does not win or lose money.

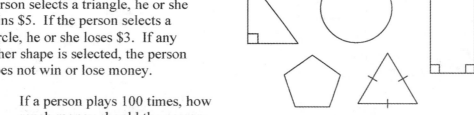

a. If a person plays 100 times, how much money should the person expect to win or lose?

b. What is the expected value of this game?

CL 10-100. Consider the solid represented by the mat plan at right.

a. Draw the front, right, and top view of this solid on graph paper.

b. Find the volume and surface area of this solid.

c. If this solid is enlarged by a linear scale factor of 3.5, what will be its new volume and surface area?

3	1	0
0	1	1
0	2	3

Right

Front

CL 10-101. Consider the descriptions of the different shapes below. Which shapes <u>must</u> be a parallelogram? If a shape does not have to be a parallelogram, what other shapes could it be?

  a. A quadrilateral with two pairs of parallel sides.

  b. A quadrilateral with two pairs of congruent sides.

  c. A quadrilateral with one pair of sides that is both congruent and parallel.

  d. A quadrilateral with two diagonals that are perpendicular.

  e. A quadrilateral with four congruent sides.

CL 10-102. In $\odot C$ at right, $\overline{AB} \cong \overline{DE}$. Prove that $\angle ACB \cong \angle DCE$.

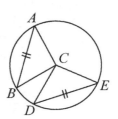

CL 10-103. Find the measure of x in each diagram below. Assume each polygon is regular.

  a. 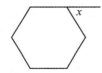   b.   c.

CL 10-104. The circle at right is inscribed in a regular pentagon. Find the area of the shaded region.

6

CL 10-105. On graph paper, graph the equation $x^2 + y^2 = 100$.

  a. What are the values of x when $y = 8$? Show how you know.

  b. What are the values of y when $x = 11$? Show how you know.

CL 10-106. Check your answers using the table at the end of the closure section. Which problems do you feel confident about? Which problems were hard? Use the table to make a list of topics you need help on and a list of topics you need to practice more.

⑤ HOW AM I THINKING?

This course focuses on five different **Ways of Thinking**: investigating, examining, choosing a strategy/tool, visualizing, and reasoning and justifying. These are some of the ways in which you think while trying to make sense of a concept or to solve a problem (even outside of math class). During this chapter, you have probably used each Way of Thinking multiple times without even realizing it!

Choose three of these Ways of Thinking that you remember using while working in this chapter. For each Way of Thinking that you choose, show and explain where you used it and how you used it. Describe why thinking in this way helped you solve a particular problem or understand something new. Be sure to include examples to demonstrate your thinking.

Answers and Support for Closure Activity #4
What Have I Learned?

Problem	Solution	Need Help?	More Practice
CL 10-98.	a. 36π b. $m\overset{\frown}{EB} = 150°$, $AD = 20\tan 15° \approx 5.36$ c. ≈ 9.55	Lessons 2.3.3, 5.1.2, 8.3.2, 10.1.1, 10.1.2, 10.1.3 Math Notes boxes	Problems 10-7, 10-15, 10-17, 10-23, 10-24, 10-26, 10-37, 10-38, 10-52, 10-59, 10-70, 10-86, 10-93
CL 10-99.	a. $140 should be won after 100 games b. $1.40 should be won per game	Lesson 10.3.1 Math Notes box	Problems 10-55, 10-64, 10-66, 10-67, 10-69, 10-75, 10-76, 10-77, 10-81, 10-92
CL 10-100.	a. Front Right Top b. $V = 11$ un^3, $SA = 42$ un^2 c. $V = 11(3.5)^3 = 471.625$ un^3, $42(3.5)^2 = 514.5$ un^2	Lessons 9.1.3 an 9.1.5 Math Notes boxes, problems 9-1, 9-2, and 9-14	Problems 9-3, 9-4, 9-5, 9-7, 9-13, 9-15, 9-16, 9-20, 9-25, 9-35, 9-37, 9-39, 9-40, 9-45, 9-46, 9-47, 9-48, 9-63, 9-73, 9-79

Problem	Solution	Need Help?	More Practice
CL 10-101.	Must be a parallelogram: (a), (c), and (e) (b) could be a kite or an isosceles trapezoid (d) could be a kite	Lessons 7.2.3, 8.1.2, and 9.2.2 Math Notes boxes, problem 7-47	Problems 7-101, 7-106, 7-116, 7-117, 7-121, 8-11, 8-56, 8-101, 9-50, 10-31
CL 10-102.	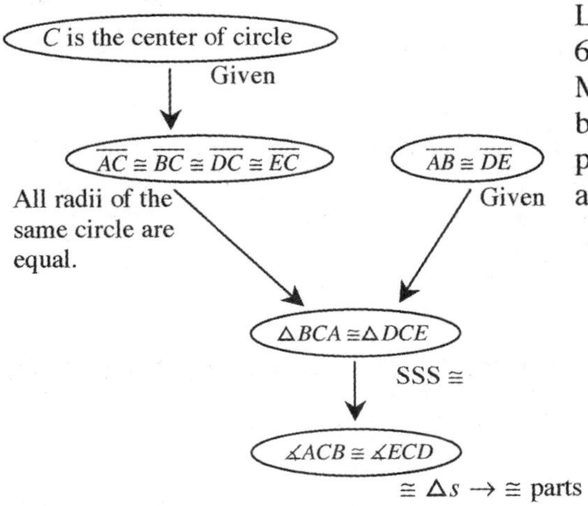	Lessons 3.2.4, 6.1.3, and 7.1.2 Math Notes boxes, problems 7-56 and 7-79	Problems 7-61, 7-78, 7-85, 7-87, 7-96, 7-104, 7-105, 8-20, 8-28, 8-58, 8-79, 8-88, 9-12, 9-31, 9-71, 9-80, 10-30, 10-36, 10-47
CL 10-103.	a. $60°$ b. $135°$ c. $36°$	Lessons 7.1.4, 8.1.1, and 8.1.4 Math Notes boxes	Problems 8-25, 8-29, 8-33, 8-34, 8-35, 8-40, 8-49, 8-55, 8-56, 8-87, 8-99, 8-109, 9-21, 9-50, 9-72, 9-83, 9-91, 10-61
CL 10-104.	Area of shaded region ≈ 8.37 un^2	Lessons 8.1.4, 8.3.1, and 8.3.2 Math Notes boxes	Problems 8-45, 8-47, 8-48, 8-67, 8-85, 8-103, 9-10
CL 10-105.	See graph at right. 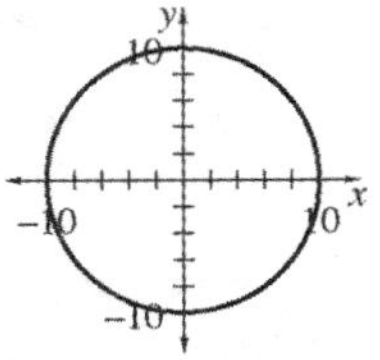 a. $x = 6$ or -6 because $6^2 + 8^2 = 100$ b. y does not exist when $x = 10$ because it is off the graph.	Problem 10-87	Problems 10-88, 10-89, 10-90

SOLIDS AND CIRCLES

11

CHAPTER 11

In Chapter 9, you learned how to find the volume and surface area of three-dimensional solids formed with blocks. Then you extended these concepts to include prisms and cylinders. In this chapter, you will complete your study of three-dimensional solids to include pyramids, cones, and spheres. You will learn how to identify the cross-sections of a solid and will **investigate** a special group of solids known as Platonic Solids.

As the word *geometry* literally means the "measurement of the Earth," it is only fitting that Section 11.2 focuses on developing the geometric tools that are used to learn more about the Earth. For example, by studying the height at which satellites orbit the Earth, you will get a chance to develop tools to work with the angle and arc measures that occur when two lines that are tangent to the same circle intersect each other.

Guiding Questions

Think about these questions throughout this chapter:

What's the relationship?

How can I measure it?

What information do I need?

Is there another way?

In this chapter, you will learn:

➤ How to find the volume and surface area of a pyramid, a cone, and a sphere.

➤ About the properties of special polyhedra, called Platonic Solids.

➤ How to find the cross-section of a solid.

➤ How to find the measures of angles and arcs that are formed by tangents and secants.

➤ About the relationships between the lengths of segments created when tangents or secants intersect outside a circle.

Chapter Outline

Section 11.1 In this section, you will learn how regular polygons can be used to form three-dimensional solids called "polyhedra." You will extend your knowledge of finding volume and surface area to include other solids, such as pyramids, cones, and spheres.

Section 11.2 By studying the coordinate system of latitude and longitude lines that help use refer to locations on the Earth, you will learn about great circles and how to find the distance between two points on a sphere. You will also **investigate** the geometric relationships created when tangents and secants intersect a circle.

11.1.1 How can I build it?

Platonic Solids

In Chapter 9, you explored three-dimensional solids such as prisms and cylinders. You developed methods to measure their sizes using volume and surface area and learned to represent three-dimensional solids using mat plans and two-dimensional (front, right, and top) views.

But what other types of three-dimensional solids can we learn about? During Section 11.1, you and your team will **examine** new types of solids in order to expand your understanding of three-dimensional shapes.

11-1. EXAMINING A CUBE

In Chapter 9, you studied the volume and surface area of three-dimensional solids, such as prisms and cylinders. A **cube** is a special type of rectangular prism because each face is a square.

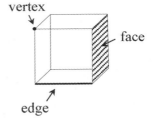

a. What are some examples of cubes you remember seeing?

b. Find the volume and surface area of a cube with an edge length of 10 units.

c. A "flat side" of a prism is called a **face**, as shown in the diagram above. Notice that the line segment where two faces meet is called an **edge**, while the point where the edges meet is called a **vertex**. How many faces does a cube have? How many edges? How many vertices? ("Vertices" is plural for "vertex.")

d. Confirm with your team that a cube has three square faces that meet at each vertex. Is it possible to have a solid where only two square faces meet at a vertex? Could a solid have four or more square faces at a vertex? Explain.

OTHER REGULAR POLYHEDRA

A three-dimensional solid made up of flat, polygonal faces is called a **polyhedron** (*poly* is the Greek root for "many," while *hedron* is the Greek root for "faces"). A cube, like the one you studied in problem 11-1, is an example of a **regular polyhedron** because all of the faces are congruent, regular polygons and the same number of faces meet at each vertex. In fact, you found that a cube is the *only* regular polyhedron with square faces.

But what if the faces are equilateral triangles? Or what if the faces are other regular polygons such as pentagons or hexagons?

Your Task: With your team, determine what other regular polyhedra are possible. First, obtain building materials from your teacher. Then work together to build regular polyhedra by testing how the different types of regular polygons can meet at a vertex. For example, what type of solid is formed when three equilateral triangle faces meet at each vertex? Four? Five? Six? Do similar tests for regular pentagons and hexagons. For each regular polyhedron, describe its shape and count its faces. Be ready to discuss your results with the class.

Discussion Points

- What is this task asking you to do?

- How should you start?

- How can your team organize the task among the members to complete the task efficiently?

Further Guidance

11-3.   For help in testing the various ways that congruent, regular polygons can build regular polyhedra, follow the directions below.

a.   Start by focusing on equilateral triangles. Attach three equilateral triangles so that they are adjacent and share a common vertex, as shown at right. Then fold and attach the three triangles so that they completely surround the common vertex. Complete the solid with as many equilateral triangles as needed so that each vertex is the intersection of three triangles. How would you describe this shape?

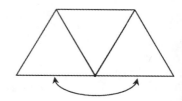

Fold so that these edges meet.

Problem continues on next page →

11-3.   *Problem continued from previous page.*

b.   Now repeat your test to determine what solids are possible when 4, 5, or more equilateral triangles meet at each vertex. If a regular polyhedron is possible, describe it and state the number of faces it has. If a regular polyhedron is not possible, explain why not.

c.   What if the faces are regular pentagons? Try building a regular polyhedron so that each vertex is the intersection of three regular pentagons. What if four regular pentagons meet at a vertex? Explain what happens in each case.

d.   End your **investigation** by considering regular hexagons. Place three or more regular hexagons at a common vertex and explain what solids are formed. If no solid is possible, explain why.

11-4.   POLYHEDRA VOCABULARY

The regular polyhedra you discovered in problem 11-2 (along with the cube from problem 11-1) are sometimes referred to as **Plato's Solids** (or **Platonic Solids**) because the knowledge about them spread about 2300 years ago during the time of Plato, a Greek philosopher and mathematician.

In addition, polyhedra are classified by the number of faces they have. For example, a cube is a solid with six faces, so it can be called a regular hexahedron (because *hexa* is the Greek root meaning "six" and *hedron* is the Greek root for "face").

Plato (490 – 430 B.C.)

Examine the table of names below. Then return to your results from problem 11-2 and determine the name for each regular polyhedron you discovered.

4 faces	Tetrahedron	9 faces	Nonahedron
5 faces	Pentahedron	10 faces	Decahedron
6 faces	Hexahedron	11 faces	Undecahedron
7 faces	Heptahedron	12 faces	Dodecahedron
8 faces	Octahedron	20 faces	Icosahedron

11-5.   Find the surface area of each of Plato's Solids you built in problem 11-2 (the regular tetrahedron, octahedron, dodecahedron, and icosahedron) if the length of each edge is 2 inches. Show all work and be prepared to share your method with the class.

11-6.   DUAL POLYHEDRA

Ivan wonders, "What happens when the centers of adjacent faces of a regular polyhedron are connected?" These connections form the edges of a solid, which can be called a **dual polyhedron**.

To **investigate** dual polyhedra, first predict the results for each regular polyhedron with your team using spatial **visualization**. Then use a dynamic geometry tool to test your prediction of what solid is formed when the centers of adjacent faces of a Platonic Solid are connected. Be sure to test all five Platonic Solids (tetrahedron, cube, octahedron, dodecahedron, and icosahedron) and record the results.

11-7.   Reflect what you learned about Plato's Solids during this lesson. What connections did you make to previous material? Write an entry in your Learning Log explaining what is special about this group of solids. Name and describe each Platonic Solid. Title this entry "Plato's Solids" and include today's date.

11-8.   Draw a hexagon on your paper.

a.   Do all hexagons have an interior angle sum of 720°?

b.   Does every hexagon have an interior angle measuring 120°? Explain your **reasoning**.

c.   Does every hexagon have 6 sides? Explain your **reasoning**.

11-9.   The **lateral surface** of a cylinder is the surface connecting the bases. For example, the label from a soup can could represent the lateral surface of a cylindrical can. If the radius of a cylinder is 4 cm and the height is 15 cm, find the lateral surface area of the cylinder. Note: It may help you to think of "unrolling" a soup can label and finding the area of the label.

11-10. For each of the relationships represented in the diagrams below, write and solve an equation for x and/or y. **Justify** your method. In part (a), assume that C is the center of the circle.

a.

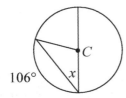

106°

b.

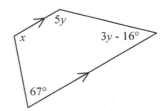

5y

3y - 16°

67°

c.

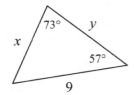

73°   y

x

57°

9

d.

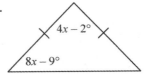

4x − 2°

8x − 9°

11-11. Garland is having trouble with the copy machine. He's trying to copy a triangle with an area of 36 square units and a perimeter of 42 units.

a. After he pressed the button to copy, Garland noticed the copier's zoom factor (the linear scale factor) was set to 200%. What is the area and perimeter of the resulting triangle?

b. Now Garland takes the result from part (a) and accidentally shrinks it by a linear scale factor of $\frac{1}{3}$! What is the area and perimeter of the resulting triangle?

11-12. Three flags are shown below on flagpoles. For each flag, determine what shape appears if the flag is spun very quickly about its pole. If you do not know the name of the shape, describe it.

a.

← pole

b.

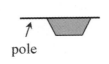

pole

c.

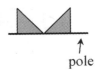

pole

11-13. **Multiple Choice:** $\triangle ABC$ has a right angle at B. If $m\angle A = 42°$ and $BC = 7$ mm, what is the approximate value of AC?

a. 9.4   b. 10.5   c. 7.8   d. 4.7

11-14.   Draw a tetrahedron on your paper.

    a.   How many faces does the tetrahedron have?

    b.   How many edges does it have?

    c.   How many vertices does it have?

11-15.   Mia found the volume of a rectangular prism to be 840 mm^3. As she was telling her father about it, she remembered that the base had a length of 10 mm and a width of 12 mm, but she could not remember the height. "Maybe there's a way you can find it by going backwards," her father suggested. Can you help Mia find the height of her prism? Explain your solution.

11-16.   On graph paper, graph a circle with center (4, 2) and radius 3 units. Then write its equation.

11-17.   **Examine** the diagram of the triangle at right.

    a.   Write an equation representing the relationship between x, y, and r.

    b.   Write an expression for $\sin\theta$. What is $\sin\theta$ if $r = 1$?

    c.   Write an expression for $\cos\theta$. What is $\cos\theta$ if $r = 1$?

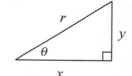

11-18.   In a circle, chord $\overline{AB}$ has length 10 units, while $m\overset{\frown}{AB} = 60°$. What is the area of the circle? Draw a diagram and show all work.

11-19.   **Multiple Choice:** Assume that the coordinates of $\triangle ABC$ are $A(5, 1)$, $B(3, 7)$, and $C(2, 2)$. If $\triangle ABC$ is rotated 90° clockwise (↻) about the origin, the coordinates of the image of B would be:

    a.   (–3, 7)   b.   (–7, 3)   c.   (7, –3)   d.   (7, 3)

11.1.2 How can I measure it?

· ·

Pyramids

In Lesson 11.1.1, you explored Plato's five special solids: the tetrahedron, the octahedron, the cube (also known as the hexahedron), the dodecahedron, and the icosahedron. You discovered why these are the only regular polyhedra and developed a method to find their surface area.

Today you will **examine** the tetrahedron from a new perspective: as a member of the **pyramid** family. As you work today with your team, you will discover ways to classify pyramids by their shape and will develop new tools of measurement.

11-20.   A **pyramid** is a polyhedron with a polygonal base formed by connecting each point of the base to a single given point (the **apex**) that is above or below the flat surface containing the base. Each triangular lateral face of a pyramid is formed by the segments from the apex to the endpoints of a side of the base and the side itself. A tetrahedron is a special pyramid because any face can act as its base.

Obtain the four Lesson 11.1.2 Resource Pages, a pair of scissors, and either tape or glue from your teacher. Have each member of your team build one of the solids. When assembling each solid, be sure to have the printed side of the net on the exterior of the pyramid for reference later. Then answer the questions below.

a.   Sketch each pyramid onto your paper. What is the same about each pyramid? What is different? With your team, list as many qualities as you can.

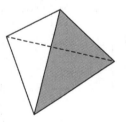

b.   A tetrahedron can also be called a **triangular-based pyramid**, because its base is always a triangle. Choose similar, appropriate names for the other pyramids that your team constructed.

c.   Find the surface area of pyramids **B** and **D**. Use a ruler to find the dimensions of the edges in centimeters.

d.   Compare pyramids **B** and **C**. Which do you think has more volume? **Justify** your **reasoning**.

11-21. THE TRANSAMERICA BUILDING

The TransAmerica building in San Francisco is built of concrete and is shaped like a square-based pyramid. The building is periodically power-washed using one gallon of cleaning solution for every 250 square meters of surface. As the new building manager, you need to order the cleaning supplies for this large task. The problem is that you do not know the height of each triangular face of the building; you only know the vertical height of the building from the base to the top vertex.

Your Task: Determine the amount of cleaning solution needed to wash the TransAmerica building if an edge of the square base is 96 meters and the height of the building is 220 meters. Include a sketch in your solution.

11-22. Read the Math Notes box for this lesson, which introduces new vocabulary terms such as "slant height" and "lateral surface area." Explain the difference between the slant height and the height of a pyramid. How can you use one to find the other?

 METHODS AND MEANINGS

Pyramid Vocabulary

If a face of a pyramid (defined in problem 11-20) or prism is not a base, it is called a **lateral face**.

The **lateral surface area** of a pyramid or prism is the sum of the areas of all faces of the pyramid or prism, not including the base(s). The area of the exterior of the TransAmerica building that needs cleaning (from problem 11-21) is an example of lateral surface area, since the exterior of the base of the pyramid cannot be cleaned.

The **total surface area** of a pyramid or prism is the sum of the areas of all faces, including the bases.

Sometimes saying the word "height" for a pyramid can be confusing, since it could refer to the height of one of the triangular faces or it could refer to the overall height of the pyramid. Therefore, we call the height of each lateral face a **slant height** to distinguish it from the **height** of the pyramid itself. See the diagram at right.

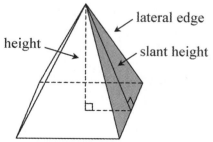

Geometry Connections

11-23.   Marina needs to win 10 tickets to get a giant stuffed panda bear. To win tickets, she throws a dart at the dartboard at right and wins the number of tickets listed in the region where her dart lands. Unfortunately, she only has enough money to play the game three times. If she throws the dart randomly, do you expect that she'll be able to win enough tickets? Assume that each dart will land on the dartboard.

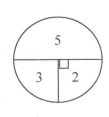

11-24.   **Examine** △ABC, △ABD, and △ABE in the diagram at right. If $\overline{CE} \parallel \overline{AB}$, explain what you know about the areas of the three triangles. **Justify** your statements.

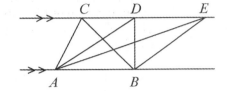

11-25.   Prove that when two lines that are tangent to the same circle intersect, the lengths between the point of intersection and the points of tangency are equal. That is, in the diagram at right, if $\overrightarrow{AB}$ is tangent to ⊙P at B, and $\overrightarrow{AC}$ is tangent to ⊙P at C, prove that $AB = AC$. Use either a flowchart or a two-column proof.

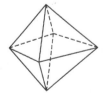

11-26.   Solve each equation below, if possible. Show all work.

a. $\frac{3}{5} = \frac{2x}{3} - 8$

b. $\frac{9x}{5000} + \frac{2}{1000} = \frac{28}{5000}$

c. $\frac{2x}{3} + \frac{x}{2} = \frac{2x}{3}$

d. $\frac{3}{2}(2x - 5) = \frac{1}{6}$

11-27.   On graph paper, plot the points $A(4, 1)$ and $B(10, 9)$.

a.   Find the distance between points A and B. That is, find AB.

b.   If point C is at $(10, 1)$, find $m\angle CAB$. Show all work.

11-28.   **Multiple Choice:** Which net below **cannot** create a regular octahedron when folded, like the one at right?

a.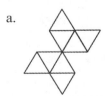

b.

c.

d.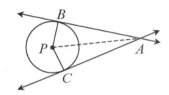

e.   None of these

11.1.3 What's the volume?

Volume of a Pyramid

Today, as you continue your focus on pyramids, look for and utilize connections to other geometry concepts. The models of pyramids that you constructed in Lesson 11.1.2 will be useful as you develop a method for finding the volume of a pyramid.

11-29.   GOING CAMPING

As Soraya shopped for a tent, she came across two models that she liked best, shown at right. However, she does not know which one to pick! They are both made by the same company and appear to have the same quality. She has come to you for help in making her decision.

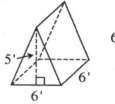

Tent A   *Tent B*

While she says that her drawings are not to scale, below are her notes about the tents:

> *Tent A is a pup tent with a rectangular base. It has a height of 5 feet, a length of 6 feet, and a width of 6 feet.*

> *Tent B is a 6-foot-tall teepee. Its base is a regular hexagon, and the greatest diagonal across the floor measures 8 feet.*

With your team, discuss the following questions in any order. Be prepared to share your discussion with the class.

- What are the shapes of the two tents?

- Without doing any calculations, which tent do you think Soraya should buy and why?

- What types of measurement might be useful to determine which tent is better?

- What do you still need to know to answer her question?

JAKE'S
SPORTING GOODS

11-30.   COMPARING SOLIDS

To analyze Tent B from problem 11-29, you need to know how to find the volume of a pyramid. But how can you find that volume?

To start, consider a simpler pyramid with a square base, such as pyramid **B** that your team built in Lesson 11.1.2. To develop a method to find the volume of a pyramid, first consider what shape(s) we can compare it to. For example, when finding the area of a triangle, you compared it to the area of a rectangle and figured out that the area of a triangle is always half the area of a rectangle with the same base and height. What shape(s) can you compare the volume of pyramid **B** to? Discuss this with your team and be prepared to share your thinking with the class.

11-31.   VOLUME OF A PYRAMID

Soraya thinks that pyramid **B** could be compared to a cube, like the one shown at right, since the base edges and heights of both are 6 cm.

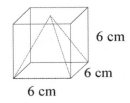

6 cm

6 cm

6 cm

a.   What fraction of the cube with edge length 6 cm is pyramid **B**? Discuss this with your team and make an estimate.

b.   Soraya remembers comparing pyramids **B** and **C** in Lesson 11.1.2. She decided to compare the volumes by using a model. She constructed a pyramid using foam layers as shown at right. What is the shape of each foam layer? Note: The name for the shape of a layer of a three-dimensional solid is called a **cross-section**.

c.   Soraya then slid all of the layers of the pyramid so that the top vertex was directly above one of the corners of the base, like Pyramid C from problem 11-20. Since she did not add or take away any foam layers, how does the volume of this pyramid compare with the pyramid in part (b) above?

d.   Test your estimate from part (a) by using as many pyramid **C**s as you need to assemble a cube. Was your estimate accurate? Now explain how to find the volume of a pyramid.

e.   Do you think your method for part (d) works with all pyramids? Why or why not?

11-32. When the top vertex of a pyramid is directly above (or below) the center of the base, the pyramid is called a **right pyramid**, while all other pyramids are referred to as **oblique pyramids**. **Examine** your models (**A**, **B**, **C**, and **D**) from problem 11-20 and decide which are right pyramids and which are oblique pyramids.

11-33. Now return to problem 11-29 and help Soraya decide which tent to buy for her backpacking trip. To make this decision, compare the volumes, base areas, and surface areas of both tents. Be ready to share your decision with the class.

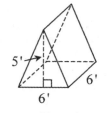
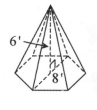

Tent A   *Tent B*

11-34. Write an entry in your Learning Log and explain how to find the volume of a pyramid. Be sure to include an example. Title this entry "Volume of a Pyramid" and include today's date.

METHODS AND MEANINGS

Cross-Sections of Three-Dimensional Solids

The intersection of a three-dimensional solid and a plane is called a **cross-section** of the solid. The result is a two-dimensional diagram that represents the flat surface of a slice of the solid.

One way to **visualize** a cross-section is to imagine the solid sliced into thin slices like a ream of paper. Since a solid can be sliced in any direction and at any angle, you need to know the direction of the slice to find the correct cross-section. For example, the cylinder at right has several

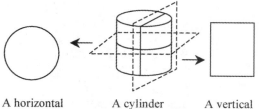

A horizontal cross-section is a circle.

A cylinder

A vertical cross-section is a rectangle.

different cross-sections depending on the direction of the slice. When this cylinder is sliced vertically, the resulting cross-section is a rectangle, while the cross-section is a circle when the cylinder is sliced horizontally.

11-35. Review the information about cross-sections in the Math Notes box for this lesson. Then answer the questions below.

    a.   Draw a cube on your paper. Is it possible to slice a cube and get a cross-section that is not a quadrilateral? Explain how.

    b.   Barbara has a solid on her desk. If she slices it horizontally at any level, the cross-section is a triangle. If she slices it vertically in any direction, the cross-section is a triangle. What could her shape be? Draw a possible shape.

11-36. Find the volume and surface area of a square-based pyramid if the base edge has length 6 units and the height of the pyramid is 4 units. Assume the diagram at right is not to scale.

11-37. The solid at right is a regular octahedron.

    a.   Trace the shape on your paper. How many faces does it have? How many edges? Vertices?

    b.   If an octahedron is sliced horizontally, what shape is the resulting cross-section?

11-38. Assume that the prisms at right are similar.

    a.   Solve for x and y.

    b.   What is the ratio of the corresponding sides of Solid B to Solid A?

    c.   If the base area of Solid A is 27 square units, find the base area of Solid B.

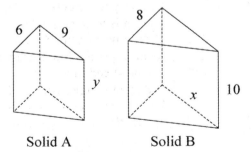

Solid A   Solid B

11-39. In the diagram at right, assume that $m\angle ECB = m\angle EAD$ and point E is the midpoint of $\overline{AC}$. Prove that $\overline{AD} \cong \overline{CB}$.

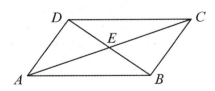

11-40. **Multiple Choice:** The graph of $x^2 + y^2 = 4$ is:

a. a parabola with y-intercept $(0, 4)$

b. a circle with radius 4 and center $(0, 0)$

c. a parabola with x-intercepts $(-2, 0)$ and $(2, 0)$

d. a circle with radius 2 and center $(0, 0)$

e. None of these

11-41. On graph paper, graph the equation $x^2 + (y - 3)^2 = 25$. Name the x- and y-intercepts.

11-42. While volunteering for a food sale, Aimee studied a cylindrical can of soup. She noticed that it had a diameter of 3 inches and a height of 4.5 inches.

a. Find the volume of the soup can.

b. If Aimee needs to fill a cylindrical pot that has a diameter of 14 inches and a height of 10 inches, how many cans of soup will she need?

c. What is the area of the soup can label?

11-43. Find the area and circumference of $\odot C$ at right. Show all work.

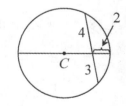

11-44. STEP RIGHT UP!

At a fair, Cyrus was given the following opportunity. He could roll the die formed by the net at right one time. If the die landed so that a shaded die faced up, then Cyrus would win $10. Otherwise, he would lose $5. Is this game fair? Explain how you know.

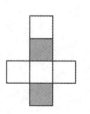

11-45.   Write and solve an equation from the geometric relationships provided in the diagrams below.

a.

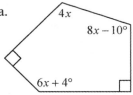

b.

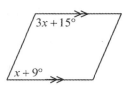

c.

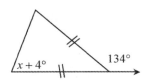

d.

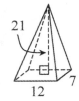

11-46.   **Multiple Choice:** Calculate the volume of the rectangle-based pyramid at right.

a.   84 un^3 b.   648 un^3 c.   882 un^3

d.   1764 un^3 e.   None of these

11.1.4 What if it's a cone?

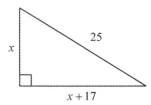

Surface Area and Volume of a Cone

Today you will continue to use what you know about the volume and surface area of prisms and pyramids and will extend your understanding to include a new three-dimensional shape: a cone. As you work with your team, look for connections to previous course material.

11-47.   Review what you learned in Lesson 11.1.3 by finding the volume of each pyramid below. Assume that the pyramid in part (a) corresponds to a rectangular-based prism and that the base of the pyramid and prism in part (b) is a regular hexagon.

a.

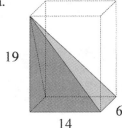

b.

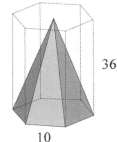

c.

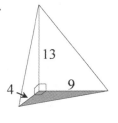

11-48. While finding the volumes of the pyramids in problem 11-47, Jamal asked, "But what if it is a cone? How would you find its volume?" Note that a **cone** is a three-dimensional figure that consists of a circular face, called the **base**, a point called the **apex**, that is not in the flat surface (plane) of the base, and the lateral surface that connects the apex to each point on the circular boundary of the base.

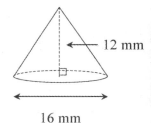

a. Discuss Jamal's question with your team. Then write a response explaining how to find the volume of a cone.

b. Find the volume of the cone at right. Show all work.

12 mm

16 mm

11-49. HAPPY BIRTHDAY!

Your class has decided to throw your principal a surprise birthday party tomorrow. The whole class is working together to create party decorations, and your team has been assigned the job of producing party hats. Each party hat will be created out of special decorative paper and will be in the shape of a cone.

Your Task: Use the sample party hat provided by your teacher to determine the size and shape of the paper that forms the hat. Then determine the amount of paper (in square inches) needed to produce one party hat and figure out the total amount of paper you will need for each person in your class to have a party hat.

11-50. The Math Club has decided to sell giant waffle ice-cream cones at the Spring Fair. Lekili bought a cone, but then she got distracted. When she returned to the cone, the ice cream had melted, filling the cone to the very top!

If the diameter of the base of the cone is 4 inches and the slant height is 6 inches, find the volume of the ice cream and the area of the waffle that made the cone.

11-51. Reflect on what you learned during this lesson and write an entry in your Learning Log on the surface area and volume of a cone. What connections did you make to previous material? Be sure to include an example. Title this entry "Surface Area and Volume of a Cone" and include today's date.

METHODS AND MEANINGS

Volume of a Pyramid

In general, the volume of a pyramid is one-third of the volume of the prism with the same base area and height. Thus:

$$V = \tfrac{1}{3}(\text{base area})(\text{height})$$

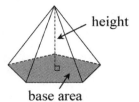

height

base area

Review & Preview

11-52. Find the volume and total surface area of each solid below. Show all work.

a.

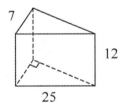

7

12

25

b.

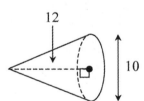

12

10

11-53. **Examine** the diagram of the cone at right.

a. How could you slice the cone so that the cross-section is a triangle?

b. What cross-section do you get if you slice the cone horizontally?

c. Lois is thinking of a shape. She says that no matter how you slice it, the cross-section will always be a circle. What shape is she thinking of? Draw and describe this shape on your paper.

11-54.   For each triangle below, decide if it is similar to the
         triangle at right. If it is similar, **justify** your
         conclusion and complete the similarity statement
         $\triangle ABC \sim \triangle$_____ . If the triangle is not similar,
         explain how you know. Assume that the diagrams
         are not drawn to scale.

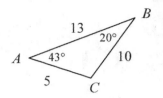

a.

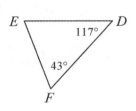

b.

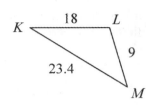

c.

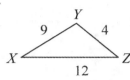

11-55.   On graph paper, graph the system of equations at right.
         Then list all points of intersection in the form (x, y).

$$x^2 + y^2 = 25$$
$$y = x + 1$$

11-56.   **Examine** the diagram at right. State the
         relationship between each pair of angles listed
         below (such as "vertical angles") and state
         whether the angles are congruent,
         supplementary, or neither.

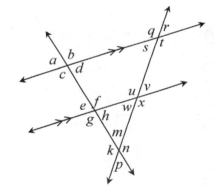

a. $\angle e$ and $\angle a$

b. $\angle t$ and $\angle u$

c. $\angle v$ and $\angle x$

d. $\angle g$ and $\angle v$

11-57.   **Multiple Choice:** In the diagram at right, the value of y is:

a. $\sin\theta$ b. $\cos\theta$ c. $\tan\theta$

d. x e.   None of these

11.1.5 What's the relationship?

Surface Area and Volume of a Sphere

This lesson will complete your three-dimensional shape toolkit. You will learn about a new shape that you encounter often in your daily life: a **sphere**. You will also make connections between a cylinder, cone, and sphere of the same radius and height.

As you work with your team, keep the following focus questions in mind:

What's the relationship?

What other tools or information do I need?

11-58. Alonzo was blowing bubbles to amuse his little sister. He wondered, "Why are bubbles always perfectly round?"

a. Discuss Alonzo's question with the class. Why are free-floating bubbles always shaped like a perfectly round ball?

b. The shape of a bubble is called a **sphere**. What other objects can you remember seeing that are shaped like a sphere?

c. What shapes are related to spheres? How are they related?

11-59. GEOGRAPHY LESSON, Part One

Alonzo learned in his geography class that about 70% of the Earth's surface is covered in water. "That's amazing!" he thought. This information only made him think of new questions, such as "What is the area of land covered in water?", "What percent of the Earth's surface is the United States?", and "What is the volume of the entire Earth?"

Discuss Alonzo's questions with your team. Decide:

• What facts about the Earth would be helpful to know?

• What do you still need to learn to answer Alonzo's questions?

11-60.   In order to answer his questions, Alonzo decided to get out his set of plastic
          geometry models. He has a sphere, cone, and cylinder that each has the same radius
          and height.

     a.   Draw a diagram of each shape.

     b.   If the radius of the sphere is r, what is the
           height of the cylinder? How do you know?

     c.   Alonzo's models are hollow and are
           designed to hold water. Alonzo was
           pouring water between the shapes,
           comparing their volumes. He discovered
           that when he poured the water in the cone
           and the sphere into the cylinder, the water
           filled up the cylinder without going over!
           Determine what the volume of the sphere
           must be if the radius of the sphere is r units.
           Show all work.

11-61.   Now that Alonzo knows that spheres, cylinders, and cones with the same height and
          radius are related, he decides to **examine** the surface area of each one. As he paints
          the exterior of each shape, he notices that the lateral surface area of the cylinder and
          the surface area of the sphere take exactly the same amount of paint! If the radius of
          the sphere and cylinder is r, what is the surface area of the sphere?

11-62.   GEOGRAPHY LESSON, Part Two

          Now that you have **strategies** for finding the volume and surface area of a sphere,
          return to problem 11-59 and help Alonzo answer his questions. That is, determine:

     •   the area of the Earth's surface that is covered in water.

     •   the percent of the Earth's surface that lies in the United States.

     •   the volume of the entire Earth.

          Don't forget that in Chapter 10, you determined that the radius of the Earth is about
          4,000 miles! Alonzo did some research and discovered that the land area of the
          United States is approximately 3,537,438 square miles.

11-63.   Write an entry in your Learning Log describing the relationships
          between the volumes of a cube, cylinder, and sphere with the same
          radius and height. Also be sure to explain how to find the surface
          area and volume of a sphere and include an example of each. Title
          this entry "Surface Area and Volume of a Sphere" and include
          today's date.

Ⓜ️ETHODS AND MEANINGS

Volume and Lateral Surface of a Cone

Finding the volume of a cone (defined in problem 11-48) is very similar to finding the volume of a pyramid. The volume of a cone is one-third of the volume of the cylinder with the same radius and height. Therefore, the volume of a cone can be found using the formula shown below, where r is the radius of the base and h is the height of the cone.

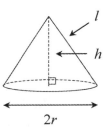

$$V = \tfrac{1}{3}(\text{Base Area})(\text{Height}) = \tfrac{1}{3}\pi r^2 h$$

To find the lateral surface area of a cone, imagine unrolling the lateral surface of the cone to create a sector. The radius of the sector would be the slant height, l, of the cone, and the arc length would be the circumference of the base of the cone, $2\pi r$.

Therefore, the area of the sector (the lateral surface area of the cone) is:

$$LA = \tfrac{2\pi r}{2\pi l}\pi l^2 = \pi r l$$

Review & Preview

11-64. As Shannon peeled her orange for lunch, she realized that it was very close to being a sphere. If her orange has a diameter of 8 centimeters, what is its approximate surface area (the area of the orange peel)? What is the approximate volume of the orange? Show all work.

11-65. Review what you know about polyhedra as you answer the questions below. Refer to the table in problem 11-4 if you need help.

   a. Find the total surface area of a regular icosahedron if the area of each face is 45 mm^2. Explain your method.

   b. The total surface area of a regular dodecahedron is 108 cm^2. What is the area of each face?

   c. A regular tetrahedron has an edge length of 6 inches. What is its total surface area? Show all work.

11-66.   Hokiri's ladder has two legs that are each 8 feet long. When the ladder is opened safely and locked for use, the legs are 4 feet apart on the ground. What is the angle that is formed at the top of the ladder where the legs meet?

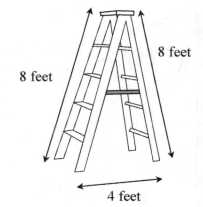

8 feet

8 feet

4 feet

11-67.   Find the area of the region that represents the solution of the inequality $x^2 + y^2 \le 72$.

11-68.   Solve each system of equations below. Write the solution in the form (x, y). Show all work.

a. $y + 3x = 14$
        $y - 3x = 6$

b. $y = 6 - 3x$
        $2x + y = 7$

11-69.   **Multiple Choice:** The probability of winning \$3 on the spinner at right is equal to the chance of winning \$5. Find the expected value for one spin.

a.   \$3.00   b.   \$4.50   c.   \$4.67

d.   \$6.00   e.   None of these

11.2.1 Where's this location?

. . . .

Coordinates on a Sphere

As you learned in Chapter 1, the word *geometry* literally means "measurement of the Earth." In fact, so far in this course, you have used your geometric tools to learn more about Earth. For example, in Lesson 11.1.5, you learned that the United States only makes up 1.8% of the Earth's surface. Also, in Lesson 10.1.1, you learned how Eristothenes used shadows to estimate the Earth's radius.

Today, you will **examine** other earthly questions that can be answered using geometry. Since we can approximate the shape of the earth as a sphere, you will be able to use many of the tools you have used previously. As you work with your team, consider the following focus questions:

What **strategy** or tool can I use?

Is there another way?

Does this **strategy** always work?

11-70.   YOU ARE HERE

In order to help a person describe a location on
the Earth, scientists have developed a reference
grid on the planet's surface, referred to as
longitude and **latitude lines**. While these
reference markings are referred to as "lines,"
they are technically circles that wrap around the
Earth.

Lines of longitude extend north and south, while
lines of latitude extend east and west, as shown in
the diagrams below. These lines help to mark off
arc measures on the planet's surface. In the

Equator

diagrams below, the lines of latitude are marked every 15° while the lines of
longitude are marked every 30°. The most famous line of latitude is the **equator**,
which separates the Earth into two **hemispheres** (half a sphere).

a.   The equator is an example of
      a **great circle**, which means
      that it is a circle that lies on
      the sphere and has the same
      diameter as the sphere.
      Compare the equator with the
      other lines of latitude. What
      do you notice?

Lines of Latitude   **Lines of Longitude**

b.   Is it possible for two great circles
      on the same sphere to intersect?
      If so, draw an example on your
      paper. If not, explain why not.

North Pole

c.   On the sphere provided by your teacher,
      carefully draw circles to represent the lines of
      latitude (every 30°) and longitude (every 30°)
      on the Earth. Highlight the equator by making
      it darker or a different color than the other
      lines of latitude. Also choose one line of
      longitude to represent 0° (called the **prime
      meridian**, which passes through Greenwich,
      England, on the eastern edge of London) and
      highlight it as well.

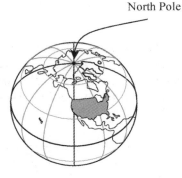

d.   Norman is exactly 1 mile north of Sula. If they both travel at the same rate due
      west, will their paths cross? Why or why not? Assume that people can travel
      over water and all types of terrain.

e.   Erin is exactly 1 mile east of Wilber. If they both travel due south at the same
      rate, will their paths cross? Why or why not?

11-71.   DEAR PEN-PAL

Brianna, who lives in New Orleans, has
been writing to her pen-pal in
Jacksonville, Florida. "Gosh," she
wonders, "How far away is my friend?"

a.   On your "globe" from problem 11-70,
locate Brianna's home. (New Orleans,
LA, is approximately 90° west of the
prime meridian and 30° north of the
equator.) Mark it with a pushpin.

b.   Now, with a second pushpin, mark the location of Brianna's friend, if
Jacksonville is 82° west of the prime meridian and 30° north of the equator.
Use a rubber band to locate the circle with the smallest radius that passes
through these two locations.

c.   What is the measure of the arc connecting these two cities? Show how you
know.

d.   Brianna thinks that if she knew the
circumference of the circle marked with the
rubber band, then she could use the arc measure
to approximate the distance between the two
cities. The shaded circle in the diagram at right
represents the cross-section of the earth 30°
above the equator. If the radius of the earth is
approximately 4000 miles, find the
circumference of the shaded circle.

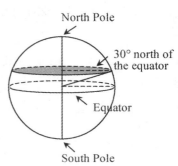

e.   Find the distance between New Orleans and Jacksonville.

11-72.   Obtain a Lesson 11.2.1 Resource Page from your teacher.
On it, mark and label the following locations.

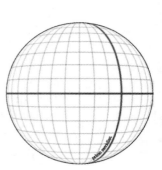

a.   London, England, which is on the prime meridian
and is approximately 51° **north** of the equator.

b.   Narsarssuaq, Greenland, which is approximately
45° **west** of the prime meridian and 61° **north** of
the equator.

c.   Quito, Equador, which is on the equator and is
approximately 79° **west** of the prime meridian.

d.   Cairo, Egypt, which is approximately 31° **east** of the prime meridian and 30°
north of the equator.

e.   Buenos Aires, Argentina, which is approximately 58° **west** of the prime
meridian and 35° **south** of the equator.

11-73.   EXTENSION

a.   If a polar bear travels
1 mile south from the
North Pole, travels
one mile east, and
then travels one mile
north, where does it
end up? Explain
what happens and
why.

b.   Is there another location the polar bear could have started from so that it still
ends up where it started after following the same directions? Explain.

LOOKING DEEPER

Meridian and Time Zones

MATH NOTES

The reference lines connecting the north and
south poles are called **lines of longitude**, as shown in
the diagram at right. These lines help navigators
determine how many degrees east or west they have
traveled.

Another name for these lines of longitude is **meridian**,
which is Latin from "medius" (which means "middle")
and "diem" (which means "day"). Meridian also used
to refer to noon, since it was the time the sun was
directly overhead. In the morning, it was "ante meridian" or before noon. This
is where the abbreviation **a.m.** comes from. Likewise, **p.m.** is short for "post
meridian," which means "after noon."

Lines of Longitude

11-74. The moon is an average distance of 238,900 miles away from the Earth. While that seems very far, how far is it?

   a. Compare that distance with the circumference of the Earth's equator. Assume that the Earth's radius is 4000 miles. How many times greater than the Earth's circumference is the distance to the moon?

   b. One way to estimate the distance between the Earth and the sun is to consider the triangle formed by the sun, Earth, and moon when the moon appears to be half-full. (See the diagram at right.) When the moon appears from earth to be half-full, it can be assumed that the moon forms a 90° angle with the sun and the Earth.

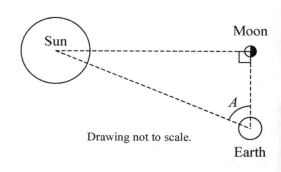

Drawing not to scale.

   Using special equipment, Ray found the measure of angle A to be 89.95°. If the moon is 238,900 miles away from the Earth, then how far is the sun from the Earth?

11-75. The length of chord $\overline{AB}$ in $\odot D$ is 9 mm. If the $m\overset{\frown}{AB} = 32°$, find the length of $\overset{\frown}{AB}$. Draw a diagram.

11-76. On your paper, draw a diagram of a square-based pyramid if the side length of the base is 9 cm and the height of the pyramid is 12 cm.

   a. Find the volume of the pyramid.

   b. If a smaller pyramid is similar to the pyramid in part (a), but has a linear scale factor of $\frac{1}{3}$, find its volume.

11-77. **Examine** the spinner at right. Assume that the probability of spinning a –8 is equal to that of spinning a 0.

   a. Find the spinner's expected value if the value of region A is 8.

   b. Find the spinner's expected value if the value of region A is –4.

   c. What does the value of region A need to be so that the expected value of the spinner is 0?

Geometry Connections

11-78.   In the picture of a globe at right, the lines of
          latitude are concentric circles. Where else might
          you encounter concentric circles?

11-79.   **Multiple Choice:** The volume of a solid is V. If the
          solid is enlarged proportionally so that the perimeter
          increases by a factor of 9, what is the volume of the
          enlarged solid?

          a. $9V$ b. $\frac{81}{4}V$ c. $81V$ d. $729V$

11.2.2 What's the relationship?

Tangents and Arcs

Today, you will develop new geometric tools as you continue to study the Earth and its
measure.

11-80.   EYE IN THE SKY

Satellite

          Did you know that as of 1997, over 8000 operating
          satellites orbited the Earth performing various
          functions such as taking photographs of our planet?
          One way scientists learn more about the Earth is to
          carefully **examine** photographs that are taken by an
          orbiting satellite.

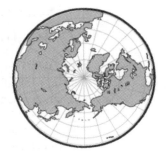

          However, how much of the Earth can a satellite see?
          What does this depend on? In other words, what
          information would you need to know in order to figure
          out how much of the planet is in view of a satellite in
          space? Discuss this with your team and be ready to
          share your ideas with the rest of the class.

11-81.   On the Lesson 11.2.2 Resource Page obtained from your teacher, locate Satellites A,
          B, and C.

          a.   On the resource page, draw an angle from Satellite A that shows the portion of
                the Earth's equator that is visible from the satellite. What is the relationship of
                the sides of the angle and the circle that represents the equator of the Earth?

Problem continues on next page →

11-81.   *Problem continued from previous page.*

  b.   Draw a quadrilateral *ADEF* that connects Satellite A, the points of tangency, and the center of the Earth (point *E*). If the measure of the angle at Satellite A is 90°, what is the measure of the equator's arc that is in view? Explain how you know.

  c.   What is the relationship of *AD* and *AF*? Prove the relationship using congruent triangles.

  d.   If $m\angle A = 90°$ and the radius of the Earth is 4000 miles, how far above the surface of the planet is Satellite A?

11-82.   What if the satellite is placed higher in orbit? Consider this as you answer the questions below.

  a.   Using a different colored pen or pencil, draw the viewing angle from Satellite B on the Lesson 11.2.2 Resource Page. Label the points of tangency *G* and *H*. Will Satellite B see more or less of the Earth's equator than Satellite A?

  b.   If $m\angle B = 60°$, find the length of the equator in view of Satellite B. Assume that the radius of the Earth is 4000 miles.

  c.   Use a third color to draw the viewing angle from Satellite C on the resource page. Label the points of tangency *J* and *K*. If $m\angle C = 45°$, find the $m\overset{\frown}{JK}$ and $m\overset{\frown}{JZK}$.

  d.   Is it possible for a satellite to see 50% of the Earth's equator? Why or why not?

11-83.   HOW ARE THEY RELATED?

  In problems 11-81 and 11-82, you found the measures of angles and arcs formed by two tangents to a circle that intersect each other.

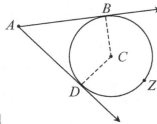

  a.   Copy the diagram at right onto your paper. Using intuition, describe how the measure of the angle formed by the tangents ($m\angle A$) seems to be related to the measures of the major and minor arcs formed by the points of tangency ($\overset{\frown}{BD}$ and $\overset{\frown}{BZD}$).

  b.   If $m\angle A = a$, find $m\overset{\frown}{BD}$ and $m\overset{\frown}{BZD}$ in terms of *a*. Compare the measure of the angle with the measure of the major and minor arcs. What do you notice?

  c.   Write an entry in your Learning Log describing the relationship between the angles and arcs formed by two intersecting tangents to a circle. Also record what you found out about the lengths of the tangents from the point of tangency to their point of intersection. Title this entry "Tangents and Arcs" and include today's date.

METHODS AND MEANINGS

Volume and Lateral Surface of a Sphere

A **sphere** is a three-dimensional solid formed by points that are equidistant from its center.

radius

center

The **volume of a sphere** is twice the volume of a cone with the same radius and height. Since the volume of a cone with radius r and height $2r$ is $V = \frac{1}{3}\pi r^2 (2r) = \frac{2}{3}\pi r^3$, the volume of a sphere with radius r is:

$$V = \frac{4}{3}\pi r^3$$

The **surface area of a sphere** is four times the area of a circle with the same radius. Thus, the surface area of a sphere with radius r is:

$$SA = 4\pi r^2$$

Review & Preview

11-84. While making his lunch, Alexander sliced off a portion of his grapefruit. If the area of the cross-section of the slice (shaded at right) was 3 in^2, and if the diameter of the grapefruit was 5 inches, find the distance between the center of the grapefruit and the slice. Assume the grapefruit is a sphere.

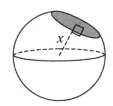

11-85. The approximate surface areas of the seven Earth continents are shown in the table at right. If the radius of the Earth's moon is approximately 1080 miles, how would its surface area compare with the size of the continents?

Continent	Area (sq. miles)
Asia	17,212,048.1
Africa	11,608,161.4
North America	9,365,294.0
South America	6,879,954.4
Antarctica	5,100,023.4
Europe	3,837,083.3
Australia/Oceania	2,967,967.3

11-86.   Find the area of the regular decagon if the length of each side is 20 units.

11-87.   The solid at right is an example of a **truncated pyramid**. It is formed by slicing and removing the top of a pyramid so that the slice is parallel to the base of the pyramid. If the original height of the square-based pyramid at right was 12 cm, find the volume of this truncated pyramid. (Hint: you may find your results from problem 11-76 useful.)

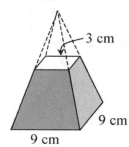

3 cm

9 cm

9 cm

11-88.   **Examine** the triangles at right. Are they similar? Are they congruent? Explain how you know. Then write an appropriate similarity or congruence statement.

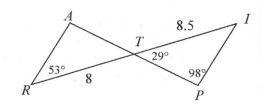

11-89.   **Multiple Choice:** Which shape below has the <u>least</u> area?

a.   A circle with radius 5 units

b.   A square with side length 9 units

c.   A trapezoid with bases of length 8 and 10 units and height of 9 units

d.   A rhombus with side length 9 units and height of 8 units.

11.2.3 What is the measure?
· ·
Secant and Tangent Relationships

In Lesson 11.2.2, you studied the angles and arcs formed by tangents when a satellite orbits the Earth, as shown in the diagram at right. Today, you will consider a related question: What if the sides of the angle intersect the circle more than once? What are the relationships between the angles and arcs formed when this happens? And what can you learn about the lengths of the segments created by the points of intersection?

Satellite

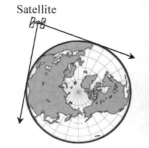

As you work with your team, carefully record your team's conjectures. And while you work, keep the following questions in mind:

What patterns do I see?

Is this relationship always true?

11-90.   Review what you learned in Lesson 11.2.2 by solving for the given variables in the
diagrams below. Show all work.

a.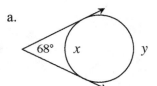

b.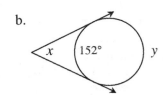

c.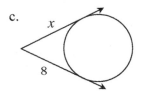

11-91.   While a tangent is a line that intersects a circle (like ⊙C in
the diagram at right) at exactly one point, a **secant** is a line
that intersects a circle twice. $\overleftrightarrow{PR}$ is an example of a secant,
while $\overleftrightarrow{QS}$ is an example of a tangent.

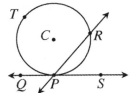

   a.   What happens to the measure of the angles and arcs
when a secant intersects the circle at the point of tangency?
Namely, how are the angles located at P in the diagram above
related to $m\overarc{PR}$ and $m\overarc{PTR}$? First make an educated guess.
Then test your ideas out using a dynamic geometry tool. Write a
conjecture and be ready to share it with the class.

   b.   Uri wants to prove his conjecture from part (a) for a
non-special secant (meaning that $\overleftrightarrow{PR}$ is not a
diameter). He decided to extend a diameter from
point P and to create an inscribed angle that intercepts
$\overarc{PR}$. With your team, **examine** Uri's diagram
carefully and consider all the relationships you can
identify that could be useful.

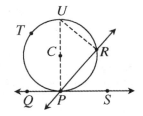

      To get you started, use the list below.

         i.   What is $m\angle URP$?

         ii. How is $m\angle RUP$ related to $m\overarc{PR}$?

         iii. What is the sum of the angles in $\triangle PRU$?

         iv. How are $\angle UPR$ and $\angle RPS$ related?

   c.   Using the relationships you explored in part (b), prove that if $m\angle RPS = x$ in
the diagram from part (b), then $m\overarc{PR} = 2x$. Remember to **justify** each step.

11-92.   Uri now has this challenge for you:
*What happens when secants and
tangents intersect outside a circle?* To
consider this, you need to **examine** two
separate cases: One is when a secant
and tangent intersect outside a circle
(case *i* below). The other is when two
secants intersect outside a circle (case *ii*
below). As with your earlier
investigations,

- First make a prediction about
  the relationship between the
  measures of *x*, *a*, and *b* for each
  case.

- Then use your dynamic geometry tool to test your conjectures.

- For each case, write an algebraic statement (equation) that
  relates *x*, *a*, and *b*. Be ready to share each equation with the
  rest of the class.

i. 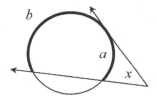   *ii.*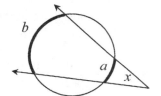

11-93.   Now prove your conjectures from problem 11-92. For each diagram, add a line
segment that will help to create an inscribed angle. Then use angle relationships
(such as the sum of the angles of a triangle must be 180°) to then find the measures
of all the angles in terms of *x*, *a*, and *b*. Be sure to show that in each case, $x = \frac{b-a}{2}$.
Remember to **justify** each statement.

i. 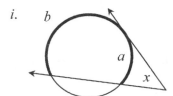   *ii.*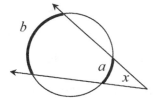

11-94.   Camille is interested in the lengths of segments that
         are created by the points of intersection. She
         remembers proving in Lesson 11.2.2 that the lengths
         of the tangents between their intersection and the
         points of tangency are equal, as shown in the
         diagram at right. She figures that there must be
         some relationships in the lengths created by the
         intersections of secants, too.

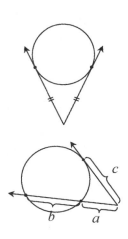

   a.   The first case she wants to consider is when a
         tangent and secant intersect outside a circle,
         as shown in the figure at right. Copy this
         diagram onto your paper.

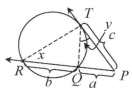

   b.   "To find a relationship, I think we need to add
         some line segments to create some inscribed
         angles and triangles," Camille tells her team.
         She decides to add the line segments shown at
         right. Show why the angles marked x and y
         must be congruent.

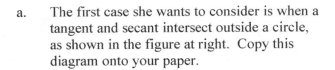

   c.   "If some of these triangles are similar, I can use that to find a relationship
         between these side lengths," Camille explains. Help her prove that
         $\triangle PQT \sim \triangle PTR$.

   d.   Use the fact that $\triangle PQT \sim \triangle PTR$ to write a proportion using a, b, and c.
         Simplify this equation as much as possible to find an equation that helps you
         understand the relationship between a, b, and c.

   e.   Use the same process to find the
         relationship between the lengths created
         when two secants intersect outside a circle.
         Two extra segments have been added to the
         diagram to help create similar triangles. Be
         ready to **justify** your relationship.

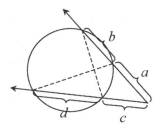

11-95.   Use all your circle relationships to solve for the variables in each of the diagrams below.

a.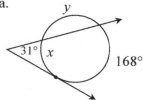

b.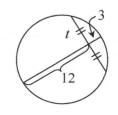

c.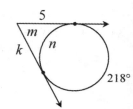

d.   *C* is the center

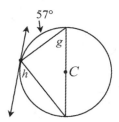

e.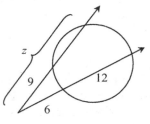

f.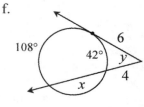

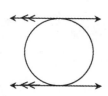
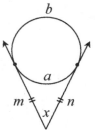

11-96.   Solve for the variables in each of the diagrams below. Assume point C is the center of the circle in part (b).

a.

b.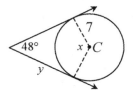

c.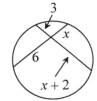

11-97.   In part (c) of problem 11-96, you used the relationship between the segment lengths formed by intersecting chords to find a missing length. But how are the arc measures of two random intersecting chords related? **Examine** the diagram at right.

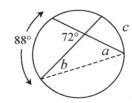

   a.   Solve for a, b, and c using what you know about inscribed angles and the sum of the angles of a triangle.

   b.   Compare the result for c with 88° and 72°. Is there a relationship?

11-98.   Perhaps you think the Earth is big? Consider the sun!

   a.   Assume that the radius of the Earth 4000 miles. The sun is approximately 109 times as wide. Find the sun's radius.

   b.   The distance between the Earth and the moon is 238,900 miles. Compare this distance with the radius of the sun you found in part (a).

   c.   If the sun were hollow, how many Earths would fill the inside of it?

11-99.   Write the equation for the graph at right.

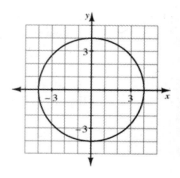

11-100.   On your paper, draw a diagram of a square-based
pyramid. If the base has side length 6 units and the
height of the pyramid is 10 units, find the total
surface area. Show all your work.

11-101.   **Multiple Choice:** Which of the following cannot be the measure of an exterior angle
of a regular polygon?

a.   18°   b.   24°   c.   28°   d.   40°

11-102.   Solve for the variables in each of the diagrams below. Assume that point C is the
center of the circle in part (b).

a.

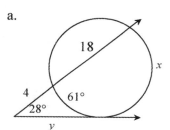

b.

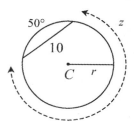

c.

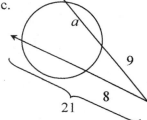

11-103.   Which has greater volume: a cylinder with radius 38 units and height 71 units or a
rectangular prism with dimensions 34, 84, and 99 units? Show all work and support
your **reasoning**.

11-104.   Copy the diagram at right onto your paper. Use the
process from problem 11-97 to find the measure of x.
Show all work.

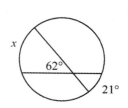

11-105.   Mr. Kyi has placed 3 red, 7 blue, and 2 yellow beads in a hat. If a person selects a red bead, he or she wins $3. If that person selects a blue bead, he or she loses $1. If the person selects a yellow bead, he or she wins $10. What is the expected value for one draw?

11-106.   A solar eclipse occurs when the moon passes between the Earth and the sun and is perfectly aligned so that it blocks the Earth's view of the sun.

Note: This diagram is not to scale.

How do scientists figure out what areas of the Earth will see an eclipse? To find out, copy the diagram above onto your paper. Then use tangents representing the sun's rays to find the portion of the Earth's equator that will see the total eclipse.

11-107.   **Multiple Choice:** The Mona Lisa, by Leonardo da Vinci, is arguably the most famous painting in existence. The rectangular artwork, which hangs in the Musée du Louvre, measures 77 cm by 53 cm. When the museum created a billboard with an enlarged version of the portrait for advertisement, they used a linear scale factor of 20. What was the area of the billboard?

a.   4081 cm^2 b.   32,638,000 cm^2

c.   81,620 cm^2 d.   1,632,400 cm^2

e.   None of these

Chapter 11 Closure   What have I learned?

Reflection and Synthesis

The activities below offer you a chance to reflect on what you have learned during this chapter. As you work, look for concepts that you feel very comfortable with, ideas that you would like to learn more about, and topics you need more help with. Look for **connections** between ideas as well as **connections** with material you learned previously.

①   TEAM BRAINSTORM

With your team, brainstorm a list for each of the following three topics. Be as detailed as you can. How long can you make your list? Challenge yourselves. Be prepared to share your team's ideas with the class.

Topics: What have you studied in this chapter? What ideas and words were important in what you learned? Remember to be as detailed as you can.

Problem Solving: What did you do to solve problems? What different **strategies** did you use?

Connections: How are the topics, ideas, and words that you learned in previous courses are **connected** to the new ideas in this chapter? Again, make your list as long as you can.

The following is a list of the vocabulary used in this chapter. The words that appear in bold are new to this chapter. Make sure that you are familiar with all of these words and know what they mean. Refer to the glossary or index for any words that you do not yet understand.

arc	base	circle
cone	**cross-section**	**cube**
cylinder	diameter	**edge**
equator	**face**	**great circle**
height	**hemisphere**	lateral face
latitude	**longitude**	oblique
octahedron	**platonic solid**	**polyhedron**
pyramid	radius	secant
slant height	**sphere**	surface area
tangent	**tetrahedron**	volume

Make a concept map showing all of the **connections** you can find among the key words and ideas listed above. To show a **connection** between two words, draw a line between them and explain the **connection**, as shown in the example below. A word can be **connected** to any other word as long as there is a **justified connection**. For each key word or idea, provide a sketch of an example.

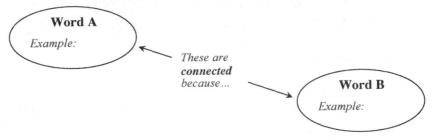

Your teacher may provide you with vocabulary cards to help you get started. If you use the cards to plan your concept map, be sure either to re-draw your concept map on your paper or to glue the vocabulary cards to a poster with all of the **connections** explained for others to see and understand.

While you are making your map, your team may think of related words or ideas that are not listed above. Be sure to include these ideas on your concept map.

③ SUMMARIZING MY UNDERSTANDING

This section gives you an opportunity to show what you know about certain math topics or ideas. Your teacher will give you directions for exactly how to do this.

④   WHAT HAVE I LEARNED?

This section will help you evaluate which types of problems you have seen with which you feel comfortable and those with which you need more help. This section will appear at the end of every chapter to help you check your understanding. Even if your teacher does not assign this section, it is a good idea to try these problems and find out for yourself what you know and what you need to work on.

Solve each problem as completely as you can. The table at the end of this closure section has answers to these problems. It also tells you where you can find additional help and practice on problems like these.

CL 11-108. Use all your circle relationships to solve for the variables in each of the diagrams below. Assume that C is the center of the circle for parts (b) and (c).

a.
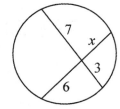

b.   The area of $\odot C$ is 25π un^2
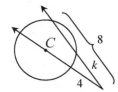

c.
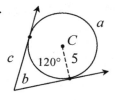

d.
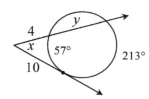

CL 11-109. The radius of the moon is approximately 1738 km. Draw a diagram of the moon on your paper.

a.   If all the Earth's water were distributed on the surface of the moon, it would be about 33.6 km deep! How much water is on the Earth?

b.   If all of this water were to be collected and reshaped into a gigantic spherical drop out in space, what would its radius be?

CL 11-110. On the same set of axes, graph the equations below. Name all points of intersection.

$$x^2 + y^2 = 100$$
$$y = \tfrac{1}{2}x + 5$$

CL 11-111. **Examine** the spinner at right.

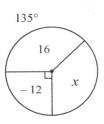

a.   Find the expected value of the spinner if $x = 4$.

b.   Find the expected value of the spinner if $x = -8$.

c.   Find x so that the expected value of the spinner is 6.

CL 11-112. Find the volume of a pyramid if its base is a regular pentagon with perimeter 20 units and if its height is 7 units.

CL 11-113. **Examine** the triangles below. Based on the markings and measurements provided in the diagrams, which are similar to $\triangle ABC$ at right? Which are congruent? Are there any that you cannot determine? **Justify** your conclusion and, if appropriate, write a similarity or congruence statement. **Note:** The diagrams are not drawn to scale.

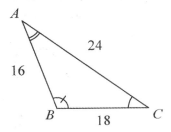

a. 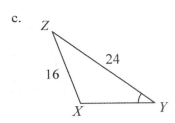 b. c.

CL 11-114. Talila is planning on giving her geometry teacher a gift. She has two containers to choose from:

• A cylinder tube with diameter 6 inches and height 10 inches

• A rectangular box with dimensions 5 inches by 6 inches by 9 inches

a.   Assuming that her gift can fit in either box, which will require the least amount of wrapping paper?

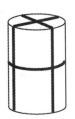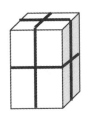

b.   She plans to tie two loops of ribbon about the package as shown at right. Which package will require the least amount of ribbon? Ignore any ties or bows.

CL 11-115. A big warehouse carrying tents has a miniature model that is similar to the full-sized tent. The tent is a triangular-based prism and the miniature model has dimensions shown in the diagram at right.

a. How much fabric does the small tent use? That is, what is its surface area?

b. What is the volume of the small model?

c. If the volume of the full-sized model is 72 ft^3, how tall is the full-sized tent?

d. How much fabric does the full-sized tent use?

CL 11-116. Check your answers using the table at the end of the closure section. Which problems do you feel confident about? Which problems were hard? Use the table to make a list of topics you need help on and a list of topics you need to practice more.

⑤   HOW AM I THINKING?

This course focuses on five different **Ways of Thinking**: investigating, examining, visualizing, choosing a strategy/tool, and reasoning and justifying. These are some of the ways in which you think while trying to make sense of a concept or to solve a problem (even outside of math class). During this chapter, you have probably used each Way of Thinking multiple times without even realizing it!

Choose three of these Ways of Thinking that you remember using while working in this chapter. For each Way of Thinking that you choose, show and explain where you used it and how you used it. Describe why thinking in this way helped you solve a particular problem or understand something new. Be sure to include examples to demonstrate your thinking.

Answers and Support for Closure Activity #4
What Have I Learned?

Problem	Solution	Need Help?	More Practice
CL 11-108.	a. $x = 3.5$ b. $k = 7$ c. $a = 240°$, $b = 60°$, $c = 5\sqrt{3}$ d. $x = 78°$, $y = 21$	Lessons 10.1.2, 10.1.3, 10.1.4, and 11.2.3 Math Notes box, problem 10-35	Problems 10-7, 10-15, 10-26, 10-37, 10-52, 10-59, 10-93, 11-43, 11-95, 11-96, 11-97, 11-102, 11-104
CL 11-109.	a. $1,300,222,453$ km b. 677.1 km	Lesson 11.2.2 Math Notes box	Problems 11-62, 11-64, 11-98
CL 11-110.	(6, 8) and (–10, 0)	Lesson 10.3.1	Problems 10-88, 10-89, 10-90, 11-16, 11-40, 11-41, 11-55, 11-67, 11-99
CL 11-111.	a. 4.5 b. 0 c. $x = -8$	Lesson 10.3.1 Math Notes box	Problems 10-55, 10-64, 10-66, 10-67, 10-69, 10-75, 10-76, 10-77, 10-81, 10-92, 11-23, 11-69, 11-77, 11-105
CL 11-112.	$V \approx 64.23$ un^3	Lessons 8.1.4, 8.1.5, 8.3.1, 11.1.2, and 11.1.4 Math Notes boxes	Problems 8-45, 8-47, 8-48, 8-67, 8-85, 9-9, 10-41, 11-31, 11-36, 11-46, 11-76

Problem	Solution	Need Help?	More Practice
CL 11-113.	a. $\triangle ABC \sim \triangle RTS$ (AA $\sim$) b. $\triangle ABC \cong \triangle MPK$ (AAS $\cong$) c. Cannot be determined because there are two possible triangles when SSA is given.	Lessons 3.2.1, 3.2.2, and 3.2.5 Math Notes boxes	Problems 7-6, 7-14, 7-28, 7-53, 7-77, 7-87, 7-104, 8-32, 8-54, 8-80, 9-12, 9-61, 10-32, 10-96, 11-54
CL 11-114.	a. The cylinder needs less paper ($SA = 78\pi$ in²) b. The prism requires less ribbon (80 inches)	Lessons 8.3.2, 9.1.2, and 9.1.3 Math Notes boxes	Problems 9-15, 9-17, 9-25, 9-26, 9-27, 9-28, 9-33, 9-40, 9-59, 9-89, 10-6, 10-41, 10-95, 11-9, 11-15, 11-42, 11-103
CL 11-115.	a. SA ≈ 31.0 ft² b. V ≈ 9 ft³ c. linear scale factor = 2, height = 6 ft. d. $SA \approx 124$ ft²	Lessons 9.1.2, 9.1.3, 9.1.5 Math Notes boxes, problems 9-35 and 9-36	Problems 9-37, 9-39, 9-40, 9-45, 9-46, 9-47, 9-48, 9-73, 10-51, 10-60, 11-11, 11-38, 11-76, 11-107

CHAPTER 12

Conics and Closure

As this course draws to a close, it is appropriate to reflect on what you have learned so far and to look for connections between topics in both algebra and geometry.

For example, in Section 12.1, you will extend your understanding of the cross-sections of a cone, called "conic sections." You will learn about the geometric properties of conic sections and will discover how to represent them algebraically.

Then, in Section 12.2, four activities offer a chance for you to apply your geometric **tools** in new ways. You will find new connections between familiar geometric ideas and learn even more special properties about familiar shapes.

In this chapter, you will learn:

> ➤ How to identify the cross-section of a solid.

> ➤ How to represent the cross-sections of a cone (the "conic sections") algebraically.

> ➤ The geometric definitions of a circle, a parabola, an ellipse, and a hyperbola.

Guiding Questions

Think about these questions throughout this chapter:

What's the cross-section?

How can I draw it?

What's the relationship?

What information do I need?

Is there another way?

Chapter Outline

Section 12.1 By studying the different cross-sections of a cone, you will discover how geometry and algebra can each define a shape. You will learn how to construct several conic sections using tools, such as string and tracing paper, and will develop geometric definitions for a circle, parabola, ellipse, and hyperbola.

Section 12.2 As you complete the course closure activities, you will apply the mathematics you have learned throughout this course. For example, you will discover a special ratio that often occurs in nature, find new relationships that exist in basic polyhedra, learn about a shape created when the midpoints of the sides of a quadrilateral are connected, and determine where a goat should be tethered to a barn so that it has the lowest probability of eating a poisoned weed.

12.1.1 What's the cross-section?

· ·

Introduction to Conic Sections

In Section 11.1, you explored the cross-sections of several types of solids. In fact, you learned that a sphere is special because it is the only solid that has a circular cross-section no matter which direction it is sliced. But what about the cross-sections of a cone? What different cross-sections can be found? And what can be learned about these cross-sections?

In Section 12.1, you and your team will explore the various cross-sections of a cone. As you explore, look for connections with other mathematical concepts you have studied previously.

12-1.   CONIC SECTIONS

Obtain the Lesson 12.1.1
Resource Page from your teacher
and construct a cone using
scissors and tape. Then, with
your team, explore the different
cross-sections of a cone (called
conic sections). Imagine slicing
a cone as many different ways as
you can. Draw and describe each
cross-section on your paper. Do
you know the names for any of
these shapes?

12-2.   **Examine** your conic sections
from problem 12-1.

a.   If you have not done so
already, determine how you
can slice the cone so that
the cross-section is a ray.

b.   Can the cross-section of a cone be a
single point? Explain.

c.   If you have not done so already,
describe the cross-section of the
cone shown at right when it is sliced
vertically through the top vertex.

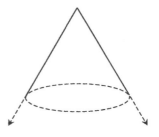

12-3. Interestingly, one of the types of conic sections is a curve you studied in algebra: the **parabola**. What more can be learned about the geometry of a parabola?

a. In Chapter 9, you constructed a parabola using tracing paper (see problem 9-78). With your team, reconstruct a parabola by carefully drawing a line (*l*) and a point not on the line (*P*) on tracing paper. Then fold the tracing paper so that line *l* passes through point *P*. Unfold the tracing paper and fold it again at a different point on line *l* so that line *l* still passes through point *P*. Continue this process until you have at least 20 creased lines forming a parabola.

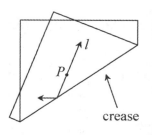

b. **Examine** where the parabola lies in relationship with the original point *P* and line *l*. Where does the point lie? Where does the line lie? Do these relationships seem to hold for the other parabolas constructed by your teammates?

12-4. FOCUS AND DIRECTRIX OF A PARABOLA

Since the point and the line help to determine the parabola, there are special names that are used to refer to them. The point is called the **focus** of the parabola, while the line is called the **directrix**.

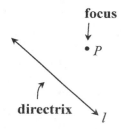

a. Together, the focus and the directrix determine the parabola. For example, can you **visualize** the parabola formed by the focus and directrix shown at right? Trace the point and line on your paper and sketch the parabola.

b. What is the relationship between the points on the parabola and its focus and directrix? Mark a point on the parabola and label it *A*. Fold the tracing paper so that *l* passes through *P* and the crease passes through *A*. Compare the distance between *P* and *A* and the distance between *A* and *l*. What do you notice? Does this work for all points on the parabola?

c. How does the distance between the focus (the point) and the directrix (the line) affect the shape of the parabola? Explore this using a dynamic geometry tool, if possible. (If a dynamic tool is not available, use tracing paper to test several different distances between the focus and directrix.) Explain the result.

12-5. Write an entry in your Learning Log describing what you learned during this lesson. Include information about the cross-sections of a cone and the geometric relationships in a parabola. What questions do you have about the other conic sections? Title this entry "Conic Sections" and include today's date.

12-6.   Cawker City, Kansas, claims to have the world's largest ball of twine. Started in 1953 by Frank Stoeber, this ball has been created by wrapping more than 1300 miles of twine. In fact, this giant ball has a circumference of 40 feet. Assuming the ball of twine is a sphere, find the surface area and volume of the ball of twine.

12-7.   The equations below are the types of equations that you will need to be able to solve automatically in a later course. Try to solve these in 10 minutes or less. The solutions are provided after problem 12-11 for you to check your answers.

   a. $2x - 5 = 7$ b. $x^2 = 16$ c. $2(x-1) = 6$

   d. $\frac{x}{5} = 6$ e. $2x^2 + 5 = x^2 + 14$ f $(x-3)(x+5) = 0$

12-8.   **Examine** the pen or pencil that you are using right now. Imagine slicing it in different directions. On your paper, draw at least three different cross-sections of the pen or pencil.

12-9.   On graph paper, graph $x^2 + y^2 = 9$.

   a.   Consider the inequality $x^2 + y^2 \leq 9$. Does the point (0, 0) make this inequality true? What is the graph of $x^2 + y^2 \leq 9$? Explain.

   b.   Now consider the inequality $x^2 + y^2 > 9$. Does the point (0, 0) make this inequality true? What region is shaded? Describe the graph of this inequality.

12-10.   Remember that the **absolute value function** finds the distance on a number line between a number and zero. For example, the absolute value of –6 (written $\left|-6\right|$) equals 6, while $\left|2\right| = 2$.

   On graph paper, copy and complete the table below and graph the function $y = \left|x\right| + 2$.

x	−4	−3	−2	−1	0	1	2	3	4
y	6				2				

12-11.   **Multiple Choice:** In the diagram at right, the value of x is:

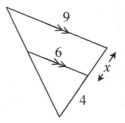

a.   1   b.   2   c.   3

d.   4   e.   None of these

Solutions to problem 12-7: a: 6, b: 4 or −4, c: 4, d: 30, e: 3 or −3, f: 3 or −5

12.1.2 How can I graph it?

Graphing Parabolas Using The Focus and Directrix

In Lesson 12.1.1, you **investigated** the geometric properties of a parabola, one of the cross-sections of a cone. Today you and your team will explore other conic sections as you continue to find ways to connect geometry and algebra.

12-12.   GRAPHING WITH A FOCUS AND DIRECTRIX

In the past, you have graphed conics, such as circles and parabolas, using rectangular graph paper and an equation. However, another way to graph conic sections is to use **focus-directrix paper**, that is designed with lines and concentric circles like the example shown in Figure A at right.

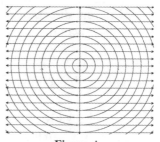

Figure A:
Focus and directrix paper

How can you graph parabolas using this paper? Obtain at least two sheets of focus-directrix paper from your teacher and follow the directions below.

a.   In problem 12-4, you discovered that each point on a parabola is an equal distance from the focus and directrix. To graph a parabola, highlight the center of the concentric circles on your focus-directrix grid with a colored marker. This will be the focus of the parabola. Then highlight a line that is two units away from the focus, as shown in the Figure B at right.

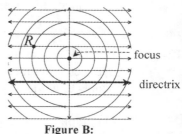

Figure B:
Point R on grid

b.   **Examine** point R on the focus-directrix grid in Figure B. Notice that the circles help you count the distance between R and the focus (the center of the circles). Explain how you know that the point R is 3 units from the focus and 3 units from the directrix.

Problem continues on next page →

12-12.   *Problem continued from previous page.*

    c.   Use the circles and lines to plot a point that is 1 unit away from the focus and the directrix. Is there another point that is also 1 unit away from both the focus and directrix?

    d.   Likewise, find two points that are 2 units away from both the focus and the directrix. Continue plotting points that are equidistant from the focus and the directrix until the parabola appears. Compare your parabola with those of your teammates to double-check for accuracy.

12-13.   What else can you learn about graphing parabolas using focus-directrix paper? The left column of the table below contains several **investigative** questions to explore using focus-directrix paper. For each question, first **visualize** the resulting parabola and discuss your prediction with your team. Then **test** the situation on a fresh focus-directrix grid. The right-hand column contains a suggested way to test your idea, although your team may design its own way to **investigate** the question.

Investigative Questions	Try it out!
a. What would happen to the parabola from problem 12-12 if the directrix were moved so that it is above the focus?	On a new focus-directrix grid, place the directrix on the line that is 2 units above the focus. Then plot the points of the resulting parabola, making sure each point is the same distance from the focus and directrix. Describe what happens.
b. What would happen to the parabola from problem 12-12 if the directrix were moved so that it is <u>farther</u> from the focus?	On a new focus-directrix grid, place the directrix so that it is 6 units away from the focus. Then plot the points of the resulting parabola, making sure each point is the same distance from the focus and directrix. Describe what happens.
c. What would happen to the parabola from problem 12-12 if the directrix were moved so that it is <u>closer</u> to the focus?	On a new focus-directrix grid, place the directrix so that it is 1 unit away from the focus. Then plot the points of the resulting parabola, making sure each point is the same distance from the focus and directrix. Describe what happens.

12-14.   With your team, brainstorm your own **investigative** question you would like to explore. You may want to start the questions with "What if…" or "What happens when…" to help you get started. Share your questions with the class.

12-15.   Celia asks this question: "What if the points are *closer* to the focus than the directrix?" For example, what if the distance between each point and the focus is <u>half</u> the distance between that point and the directrix? Consider this as you answer the questions below.

a.   On a new sheet of focus-directrix paper, highlight the center (focus) and a line that is 6 units away from the center.

b.   For every unit a point is away from the focus, it needs to be 2 units away from the directrix. Find the first point that is 2 units away from the focus and 4 units away from the directrix. Then find another point that is 1 *more* unit away from the focus and 2 *more* units away from the directrix. (This point should be a total of 3 units away from the focus and 6 units away from the directrix.) Continue this pattern until the graph is complete. What shape do you see?

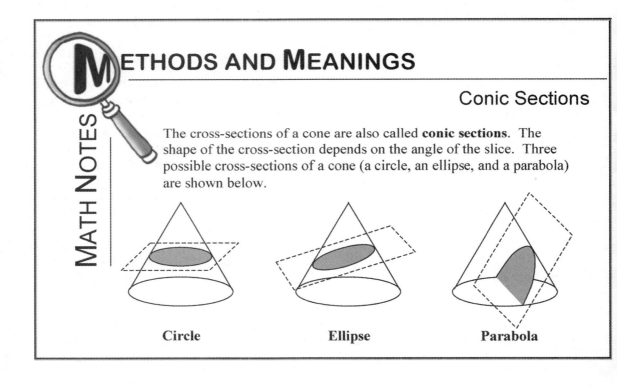

MᴇTHODS AND Mᴇᴀɴɪɴɢs

Conic Sections

MATH NOTES

The cross-sections of a cone are also called **conic sections**. The shape of the cross-section depends on the angle of the slice. Three possible cross-sections of a cone (a circle, an ellipse, and a parabola) are shown below.

Circle   **Ellipse**   **Parabola**

Review & Preview

12-16.   A solid with volume 820 cm^3 is reduced proportionally with a linear scale factor of $\frac{1}{2}$. What is the volume of the result?

12-17.   On graph paper, graph the equations below.

   a. $x^2 + y^2 = 4.5^2$

   b. $x^2 + y^2 = 75$

12-18.   Use the relationships in each diagram below to solve for the given variables.

   a.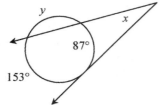

   b.   The area of $\odot K$ is 36π un^2.

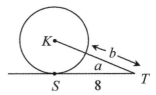

   c.   The diameter of $\odot C$ is 13 units. w is the length of $\overline{AB}$.

   d.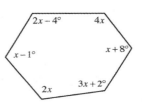

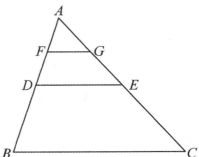

12-19.   In the triangle at right, $\overline{DE}$ is a midsegment of $\triangle ABC$ and $\overline{FG}$ is a midsegment of $\triangle ADE$. If $DE = 7$ cm, find BC and FG.

12-20.   Find the volume of a cone if the circumference of the base is 28π inches and the height is 18 inches.

12-21.   **Multiple Choice:** As Carol shopped for a spring picnic, she spent $2.00 for each liter of soda and $3.50 for each bag of chips. In all, she bought 18 items for a total of $43.50. Assuming she only bought chips and soda, how many bags of chips did she buy?

   a.   9   b.   5   c.   15   d.   3

12.1.3 What shape does it make?

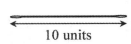

. . . .

Circles and Ellipses

In Lesson 12.1.1, you **investigated** the geometric properties of a parabola, one of the cross-sections of a cone. Today you and your team will explore other conic sections as you look for ways to connect geometry and algebra.

12-22. What shapes can you make using string? To find out, obtain a piece of cardboard, some thumbtacks, a ruler, and a piece of string from your teacher. Then follow the directions below.

10 units

a. Attach a piece of graph paper to the cardboard. Form two loops on the string so that, when pulled apart, the ends of the loops are 10 units apart. Attach one loop to the center of the cardboard using a thumbtack. If you place your pencil in the other loop and keep the string taut (tight), what shape will you create? Explain how you know and then test your idea by drawing the shape on the graph paper.

b. What if the string is attached to the cardboard at the ends of both loops? Attach both loops of the string from part (a) to the cardboard using two thumbtacks spaced 8 units apart. Predict what shape a pencil will create as it pulls the string tight in all directions.

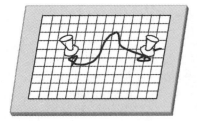

Then test your prediction by drawing the shape on your graph paper. Describe the result. Where have you seen this shape before?

c. What happens to the shape if the thumbtacks are moved so that they are farther apart? What happens when the thumbtacks are closer together? What happens when the thumbtacks are at the same point? Explore these questions with your team and be prepared to share your conclusions with the class.

12-23.   ELLIPSE

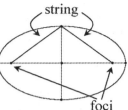
string

foci

The shape that you created in problem 12-22 is called an **ellipse**. Each thumbtack represents a **focus** of the ellipse, so while a parabola only has one focus, an ellipse has two **foci** (plural for "focus").

Examine the ellipse that you created in problem 12-22. How wide is it (in graph paper units)? How tall? How are these lengths related to the length of the string (between the loops)?

12-24.   On focus-directrix paper, graph each set of points that are described below. Use a new focus-directrix grid for each part.

a.   Graph the set of points that are 6 units away from the focus.

b.   The directrix is 8 units away from the focus. Graph the set of set of points that are equidistant (i.e. the same distance) from the focus and the directrix.

c.   The directrix is 12 units away from the focus. Graph the result if the distance between each point of the graph and the focus is half the distance between that same point on the graph and the directrix.

Review & Preview

12-25.   Find the volume of each shape below. Assume that all corners in part (b) are right angles.

a.   cone

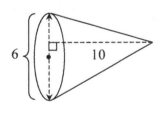
6   10

b.

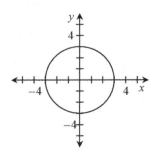
18   9   12   10   21

12-26.   **Examine** the graph of the circle at right.

a.   Find the equation of the circle.

b.   On graph paper, sketch the graph of the equation $x^2 + y^2 = 49$. What is the radius?

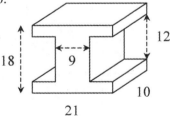

12-27.   **Examine** the diagram at right.

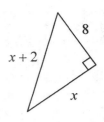

a.   Write an equation using the geometric relationships in the diagram. Then solve your equation for *x*.

b.   Find the measures of the acute angles of the triangle. What **tool** did you use?

12-28.   Jinning is going to flip a coin. If the result is "heads," he wins $4. If the result is "tails," he loses $7.

a.   What is his expected value per flip?

b.   If he flips the coin 8 times, how much should he win or lose?

12-29.   Use the diagram of $\odot C$ at right to answer the questions below.

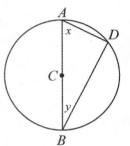

a.   If $m\angle x = 28°$, what is $m\overarc{AD}$?

b.   If $AD = 5$ and $BD = 5\sqrt{3}$, what is the area of $\odot C$?

c.   If the radius of $\odot C$ is 8 and if $m\overarc{BD} = 100°$, what is BD?

12-30.   **Multiple Choice:** Based on the markings in the diagrams at right, which statement is true?

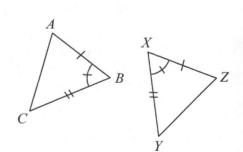

a. $\triangle ABC \cong \triangle XYZ$

b. $\triangle ABC \cong \triangle YXZ$

c. $\triangle ABC \cong \triangle ZXY$

d. $\triangle ABC \cong \triangle ZYX$

e.   None of these

12.1.4 How can I construct it?

The Hyperbola

12-31. Review what you have learned about ellipses as you answer the questions below. You may find the information in the Math Notes box useful.

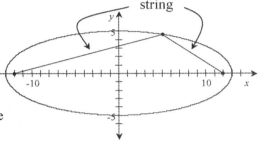

a. Maya used string and thumbtacks to draw the ellipse at right. How wide is her ellipse? How long is the string she used? How can you tell?

b. Maya's thumbtacks are placed at $(12, 0)$ and $(-12, 0)$. What are these points called?

c. How could Maya change her thumbtacks so that the ellipse is 26 units tall and 10 units wide?

12-32. CONSTRUCTING AN ELLIPSE

Maya thinks that an ellipse is closely related to a circle. For one thing, they are both cross-sections of a cone. Also, when the two foci of an ellipse coincide (lie on top of each other), the ellipse becomes a circle. Therefore, Maya suspects that there must be a way to use a circle to construct an ellipse with tracing paper.

a. Use a compass to construct a circle with a radius of approximately 2 inches on a piece of tracing paper. Label its center C.

b. Find and label a point P inside the circle (other than the center). Then fold the tracing paper so that the circle passes through P. Unfold and then fold in a different location so that the circle still passes through P. Continue this process until an ellipse emerges.

c. Where are the foci of the ellipse?

d. Why does this construction work? Pick a point on the circle and label it A. Draw the radius $\overline{AC}$. Study what happens as you fold the circle so that point A lies on point P. Explain why the sum of the distances between each point on the ellipse and the foci must be constant.

12-33. Maya asks, "What if the point is outside the circle?"

Your Task: Repeat the folding process that you used in problem 12-32 to explore Maya's question with your team. Each time you fold the tracing paper, be sure a different point on the circle passes through point P. Use fresh tracing paper for each construction. Write down what happens and be prepared to share your findings with the class.

12-34.   THE HYPERBOLA

The shape you constructed in problem 12-33
is called a **hyperbola**. A hyperbola is
sometimes described as having two curves
facing away from each other.

a.   A hyperbola has two foci. **Examine** the
hyperbola that you constructed in
problem 12-33. Where do you think the
foci might lie? Explain your thinking.

b.   In an ellipse, the sum of the distances
between each point on the ellipse and its
foci must be constant. One way to
remember this is to imagine constructing
the ellipse with a string that is attached
at both foci.

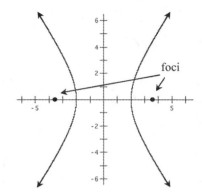

Example of a hyperbola

But what about a hyperbola? How are the distances between
each point on the hyperbola and the foci related? Explore this
idea with a dynamic geometry tool, if possible. (If a dynamic
tool is not available, ask your teacher for the Lesson 12.1.4
Resource Page or download a copy from www.cpm.org.)
Describe the relationship between the distances from each focus to each point
on the hyperbola.

12-35.   Maya is still wondering about her
construction. "What if the point lies
<u>on</u> the circle? What conic would be
created then?" Use the dynamic
geometry tool to **investigate** her
question. Explain what happens.

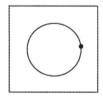

METHODS AND MEANINGS

MATH NOTES

Ellipses

One of the cross-sections of a cone is an **ellipse**. An ellipse is often described as an oval or a circle that is "stretched."

An ellipse has two **foci** that lie on its longest line of symmetry. The sum of the distances between each point on the ellipse and the foci must be constant. For example, if A and B are the foci of the ellipse at right, then the sum of the lengths of $\overline{AD}$ and $\overline{BD}$ must be constant.

The sum of the distances between each point on the ellipse and the foci is also equal to the length of the widest distance across the ellipse.

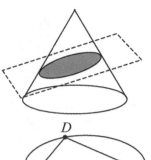

Review & Preview

12-36.   Find the surface area of the solids below. Assume that the solid in part (a) is a prism with a regular octagonal base and the pyramid in part (b) is a square-based pyramid. Show all work.

a.

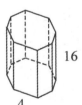

16

4

b.

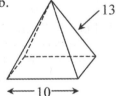

13

$\longleftarrow$ 10 $\longrightarrow$

12-37.   Solve each equation below for the given variable. Check your solution by verifying that your solution makes the original equation true.

a. $\frac{2}{3}(15u - 6) = 14u$

b. $(5 - x)(3x + 8) = 0$

c. $2(k - 5)^2 = 32$

d. $2p^2 + 7p - 9 = 0$

12-38.   **Examine** the diagram at right.

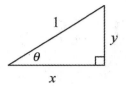

a.   Explain why $y = \sin\theta$ and $x = \cos\theta$.

b.   According to this diagram, what is $(\sin\theta)^2 + (\cos\theta)^2$?
Explain how you know.

c.   Is this relationship true for all angles? Use your calculator to find
$(\sin 23°)^2 + (\cos 23°)^2$ and $(\sin 81°)^2 + (\cos 81°)^2$. Write down your findings.

12-39.   For each geometric relationship below, determine whether a or b is larger, or if they
are equal. Assume that the diagrams are not drawn to scale. If there is not enough
information, explain what information is missing.

a.

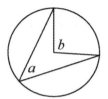

b.

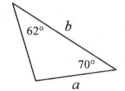

c.

area of the   area of the
triangle is a.   square is b.

12-40.   On graph paper, graph the function $y = x^2 - 3x - 4$.

a.   What is y when $x = 3$? -2? $\frac{1}{2}$?   b.   What is x when $y = -4$? 0?

12-41.   **Multiple Choice:** What is the measure of each interior angle of a regular octagon?

a. $135°$ b. $120°$ c. $180°$ d. $1080°$

12.1.5 What will it look like?

Conic Equations and Graphs

To complete this study of conics, today you will examine the types of equations that represent the different conic sections. You will review your understanding of equations for circles and parabolas and will extend your understanding to include equations for ellipses and hyperbolas. Then you will have an algebraic and geometric understanding of each of the conic sections.

12-42.   How can you tell what an equation will look like when it is graphed? In this problem, you and your team will review what you already know about the equations of conic sections.

      a.   **Examine** the equations below. Which one is the equation of a line? Of a parabola? Of a circle? How can you tell?

          (1) $x^2 + y^2 = 25$ (2) $y = x^2 - 5$ (3) $y = x + 4$

      b.   On a piece of graph paper, graph the equations at right. Then name all points of intersection in the form (x, y).

$$x^2 + y^2 = 25$$
$$y = x^2 - 5$$

      c.   Is the circle you graphed in part (b) a function? What about the parabola? You may want to review the idea of "function" in the Math Notes box for this lesson.

12-43.   GRAPH INVESTIGATION

Since the graph of the equation $x^2 + y^2 = 4$ will be a circle with radius 2 and center at $(0, 0)$, what happens when the equation is changed to become $5x^2 + y^2 = 4$ or $x^2 - 2y^2 = 4$?

Your Task: Use a graphing tool such as a graphing calculator to investigate the graphs that can be found by altering the circle equation. Start with the equation $ax^2 + by^2 = 1$ and find out what happens as you change the values of a and/or b. Write down any ideas or conjectures you find during this **investigation** and be ready to share them with the class.

12-44.   GRAPHING HYPERBOLAS

In Lesson 12.1.2, you graphed a parabola by using the fact that each point on the graph was an equal distance to both the focus and directrix. Then, when you graphed a curve so that each point was closer to the focus than the directrix, you got an ellipse! What happens when each point is twice as far from the focus as it is from the directrix?

Obtain a sheet of focus-directrix paper from your teacher. Highlight the center of the circles to be the focus, and highlight a line that is three units away from the focus to be the directrix, as shown in the graph at right.

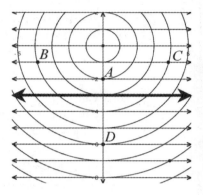

a.   Points A, B, C, and D are all points that are twice as far from the focus than they are from the directrix. Plot these four points on your graph and confirm that the distance from each point to the focus is twice its distance to the directrix.

b.   Continue plotting points that fit this pattern. Remember that each point you plot must be twice as far from the focus than the directrix. Also, notice in the case of point D above, the points can lie on both sides of the directrix. What curve appears?

12-45.   RETURN TO THE CONE

The hyperbola seems linked to the conic sections you found in problem 12-1. For example, a hyperbola can be graphed using a focus and directrix, just like an ellipse and parabola. A hyperbola can also be constructed using a circle and a point outside a circle, much like the construction of an ellipse (which uses a circle and a point inside the circle). Even the equation of a hyperbola (such as $x^2 - y^2 = 1$) looks a lot like the equation of a circle or an ellipse.

The reason why a hyperbola did not appear when you found the cross-sections of a cone is because a hyperbola needs to have two branches curving away from each other. A way to get this cross-section is by using a **double-cone**, a shape created with two cones placed in opposite directions with vertices together, as shown at right. With your team, explain how to slice this double-cone to create a cross-section that is a hyperbola.

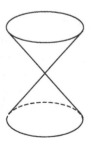

METHODS AND MEANINGS

Functions and Relations

A **relation** establishes a correspondence between its inputs and outputs (in math language called "sets"). For equations, it establishes the relationship between two variables and determines one variable when given the other. Some examples of relations are:

$$y = x^2, \ y = \frac{x}{x+3}, \ y = -2x + 5$$

A **relation** is called a **function** if there exists <u>no more than one</u> output for each input. If a relation has two or more distinct outputs for a single input value, it is not a function. The relation graphed at right is not a function because, for example, there are two y-values for each x-value greater than -3.

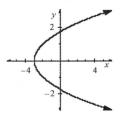

12-46.   A silo (a structure designed to store grain) is designed as a cylinder with a cone on top, as shown in the diagram at right. Assume that the base of the cylinder is on the ground.

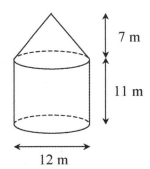

a.   If a farmer wants to paint the silo, how much surface area must be painted?

b.   What is the volume of the silo? That is, how many cubic meters of grain can the silo hold?

12-47.   A regular pentagram is a 5-pointed star that has congruent angles at each of its outer vertices. Use the fact that all regular pentagrams can be inscribed in a circle to find the measure of angle a at right.

12-48.   In Chapter 7, you discovered that the midsegment of a triangle is not only parallel to
         the third side, but also half its length. But what about the midsegment of a
         trapezoid?

         The diagram at right shows a midsegment
         of a trapezoid. That is, $\overline{EF}$ is a
         midsegment because points E and F are
         both midpoints of the non-base sides of
         trapezoid $ABCD$.

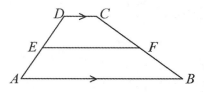

         a.   If $A(0,0)$, $B(9,0)$, $C(5,6)$, and $D(2,6)$, find the coordinates of E and F.
               Then compare the lengths of the bases ($\overline{AB}$ and $\overline{CD}$) with the length of the
               midsegment $\overline{EF}$. What seems to be the relationship?

         b.   See if the relationship you observed in part (a) holds if $A(-4,0)$, $B(2,0)$,
               $C(0,2)$, and $D(-2,2)$.

         c.   Write a conjecture about the midsegment of a trapezoid.

12-49.   For each diagram below, solve for x. Show all work.

         a.   b.   c.

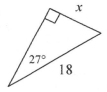   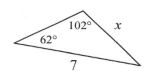   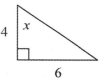

12-50.   For each relationship below, write and solve an equation for x. **Justify** your method.

         a.   b.   c.

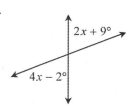   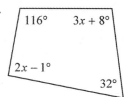   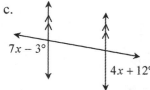

12-51.   **Multiple Choice:** The volume of the square-based pyramid
         with base edge 9 units and height 48 units is:

         a.   324 un^3 b.   1296 un^3

         c.   3888 un^3 d.   not enough information

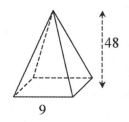

12.2.1 What's the shape?

•••
Using Coordinate Geometry and Construction to Explore Shapes

In today's activity, you will learn more about quadrilaterals as you review what you know about coordinate geometry, construction, and proof.

12-52.　Review what you have learned about the midsegment of a triangle as you answer the questions below. Assume that $\overline{DE}$ is a midsegment of $\triangle ABC$.

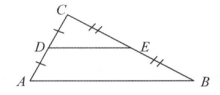

a.　What is the relationship between $\overline{DE}$ and $\overline{AB}$?

b.　What is the relationship between $\angle CDE$ and $\angle DAB$? How do you know?

c.　What is the relationship between $\triangle ABC$ and $\triangle DEC$? **Justify** your conclusion.

d.　If $DE = 4x + 7$ units and $AB = 34$ units, what is x?

12-53.　QUIRKY QUADRILATERALS

Quinn decided to experiment with the midpoints of the sides of a quadrilateral one afternoon. With a compass, he located the midpoint of each side of a quadrilateral. He then connected the four midpoints together to create a new quadrilateral inside his original quadrilateral.

a.　Without knowing anything about Quinn's original quadrilateral and without trying the construction yourself, **visualize** the result. What can you predict about Quinn's resulting quadrilateral? Share your ideas with your team.

b.　Use a compass and straightedge to repeat Quinn's experiment on an unlined piece of paper. Make sure each member of your team starts with a differently-shaped quadrilateral. Describe your results. Did the results of you and your teammates match your prediction from part (a)?

c.　Does it matter if your starting quadrilateral is convex or not? Start with a non-convex quadrilateral, like the one shown at right, and repeat Quinn's experiment. On your paper, describe your results.

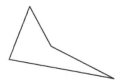

12-54.   Quinn decided to graph his quadrilateral on a set of coordinate axes and prove that his inner quadrilateral is, in fact, a parallelogram. His quadrilateral $ABCD$ uses the points $A(-3, -2)$, $B(-5, 4)$, $C(5, 6)$, and $D(1, -4)$.

a.   On graph paper, graph the quadrilateral $ABCD$.

b.   If the midpoint of $\overline{AB}$ is E, the midpoint of $\overline{BC}$ is F, the midpoint of $\overline{CD}$ is G, and the midpoint of $\overline{DA}$ is H, find and label points E, F, G, and H on $ABCD$.

c.   Connect the midpoints of the sides you found in part (b). Then find the slope of each side of quadrilateral $EFGH$ and use these slopes to prove that Quinn's inner quadrilateral is a parallelogram.

d.   Quinn wondered if his parallelogram is also a rhombus. Find EF and FG, and then decide if $EFGH$ is a rhombus. Show all work.

12-55.   PROVING THE RESULT FOR ALL QUADRILATERALS

In problem 12-54, you proved that Quinn's inner quadrilateral was a parallelogram when $A(-3, -2)$, $B(-5, 4)$, $C(5, 6)$, and $D(1, -4)$. However, what about other, random quadrilaterals?

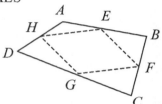

To prove this works for all quadrilaterals, start with a diagram of a generic quadrilateral, like the one above. Assume that the midpoint of $\overline{AB}$ is E, the midpoint of $\overline{BC}$ is F, the midpoint of $\overline{CD}$ is G, and the midpoint of $\overline{DA}$ is H. Prove that $EFGH$ is a parallelogram by proving that its opposite sides are parallel. It may help you to draw diagonal $\overline{AC}$ and consider what you know about $\triangle ABC$ and $\triangle ACD$. Use any format of proof.

12-56.   In $\triangle PQR$ at right, what is $m\angle Q$? Explain how you found your answer.

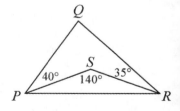

12-57.   The United State Department of Defense is located in a building called the Pentagon because it is in the shape of a regular pentagon. Known as "the largest office building in the world," it's exterior edges measure 921 feet. Find the area of land enclosed by the outer walls of the Pentagon building.

12-58.   **Examine** the triangles below. Decide if each one is a right triangle.
If the triangle is a right triangle, **justify** your conclusion. Assume
that the diagrams are not drawn to scale.

a.

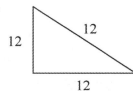

b.

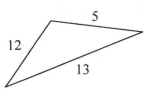

12-59.   **Examine** the Venn diagram at
right. In which region should
the figure below be placed?
Show all work to **justify** your
conclusion.

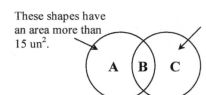

These shapes have
an area more than
15 un².

These shapes have
perimeter more
than 20 units.

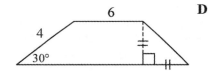

12-60.   For each equation below, decide if the equation has any real number for the given
variable. For each problem, explain how you know.

a. $4(x-3)=11$ b. $x^2=-10$

c. $3x^2-18=0$ d. $-7=\left|\,x-6\,\right|$

12-61.   **Multiple Choice:** Which number below could be the length of the third side of a
triangle with sides of length 29 and 51?

a.   10   b.   18   c.   23   d.   81

12.2.2 What's the pattern?

Euler's Formula for Polyhedra

Throughout this course, you have developed your skills of exploring a pattern, forming a conjecture, and then proving your conjecture. Today, with the assistance of materials such as toothpicks and gumdrops, you will review what you know about basic polyhedra (with no holes) as you look for a relationship between the number faces, edges, and vertices each basic polyhedron has. Once you have written a conjecture, your class will discuss how to prove that it must be true.

As you work today, consider the following questions:

Which types of basic polyhedra have we not tested yet?

What relationship can I find between the number of edges, faces, and vertices of a basic polyhedron?

Does this relationship always hold true?

12-62. POLYHEDRA PATTERNS

Does a basic polyhedron (with no holes) usually have more faces, edges, or vertices? And if you know the number of faces and vertices of a basic polyhedron, how can you predict the number of edges? Today you will answer these questions and more as you **investigate** polyhedra.

Your Task: Obtain the necessary building materials from your teacher, such as toothpicks (for edges) and gumdrops (for vertices). Your team should build *at least* six distinctly different polyhedra and each person in your team is responsible for building *at least* one polyhedron. Be sure to build some regular polyhedra (such as a tetrahedron and an octahedron), basic prisms, pyramids, and unnamed polyhedra.

Create a table like the one at right to hold your data. Once you have recorded the number of vertices, edges, and faces for

Polyhedron	Faces (F)	Vertices (V)	Edges (E)

your team's polyhedra, look for a relationship between the numbers in each row of the table. Try adding, subtracting (or both) the numbers to find a pattern. Write a conjecture (equation) using the variables F, V, and E.

12-63.   EULER'S FORMULA FOR POLYHEDRA

The relationship you discovered in problem 12-62
between the number of faces, vertices, and edges of
a basic polyhedron is referred to as **Euler's
Formula for Polyhedra**, after Leonhard Euler
(pronounced "oiler"), a mathematician from
Switzerland.[1] It states that if V is the number of
vertices, F is the number of faces, and E is the
number of edges of a basic polyhedron, then
$V + F - E = 2$.

Use Euler's Formula to answer the following questions about basic polyhedra.

a.   If a polyhedron has 5 faces and 6 vertices, how many edges must it have?

b.   What if a polyhedron has 36 edges and 14 faces? How many vertices must it
have?

c.   Could a polyhedron have 10 faces, 3 vertices, and 11 edges? Explain why or
why not.

12-64.   If V represents the number of vertices, F represents the number of faces, and
E represents the number of edges of a basic polyhedron, how can you prove that
$V + F - E = 2$? First think about this independently. Then, as a class, prove Euler's
Formula.

12-65.   For each situation below, decide if a is greater, b is greater, if they are the same
value, or if not enough information is given.

a. a is the measure of a central angle of an equilateral triangle; b is the measure
of an interior angle of a regular pentagon.

b.   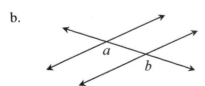   c.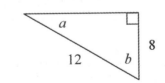

d. $a = b + 3$ e.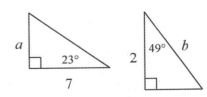

12-66. In the diagram at right, $ABCD \sim DCFE$. Solve for x and y. Show all work.

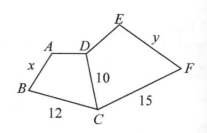

12-67. On graph paper, make a table and graph the function $f(x) = -2(x-1)^2 + 8$.

    a.   Label the x- and y-intercepts and state their coordinates.

    b.   Name the vertex.

    c.   Find $f(100)$ and $f(-15)$.

12-68. Find the area of the graph of the solution region of $x^2 + y^2 \le 49$.

12-69. Find the volume and surface area of the box formed by the shaded net at right.

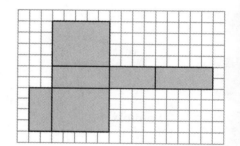

12-70. **Multiple Choice:** The radius of the front wheel of Gavin's tricycle is 8 inches. If Gavin rode his tricycle for 1 mile in a parade, approximately how many rotations did his front wheel make? (Note: 1 mile = 5280 feet).

    a.   50   b.   1260   c.   660   d.   42,240

12.2.3 What's special about this ratio?

The Golden Ratio

In Chapter 8, you discovered an important irrational number: π. Pi (π) is the ratio of any circle's circumference to its diameter. However, there is another special ratio that appears not only in geometry, but also in nature. Today, you will discover this number and will examine several different contexts in which this number appears.

12-71. While doodling one day, Alex drew the diagram at right. He started with a large rectangle (*A*). He divided this rectangle into a square (*B*) and a smaller rectangle. Then he divided the smaller rectangle into a square (*C*) and a rectangle (*D*). He noticed that *D* had a height of 1 unit (as shown in the diagram).

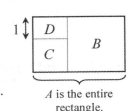

A is the entire rectangle.

a. Draw Alex's diagram on a piece of graph paper.

b. If the length of each side of square *C* is 3 units, what is the area of square *B*? What are the dimensions of rectangle *A*? **Justify** your answers.

c. If the longest dimension of rectangle *A* is 9 units, what are the dimensions of squares *B* and *C*? Show how you know.

12-72. THE GOLDEN RATIO

As Alex looked at his diagram from problem 12-71, he noticed that the dimensions of the large composite rectangle seemed to be subdivided proportionally. In other words, Figures *E* and *F*, shown at right, appeared to be similar.

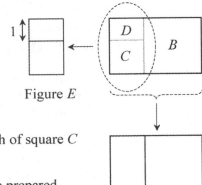

Figure *E*

Figure *F*

a. If the height of *D* is 1 unit and the side length of square *C* is x, what is the side length of square *B*?

b. If Figures *E* and *F* are similar, what is x? Be prepared to share your solution with the class.

c. The value for x that you found in part (b) has a special name: the **Golden Ratio**. It is often represented by the greek letter phi (ϕ), pronounced "fee." Read the Math Notes box about the golden ratio before moving on to problem 12-73.

12-73. GOLDEN SPIRALS

Each non-square rectangle in Alex's diagram
from problem 12-71 is an example of a **golden
rectangle** because the ratio of the longer length
to the shorter length is ϕ, the golden ratio. In
addition, Alex's process of subdividing each
golden rectangle into a square and smaller
golden rectangle can be **iterated** (repeated over
and over) creating an infinite series of nested
squares and rectangles.

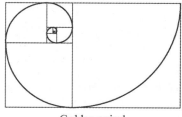

Golden spiral

When connected arcs are placed in
each of the squares, a spiral forms,
like the one shown above. One place
you can find this spiral is the human
ear, as shown at right.

Use a compass to draw a golden
spiral on the Activity 12.2.3
Resource Page provided by your
teacher. Where else (outside of
class) have you seen a spiral like
this?

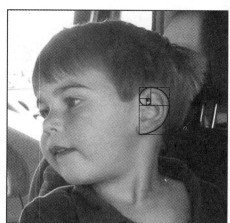

12-74. Alex wonders where else the number phi (ϕ) shows up.
Look for phi (ϕ) as you analyze the following situations.

a. **Examine** the regular decagon at right. If the side length is
1 unit, find the radius of the decagon. What do you notice?

b. Each central triangle in the regular decagon from part (a) is a **golden triangle**
because the ratio of the congruent sides to the base of each triangle is phi (ϕ).
What are the angles of a golden triangle?

c. In problem 12-73, you learned about nested golden rectangles (where each
golden rectangle is subdivided into a square and a smaller golden rectangle).
But what about nested expressions?

Consider the expression at right. The
"…" signifies that the pattern within the
expression continues infinitely. With
your team, find a way to approximate
the value of this expression. Try to find
the most accurate approximation you
can. What do you notice?

$$1 + \sqrt{1 + \sqrt{1 + \sqrt{1 + \sqrt{1 + \sqrt{1 + \ldots}}}}}$$

12-75. What if three golden rectangles intersect perpendicularly so that their centers coincide, as shown at right? If each vertex of the golden rectangles is connected with the five closest vertices, what three-dimensional shape appears? First **visualize** the result. Then, if you have a model available, test your idea with string.

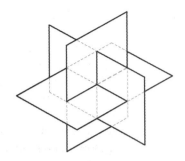

The Golden Ratio

The number phi (ϕ), pronounced "fee," has a value of $\frac{1+\sqrt{5}}{2} \approx 1.618$ and is often referred to as the **golden ratio**. This special number is often found when comparing dimensions of geometric shapes and by comparing measurements of objects in nature.

For example, phi can be found multiple ways in a regular pentagon. The ratio of the length of any diagonal of a regular pentagon to the length of a side is phi (ϕ). This can be shown by assuming the side length is 1 unit and finding the length of the diagonal. Since each interior angle of the pentagon must be 108°, then the length of the diagonal must be:

$$d = \sqrt{1^2 + 1^2 - 2(1)(1)\cos 108°} \approx 1.618$$

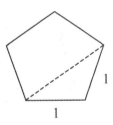

Regular pentagon

Phi also appears in nature. For example, the human body has many ratios that seem to relate to phi (ϕ). As shown in the picture at right, the ratio of the distance between the eyes and the corners of the mouth to the length of the nose is often phi (ϕ). That is, if the nose is 1 unit long, the vertical distance between the eyes and the corners of the mouth is often $\frac{1+\sqrt{5}}{2} \approx 1.618$ units.

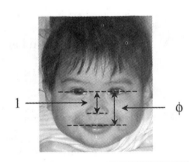

12-76.   If $\triangle ABC$ is equilateral, and if $A(3,2)$ and $B(7,2)$, find all possible coordinates of vertex C. **Justify** your answer.

12-77.   Find the area of the shaded region of the regular pentagon at right. Show all work.

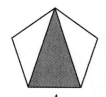

4

12-78.   On graph paper, graph the following system of inequalities. Be sure that your shaded region represents all of the points that make both inequalities true.

$$y < \tfrac{2}{3}x - 2$$
$$y \ge -5x - 2$$

12-79.   Jamila solved the quadratic $x^2 + 3x - 10 = 8$ (see her work below). When she checked her solutions, they did not make the equation true. However, Jamila cannot find her mistake. Explain her error and then solve the quadratic correctly.

$$x^2 + 3x - 10 = 8$$
$$(x + 5)(x - 2) = 8$$
$$x + 5 = 8 \quad \text{or} \quad x - 2 = 8$$
$$x = 3 \quad \text{or} \quad x = 10$$

12-80.   If the sum of the interior angles of a regular polygon is $2160°$, how many sides must it have?

12-81.   **Multiple Choice:** Assume that $A(6,2)$, $B(3,4)$, and $C(4,-1)$. If $\triangle ABC$ is rotated $90°$ counterclockwise ($\circlearrowleft$) to form $\triangle A'B'C'$, and if $\triangle A'B'C'$ is reflected across the x-axis to form $\triangle A''B''C''$, then this is the coordinates of C''.

a. $(1, 4)$ b. $(-4, 1)$ c. $(1, -4)$ d. $(4, 1)$

12.2.4   What's the probability?

Using Geometry to Find Probability

In this final activity, you will **connect** and **apply** much of your knowledge from throughout the course to solve a challenging problem.

12-82.   ZOE AND THE POISON WEED

Dimitri is getting his prize sheep, Zoe, ready for the county fair. He keeps Zoe in the pasture beside the barn and shed. What he does not know is that there is a single locoweed in this pasture, which will make Zoe too sick to go to the fair if she eats it, and she can eat it in one bite. Zoe takes about one bite of grass or plant every three minutes for six hours a day.

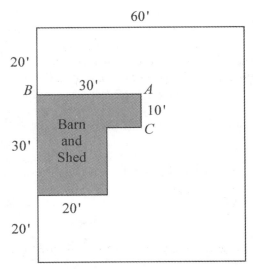

The layout of the field and building is provided at left and on the Activity 12.2.4 Resource Page provided by your teacher. Assume that the entire field (the unshaded region) has plants growing on it and that each square foot of field provides enough food for 40 bites. Also assume that each corner of the barn and field is a right angle.

Dimitri is worried that Zoe will get into trouble unless she is tethered with a rope to the building. He has decided to tether Zoe at point *A* with a 20-foot rope. Zoe is unable to enter the barn or shed while on her tether.

Your Task: If the locoweed lies in Zoe's grazing area, what is the probability that Zoe will get sick in one day?

Discussion Points

What is the problem asking you to find?

What does Zoe's grazing region look like?

What do you need to figure out in order to find the probability?

12-83.   To help find the probability that Zoe will eat the single locoweed, first consider the grazing region if she is tethered to point A with a 20-foot rope.

    a.   On your Activity 12.2.4 Resource Page, draw and label the region that Zoe can roam. Then find the area of that region.

    b.   Since each square foot of the field contains 40 bites of food, how many bites of food lie within Zoe's reach?

    c.   How many bites of food does Zoe eat each day? Show your calculations.

    d.   If the single locoweed is within this area, what is the probability that she eats the weed in one day? Be prepared to explain your answer to the class.

Further Guidance
section ends here.

12-84.   FAMILY DISCUSSION

When Dimitri discussed his idea with his family, he received other ideas! Analyze each of the ideas given below and then report back to Dimitri about which of them has the least probability that Zoe will eat the locoweed. Your analysis should include:

    •   A diagram of each proposed region on the Activity 12.2.4 Resource Page (or use the figure in problem 12-82).

    •   All calculations that help you determine the probability that Zoe will eat the poisoned weed for each proposed region.

Assume that a single locoweed lies somewhere in each region that is proposed.

    a.   **Dimitri's Father:** "Dimitri! Why do you need to waste rope? All you need is to tether your sheep with a 10-foot rope attached at point A. Take it from me: Less area to roam means there is less chance that the sheep will eat the terrible locoweed!"

    b.   **Dimitri's Sister:** "I don't agree. I think you should consider using a 30-foot rope attached to point B. The longer rope will give Zoe more freedom, but the building and fences will still limit her region. This is the best way to reduce the chance that Zoe gets sick before the fair."

Problem continues on next page →

12-84.   *Problem continued from previous page.*

   c.   **Dimitri's Mother:** "Both of those
        regions really restrict Zoe to the north-
        eastern part of the field. That means she
        won't be able to take advantage of the
        grass grown in the southern section of
        the field that is rich in nutrients because
        of better sunlight. I recommend that you
        use a 30-foot rope attached to point *C*.
        You won't be disappointed!"

12-85.   Find the area of each quadrilateral below. Show all work.

   a.   Kite   b.   Rhombus

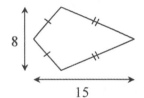

12-86.   A spinner is divided into two regions. One region, red, has a central angle of 60°.
           The other region is blue.

   a.   On your paper, sketch a picture of this spinner.

   b.   If the spinner is spun twice, what is the probability that both spins land on
        blue?

   c.   If the radius of the spinner is 7 cm, what is the area of the blue region?

   d.   A different spinner has three regions: purple, mauve, and green. If the
        probability of landing on purple is $\frac{1}{4}$ and the probability of landing on mauve
        is $\frac{2}{3}$, what is the central angle of the green region?

12-87.   Perry threw a tennis ball up into the air from the edge of a cliff. The height of the ball was $y = -16x^2 + 64x + 80$, where y represents the height in feet of the ball above ground at the bottom of the cliff, and x represents the time in seconds after the ball is thrown.

   a.   How high was the ball when it was thrown? How do you know?

   b.   What was the height of the ball 3 seconds after it was thrown? What was its height $\frac{1}{2}$ a second after it was thrown? Show all work.

   c.   When did the ball hit the ground? Write and solve an equation that represents this situation.

12-88.   **Examine** the triangles below. Which, if any, are similar? Which are congruent? For each pair that must be similar, state how you know. Remember that the diagrams are not drawn to scale.

   a.   b.   c.   d.

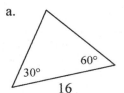   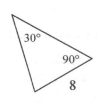   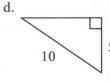

12-89.   **Examine** the mat plan of a three-dimensional solid at right.

   a.   On your paper, draw the front, right, and top views of this solid.

   b.   Find the volume of the solid.

   c.   If each edge of the solid is multiplied by 5, what will the new volume be? Show how you got your answer.

3	1	0
1	2	1
0	2	1

RIGHT

FRONT

Mat Plan

12-90.   Prove that the base angles of an isosceles triangle must be congruent. That is, prove that if $\overline{BC} \cong \overline{AC}$ in the triangle at right, then $\angle A \cong \angle B$. (Hint: Is there a convenient auxiliary line that can be added to the diagram that divides the triangle into two congruent triangles?)

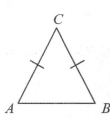

12-91.   Find the area and perimeter of the shape at right. Assume that any non-straight portions of the shape are part of a circle. Show all work.

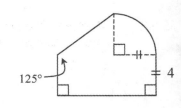

12-92. **Examine** the diagrams below. For each one, use the geometric relationships to solve for the given variable.

a. $\overrightarrow{PR}$ is tangent to $\odot C$ at P and $m\overset{\frown}{PMQ} = 314°$. Find QR.

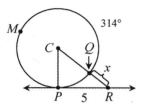

b. $\overline{AB}$ and $\overline{CD}$ intersect at E.

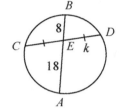

c. Radius = 7 cm

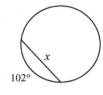

12-93. **Examine** the net at right.

a. Describe the solid that is formed by this net. What are its dimensions?

b. Find the surface area and volume of the solid formed by this net.

c. If all the dimensions of this solid are multiplied by 3, what is the SA of the resulting solid? What is the volume?

12-94. Polly has a pentagon with measures $3x - 26°$, $2x + 70°$, $5x - 10°$, $3x$, and $2x + 56°$. Find the probability that if one vertex is selected at random, then the measure of its angle is more than or equal to 90°.

12-95. Find at least three different shapes that can be cross-sections of a cube, like the one at right. For each one, draw the resulting cross-section and explain how you sliced the cube.

12-96. **Multiple Choice:** A square based pyramid has a slant height of 10 units and a base edge of 10 units. What is the height of the pyramid?

a. 5   b. $5\sqrt{3}$ c. 6   d. 8

Appendix A What's the intersection?

Points, Lines, and Planes

In this course, you will study many shapes that are "built" with other shapes. For example, the rectangle at right is formed with four sides that are called **line segments**. Understanding the parts of shapes will help you not only *understand* the shapes better, but will also help you *describe* the shapes accurately.

A-1. PLANES

A **plane** is a two-dimensional flat surface that extends without end. Even though a plane has no thickness, you can visualize it as the top surface of your desk or tabletop (if all sides of your desk extend infinitely). A graph with x- and y-axes that continue forever is a representation of a plane (see diagram at right).

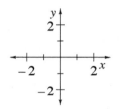

a. A plane is often represented by drawing a parallelogram, such as the one shown at right. Although the diagram seems to show edges, it is important to remember that a plane extends without end. The plane at right is named Q.

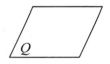

Use two pieces of cardboard to represent two planes. Remembering that planes extend infinitely and do not have borders (unlike your cardboard, which has edges), try to place your two planes so that they will never intersect (cross). Is it possible? If so, explain how the planes can be placed so that they do not intersect (or draw a diagram showing this situation). If not, explain why it is not possible.

b. What happens when two planes intersect? What does their intersection look like? How could you describe the intersection?

c. What about three planes? Is it possible to have all three planes intersect each other? Is it possible to have two intersect, with a third plane somewhere else, never intersecting the other two? And is it possible for all three planes not to intersect anywhere? Consider these questions with your team members. For each case, explain how the planes are arranged and what their intersection(s) look(s) like. Be prepared to share your ideas with the class.

A-2. **LINES**

In problem A-1, you discovered that when two planes intersect, their intersection is a line. While a plane is two-dimensional, a **line** is only one-dimensional. A line extends without end in two directions and has no thickness.

a. Where have you used or seen a line before? In what contexts?

b. If two lines intersect, how can you describe the intersection? Assume that the lines do not coincide (that is, assume that the lines do not lie directly on top of each other). Draw an example of two lines intersecting, and describe the intersection on your paper.

c. When two lines intersect, their intersection is a **point**. A point has no dimension (and therefore, no thickness). Is it possible for two lines not to intersect? If so, is there more than one way for this to happen? To help you investigate this, use straight objects (such as two pencils) to represent lines. Be sure to keep in mind that lines extend infinitely in two directions. Explain what you find.

A-3. Lines extend infinitely in two directions. However, what if a line extends infinitely in only one direction?

a. On your paper, draw an example of a part of a line that extends infinitely in only one direction. This geometric figure is called a **ray**. A ray has one dimension, like a line. Where have you seen a ray before?

Ray

b. A ray can be named using two points: the endpoint and one other point on the ray. For example, the ray above is called $\overrightarrow{AB}$. However, another way to represent a ray is on a number line, like the one shown below. This ray could be named $x \geq 2$.

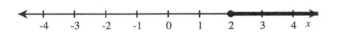

On your paper, draw a number line. Then draw the ray $x \leq 3$. If this ray is named $\overrightarrow{EF}$, what is the coordinate of point E?

c. Examine the ray at right. Name this ray at least three different ways.

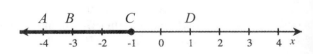

A-4.   What about the points represented by the expression $-1 \le x \le 2$? What shape would these points form?

a.   On your paper, graph this shape on a number line. Then describe this shape.

b.   A portion of a line between two points is called a **line segment**. A line segment can be named using the two endpoints. For example, the line segment at right could be called $\overline{AB}$ or $\overline{BA}$.

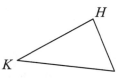

Using this notation, name the sides of the triangle at right.

c.   Examine the number line below. Name the line segment in as many ways as you can. Be ready to share your names with the class.

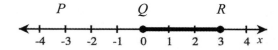

A-5.   In your Learning Log, write an entry describing what you learned today about points, lines, rays, line segments, and planes. Be sure to draw an example of each. Title this entry "Points, Lines, and Planes" and include today's date.

METHODS AND MEANINGS

Points, Lines, and Planes

MATH NOTES

A **point** is an undefined term in geometry. It has no dimension. It can be labeled with a capital letter (like point A at right) or with a coordinate (like 1).

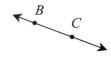

A **line** has one dimension and extends without end in two directions. A number line is an example of a line. It is often named using two points on the line (like $\overleftrightarrow{BC}$ at right).

A **line segment** is a portion of a line between (and including) two points. It can be named using its endpoints (like $\overline{DE}$ at right) or with an interval on a number line (such as $-2 \leq x \leq 4$).

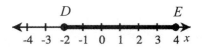

A **plane** is two-dimensional and extends without end. One way to think of a plane is as a flat surface, like the top of a table, that extends infinitely in all directions.

Review & Preview

A-6. The ray at right can be named $\overrightarrow{AB}$ or $x \geq -3$. For each shape represented on the number lines below, write the name at least two different ways.

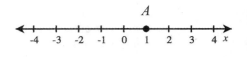

a.

b.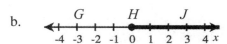

c.

d.

A-7.   In problem A-2, you showed that when two lines intersect and do not coincide (lie directly on top of each other), their intersection is a point.

    a.   Now consider three lines. If none of the lines coincide, how many arrangements are possible? Draw each case.

    b.   How can a line and a plane be arranged? For each case, describe the arrangement. If they intersect, describe the intersection.

A-8.   Draw a number line for $-4 \le x \le 4$ on your paper.

    a.   Label point A if its coordinate is 3.

    b.   Draw $\overline{EF}$ if it can be represented as $0 \le x \le 2$ and the coordinate of E is 0.

    c.   Explain where ray $\overrightarrow{FA}$ would exist. Then write another name for this ray.

A-9.   Part of this course is learning about geometry on a coordinate plane. What is the difference between how a point is represented on a number line and how it is represented on a coordinate plane?

    a.   To think about this question, first consider point A on the number line at right. What is the coordinate of A?

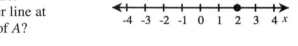

    b.   What happens when a y-axis is added to the diagram? Now how is point A represented with coordinates? Why is there a difference?

    c.   On graph paper, plot and label ray $\overrightarrow{AB}$ if A is (2, 3) and B is (4, 1).

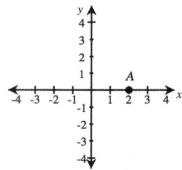

A-10.   On graph paper, find the intersection of line $\overleftrightarrow{AB}$ and ray $\overrightarrow{CD}$ if $A(4, 3)$, $B(-3, -4)$, $C(3, -4)$, and $D(1, -3)$.

Appendix B   What can I assume?

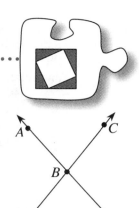

Euclidean Geometry

So far in this course, you have developed geometric ideas by assuming that certain geometric principals are true. For example, when you state that lines $\overleftrightarrow{AE}$ and $\overleftrightarrow{DC}$ intersect at point B, how can you be sure that they only intersect once? What are you assuming?

And when you became convinced that vertical angles are congruent (such as ∠ABC and ∠DBE at right), what assumptions did you make? What would be true if these assumptions were false?

To clarify issues like this, mathematicians have developed a geometric system of definitions, axioms, and theorems that includes assumptions as the basis for the mathematical ideas in the system. Perhaps the person most famous for this work is Euclid, a Greek mathematician who lived between 325 BC and 265 BC.

B-1.   THE ELEMENTS

Euclid is often referred to as the "Father of Geometry," in large part because of a famous set of books he wrote, collectively called *Elements*. In this set of books, he provided critical definitions for many basic geometric figures and relationships, such as parallel lines and obtuse angles. In the left column of part (b) below are four of the geometric shapes defined by Euclid in *Elements*.

a.   Complete this definition, which is a translation of Euclid's Definition 10: "*And when a straight-line stood upon another straight-line makes adjacent angles which are equal to one another, each of the equal angles is a right-angle, and the former straight line is called _____ to that upon which it stands.*" (Translation by Richard Fitzpatrick.)

b.   Match each geometric term in the left column with its definition (translated into English from Greek) in the right column. One definition in the right column will be left over. Decide what shape Euclid was defining in the unmatched definition.

a. Line	1. Greater than a right angle.
b. Obtuse angle	2. A quadrilateral figure that is right-angled and equilateral.
c. Boundary	3. That of which there is no part.
d. Point	4. Length without breadth.
	5. That which is the extremity of something.

B-2.   In addition to definitions, Euclid offered five **postulates** (also sometimes called **axioms**), which are statements that are assumed to be true. Euclid recognized that if these postulates were widely recognized as true, many other geometric properties and relationships could be proven true as well.

a.   One of Euclid's postulates is translated, "*A straight line segment can be drawn by joining any two points.*" Draw two points on your paper and label them *A* and *B*. How many straight lines can connect points *A* and *B*? Draw as many as you can.

b.   Another translated postulate states, "*All right angles are equal to one another.*" Do you agree with this assumption? If this postulate were not true, what would that mean?

c.   Perhaps Euclid's most famous and studied postulate was his fifth postulate, which has been translated as, "*If a straight line falling across two other straight lines makes internal angles on the same side that are less than two right angles, then these two lines, when extended to infinity, will intersect on the same side as the angles and do not meet on the other side.*"

Draw a diagram that could have accompanied this postulate. Is this assumption reasonable? What if this postulate were false?

B-3.   Another part of Book 1 of Euclid's *Elements* contains a series of Propositions (also called **theorems**), which are statements that are proven always to be true. By using definitions and postulates, Euclid set out to prove new geometric statements that, in turn, could be used to prove other new mathematical statements.

Proposition 15 may look very familiar. Euclid proved that, "*If two straight lines cut one another, the angles that are vertically opposite are equal to one another.*" He then proved this by using a combination of several propositions and postulates.

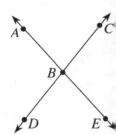

a.   In his argument, Euclid states that if $\overleftrightarrow{DC}$ intersects $\overleftrightarrow{AE}$ at *B*, then $\angle ABC$ and $\angle CBE$ together form two right angles. What do you think he meant by that statement?

b.   Euclid also used a common notion that "*things that are equal to the same thing are equal to each other.*" This is now referred to as the **Transitive Property**. Where have you used this property before?

LOOKING DEEPER

Euclid's *Elements*

In his set of books, collectively called *Elements*, Euclid defined many geometric terms to help fellow mathematicians and to create a common language about geometry. In addition, he also shared what he saw as five "common notions," listed below. Consider how you have used each of these notions in the past.

- If two things are equal to the same thing, then they are equal to each other.

- When equal things are added to equal things, then the sums are equal.

- When equal things are subtracted from equal things, then the differences are equal.

- When things coincide with one another, they are also equal to one another.

- The whole is greater than the part.

B-4.   On graph paper, draw $\triangle ABC$ if $A(2, 4)$, $B(9, 5)$, and $C(4, 10)$.

     a.   Verify that $D(3, 7)$ is a midpoint of $\overline{AC}$.

     b.   Find the equation of the line through points D and B.

     c.   Is $\overline{BD}$ a height of $\triangle ABC$? Use slope to show that $\overline{BD}$ is perpendicular to $\overline{AC}$.

B-5.   Draw a number line on your paper. If point A is at -1 and B is at 2, draw $\overline{AB}$. Describe the result.

B-6.   Consider points A and B on the number line at right. For the coordinates provided below, find the length of $\overline{AB}$. Assume that the coordinate of B is greater than or equal to the coordinate of A.

a. A is 3 and B is 10

b. A is -2 and B is 8

c. A is 6 and B is x

d. A is x and B is y

B-7.   Examine $\triangle ABC$ on the graph at right.

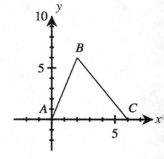

a.   Find the midpoint of $\overline{AB}$ and call it D.

b.   Find the midpoint of $\overline{BC}$ and call it E.

c.   Find the equation of $\overline{DE}$.

d.   Is $\overleftrightarrow{DE}$ parallel to $\overleftrightarrow{AC}$? Use slope to justify your conclusion.

B-8.   On a piece of graph paper, graph $y = -\frac{1}{2}x + 4$ and label its x-intercept A and its y-intercept B. Label the origin (0, 0) point C.

a.   Find the area of $\triangle ABC$.

b.   Draw a height to $\overline{AB}$ through C. What is the slope of this height? Show how you found this slope.

c.   If the height you drew in part (b) intersects side $\overline{AB}$ at point D, find the equation of the line through C and D.

Appendix C What if parallel lines intersect?

Non-Euclidean Geometry

In this course, you have learned many of the theorems set out in Euclid's book, *Elements*. Euclid, who lived between 325 BC and 265 BC, set up a system of definitions, postulates (also called axioms), and common notions that form much of the basis for plane geometry. This geometric system is now called **Euclidean geometry**, in reference to Euclid's work.

Today you will investigate a different system of geometry, called **spherical geometry**. Because it deviates from Euclidean geometry, it is a form of **non-Euclidean geometry**.

C-1.   LINES ON A SPHERE

The paths chosen by pilots often surprise travelers. For example, someone traveling from Seattle, Washington to Athens, Greece may assume that because Greece is south of Seattle, the shortest path is one that travels south as shown with the dashed line on the map at right.

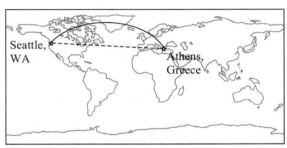

Which is the shortest path between
Seattle, WA and Athens, Greece?

However, it turns out that the shortest path actually first takes a traveler *north*, over Greenland and very close to the North Pole, as shown by the solid curve on the diagram above. This is because the shape of the Earth is close to that of a sphere, and the shortest distance between two points on a sphere is along the great circle that passes through the two points. See this path at right.

Seattle, WA, USA

Athens, Greece

Use your model of the Earth to help you think about each of the situations below. Assume the Earth's surface is smooth and spherical.

a.   Since the path on a great circle is the shortest path on the sphere between the two points, it can also be referred to as a "line." Lines of longitude are examples of lines on the surface of a sphere.

On your spherical model, think about all possible lines on the surface. Are there any two great circles that do not intersect? With your team, try to find two lines (great circles) that do not intersect. Explain your conclusion(s).

Problem continues on next page →

C-1.   *Problem continued from previous page.*

    b.   In part (a), you determined that <u>any</u> two lines on the surface of a sphere must intersect. This contradicts plane geometry (also referred to as Euclidean geometry), in which it is possible for two lines not to intersect. Since the geometry on a sphere behaves differently than the geometric system set up by Euclid, it is referred to as **non-Euclidean geometry**. The study of geometry on a sphere is also referred to as **spherical geometry**.

        In a plane, a line has infinite length. How long is a line on a sphere? Explain.

    c.   In a plane, only one line can be drawn between two points. But what about on a sphere? Examine the poles of your spherical model. How many lines pass through two poles of the sphere? What are these lines called?

C-2.   COMPARING EUCLIDEAN AND NON-EUCLIDEAN GEOMETRY

Look for differences between Euclidean and spherical geometry as you answer the questions below.

    a.   In a plane, two lines that do not coincide intersect at one point (at most). Two lines on a sphere that do not coincide intersect each other at how many points? Use your spherical model and rubber bands to help you visualize this situation.

    b.   In a plane, two lines can be perpendicular. Is it possible for two lines on a sphere to be perpendicular? If so, provide an example. If not, explain why not.

    c.   Is it possible to have a ray in spherical geometry? Why or why not?

    d.   The diagram of the Earth at right shows many lines of latitude. Are all of these lines of latitudes considered to be lines in spherical geometry? Why or why not?

Lines of Latitude

C-3.   TRIANGLES ON A SPHERE

Consider the triangle drawn on the model of the Earth at right. Note that point *P* is the North Pole, while points *A* and *B* lie on the Equator.

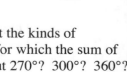

    a.   Without knowing $m\angle APB$, what can you state about the sum of the angles of $\triangle APB$? Compare this with what you know about the sum of the angles of a triangle in a plane.

    b.   Using rubber bands and your spherical model, think about the kinds of triangles you can create. Is it possible to form a triangle for which the sum of the angles is only 90°? Can the sum be 180°? What about 270°? 300°? 360°? Describe the possible sums.

C-4. In your Learning Log, explain what you learned today about non-Euclidean geometry. What surprised you? How is spherical geometry different than Euclidean geometry? Title this entry "Non-Euclidean Geometry" and include today's date.

C-5. When considering new plans for a covered baseball stadium, Smallville looked into a design that used a cylinder with a dome in the shape of a hemisphere. The radius of the proposed cylinder is 200 feet. See a diagram of this at right.

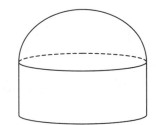

   a. One of the concerns for the citizens of Smallville is the cost of heating the space inside the stadium for the fans. What is the volume of this stadium? Show all work.

   b. The citizens of Smallville is also interested in having the outside of the new stadium painted in green. What is the surface area of the stadium? Do not include the base of the cylinder.

C-6. An ice-cream cone is filled with ice-cream. It also has a semi-spherical scoop of ice-cream on top. It turns out that the volume of ice-cream inside the cone equals the volume of the scoop on top. If the height of the cone is 6 inches and the radius of the scoop of ice-cream is 1.5 inches, find the height of the extra scoop on top. Ignore the thickness of the cone.

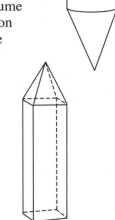

C-7. The campanile at Iowa State University is a beautiful tower that is composed of a square-based pyramid atop a tall rectangular prism. The prism sits on a 16 by 16 foot square base and extends 90 feet. The pyramid extends another 20 feet vertically. Find the surface area of the tower. Show all work.

C-8. On graph paper, graph the inequality $y \geq x - 2$. Shade the region that makes the inequality true.

   a. Is the point (3, 0) a solution to this inequality? Why or why not?

   b. Is the point (3, 1) a solution to this inequality? Why or why not?

C-9.   Examine the diagram at right. Find the values
         of a and b. Show all work.

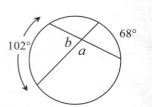

C-10.   **Multiple Choice:** Which point below will ray $\overrightarrow{AB}$ pass
         through?

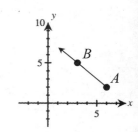

   a. $(0, 8)$

   b. $(3, 5)$

   c. $(9, -1)$

   d. $(5, 0)$

   e.   None of these

Glossary

AA ~ (Triangle Similarity)   If two angles of one triangle are congruent to the two corresponding angles of another triangle, then the triangles are similar. For example, given $\triangle ABC$ and $\triangle A'B'C'$ with $\angle A \cong \angle A'$ and $\angle B \cong \angle B'$, then $\triangle ABC \sim \triangle A'B'C'$. You can also show that two triangles are similar by showing that *three* pairs of corresponding angles are congruent (which would be called AAA~), but two pairs are sufficient to demonstrate similarity. (pp. 151 and 171)

AAS ≅ (Triangle Congruence)   If two angles and a non-included side of one triangle are congruent to the corresponding two angles and non-included side of another triangle, the two triangles are congruent. Note that AAS ≅ is equivalent to ASA ≅. (p. 299)

absolute value   The absolute value of a number is the distance of the number from zero. Since the absolute value represents a distance, without regard to direction, it is always non-negative. Thus the absolute value of a negative number is its opposite, while the absolute value of a non-negative number is just the number itself. The absolute value of x is usually written $|x|$. For example, $|-5| = 5$ and $|22| = 22$. (pp. 453 and 575)

acute angle   An angle with measure greater than 0° and less than 90°. One example is shown at right. (p. 24)

adjacent angles   For two angles to be adjacent, they must satisfy these three conditions: (1) The two angles must have a common side; (2) They must have a common vertex; and (3) They can have no interior points in common. This means that the common side must be between the two angles; no overlap between the angles is permitted. In the example at right, $\angle ABC$ and $\angle CBD$ are adjacent angles.

adjacent leg   In a right triangle, the leg adjacent to an acute angle is the side of the angle that is not the hypotenuse. For example, in $\triangle ABC$ shown at right, $\overline{AB}$ is the leg adjacent to $\angle A$. (p. 241)

alpha (α)   A Greek letter that is often used to represent the measure of an angle. Other Greek letters used to represent the measure of an angle include theta (θ) and beta (β). (p. 190)

alternate interior angles   Angles between a pair of lines that switch sides of a third intersecting line (called a transversal). For example, in the diagram at right the shaded angles are alternate interior angles. If the lines intersected by the transversal are parallel, the alternate interior angles are congruent. Conversely, if the alternate interior angles are congruent, then the two lines intersected by the transversal are parallel. (p. 91)

altitude   See *height*.

ambiguous   Information is ambiguous when it has more than one interpretation or conclusion. (pp. 270)

angle In general, an angle is formed by two rays joined at a common endpoint. Angles in geometric figures are usually formed by two segments, with a common endpoint (such as the angle shaded in the figure at right). (pp. 22 and 24)

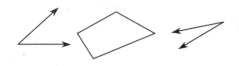

angle measure *See* measurement.

angle of depression When an object (*B*) is below the horizontal line of sight of the observer (*A*), the angle of depression is the angle formed by the line of sight to the object and the horizontal line of sight.

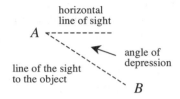

angle of elevation When an object (*B*) is above the horizontal line of sight of the observer (*A*), the angle of elevation is the angle formed by the line of sight to the object and the horizontal line of sight.

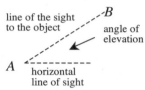

apex In a cone or pyramid, the apex is the point that is the farthest away from the flat surface (plane) that contains the base. In a pyramid, the apex is also the point at which the lateral faces meet. An apex is also sometimes called the "vertex" of a pyramid or cone. (p. 533)

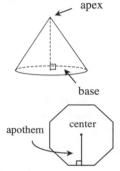

apothem A segment that connects the center of a regular polygon to a point on one of its sides, and is perpendicular to that side. (p. 410)

approximate Close, but not exact. An approximate answer to a problem is often a rounded decimal. For example, if the exact answer to a problem is $\sqrt{2}$, then 1.414 and 1.41 are approximate answers. (p. 123)

arc A connected part of a circle. Because a circle does not contain its interior, an arc is more like a portion of a bicycle tire than a slice of pizza. (pp. 426 and 485)

arc length The length of an arc (in inches, centimeters, feet, etc.) is the distance from one of the arc's endpoints to the arc's other endpoint, measured around the circle. Note that arc length is different from arc measure. Arcs of two different circles may have the same arc measure (like 90°), but have different arc lengths if one circle has a larger radius than the other one. For an example, see concentric circles. (p. 490)

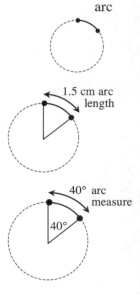

arc measure The measure in degrees of an arc's central angle. Note that arc measure is measured in degrees and is different from arc length. (p. 490)

area On a flat surface (plane), the number of non-overlapping square units needed to cover the region. *Also see* surface area. (p. 490)

area model   A tool that uses the area of rectangles to represent the probabilities of possible outcomes when considering two independent events. For example, suppose you are going to randomly select a student from a classroom. If the probability of selecting a female student from the room is $\frac{2}{3}$ and the probability of selecting a 9th grader from the room is $\frac{1}{4}$, the area of the shaded rectangle at right represents the probability that a randomly selected student is a female 9th grader ($\frac{2}{3} \cdot \frac{1}{4} = \frac{1}{6}$). A generic area model is a tool that enables you to find the probabilities of outcomes without drawing a diagram to scale. (p. 219)

	male $\frac{1}{3}$	female $\frac{2}{3}$
9th grader $\frac{1}{4}$	$\frac{1}{12}$	$\frac{1}{6}$
not 9th grader $\frac{3}{4}$	$\frac{1}{4}$	$\frac{1}{2}$

Area model

arrow diagram   A pictorial representation of a conditional statement. The arrow points toward the conclusion of the conditional (the "then" part of the "If… then" statement). For example, the conditional statement *"If two lines cut by a transversal are parallel, then alternate interior angles are congruent"* can be represented by the arrow diagrams below. (p. 84)

Lines cut by a transversal are parallel → *alternate interior angles are congruent.*

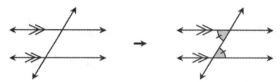

arrowheads   To indicate a line on a diagram, we draw a segment with arrowheads on its ends. The arrowheads show that our diagram indicates a line, which extends indefinitely. Marks on pairs of lines or segments such as ">>" and ">>>" indicate that the lines or segments are parallel. Both types of marks are used in the diagram above. (p. 54)

ASA ≅ (Triangle Congruence)   If two angles and the included side of one triangle are congruent to the corresponding two angles and included side of another triangle, the triangles are congruent. Note that ASA ≅ is equivalent to AAS ≅. (p. 299)

auxiliary lines   Segments and lines added to existing figures. Auxiliary lines are usually added to a figure to allow us to prove something about the figure.

axioms   Statements accepted as true without proof. Also known as "postulates."

base   (a) Triangle: Any side of a triangle to which a height is drawn. There are three possible bases in each triangle (p. 112); (b) Trapezoid: the two parallel sides (p. 107); (c) Parallelogram (and rectangle, rhombus, and square): Any side to which a height is drawn. There are four possible bases (p. 106); (d) Solid: *See* cone, cylinder, prism, and pyramid.

binomial   An expression that is the sum or difference of exactly two terms, each of which is a monomial. For example, $-2x + 3y^2$ is a binomial. (p. 104)

bisect   To bisect a geometric object is to divide it into two congruent parts. (p. 317)

center of a circle   On a flat surface, the fixed point from which all points on the circle are equidistant. *See* circle. (p. 341)

central angle An angle with its vertex at the center of a circle. (p. 490)

centroid The point at which the three medians of a triangle intersect. The centroid is also the center of balance of a triangle. The other points of concurrency studied in this course are the circumcenter and the incenter. (pp. 471 and 501)

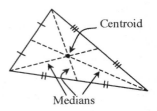

chord A line segment with its endpoints on a circle. A chord that passes through the center of a circle is called a "diameter." *See* circle. (p. 485)

circle The set of all points on a flat surface that are the same distance from a fixed point. If the fixed point (center) is O, the symbol $\odot O$ represents a circle with center O. If r is the length of a circle's radius and d is the length of its diameter, the circumference of the circle is $C = 2\pi r$ or $C = \pi d$. The area of the circle is $A = \pi r^2$. The equation of a circle with radius length r and center $(0, 0)$ is $x^2 + y^2 = r^2$. (pp. 341, 485, and 490)

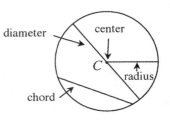

circular angle An angle with a measure of 360°. (pp. 22 and 24)

circumcenter The center of the circle that passes through the vertices of a triangle. It can be found by locating the point of intersection of the perpendicular bisectors of the sides of the triangle. The other points of concurrency studied in this course are the centroid and the incenter. (p. 501)

circumference The perimeter of (distance around) a circle. (p. 426)

circumscribe A circle circumscribes a polygon when it passes through all of the vertices of the polygon. (p. 500)

clinometer A device used to measure angles of elevation and depression. (p. 202)

$\odot C$ circumscribes the pentagon.

clockwise Clockwise identifies the direction of rotation shown in the diagram at right. The word literally means "in the direction of the rotating hands of a clock." The opposite of clockwise is counter-clockwise. (p. 34)

compass (a) A tool used to draw circles; (b) A tool used to navigate the Earth. A compass uses the Earth's magnetic field to determination which direction is north.

complementary angles Two angles whose measures add up to 90°. Angles T and V are complementary because $m\angle T + m\angle V = 90°$. Complementary angles may also be adjacent, like $\angle ABC$ and $\angle CBD$ in the diagram at far right. (p. 74)

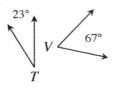

concentric circles Circles that have the same center. For example, the circles shown in the diagram at right are concentric. (p. 460)

concurrency (point of) The single point where two or more lines intersect on a plane. (p. 501)

conditional statement A statement written in "If …, then …" form. For example, "*If a rectangle has four congruent sides, then it is a square*" is a conditional statement. (p. 108)

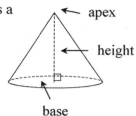

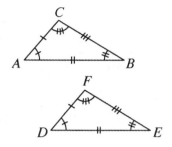

cone A three-dimensional figure that consists of a circular face, called the "base," a point called the "apex," that is not in the flat surface (plane) of the base, and the lateral surface that connects the apex to each point on the circular boundary of the base. (pp. 542 and 547)

congruent Two shapes are congruent if they have exactly the same shape and size. Congruent shapes are similar and have a scale factor of 1. The symbol for congruence is ≅. (pp. 159 and 291)

congruence statement A statement indicating that two figures are congruent. The order of the letters in the names of the shapes indicates which sides and angles are congruent to each other. For example, if $\triangle ABC \cong \triangle DEF$, then $\angle A \cong \angle D$, $\angle B \cong \angle E$, $\angle C \cong \angle F$, $\overline{AB} \cong \overline{DE}$, $\overline{BC} \cong \overline{EF}$, and $\overline{AC} \cong \overline{DF}$. (p. 346)

conic section A curve that is the intersection of a plane with a double cone. Conic sections include parabolas, circles, ellipses, and hyperbolas. Conic sections that degenerate (collapse) into a point or line are excluded. (p. 578)

conjecture An educated guess. Conjectures often result from noticing a pattern during an investigation. Conjectures are also often written in conditional ("If…, then…") form. Once a conjecture is proven, it becomes a theorem. (pp. 10 and 304)

construction The process of using a straightedge and compass to solve a problem and/or create a geometric diagram. (pp. 459 and 468)

converse The converse of a conditional statement can be found by switching the hypothesis (the "if" part) and the conclusion (the "then" part). For example, the converse of "*If P, then Q*" is "*If Q, then P.*" Knowing that a conditional statement is true does not tell you whether its converse is true. (p. 304)

convex polygon A polygon is convex if any pair of points inside the polygon can be connected by a segment without leaving the interior of the polygon. (p. 396)

coordinate geometry The study of geometry on a coordinate grid. (p. 395)

corresponding angles (a) When two lines are intersected by a third line (called a transversal), angles on the same side of the two lines and on the same side of the transversal are called corresponding angles. For example, the shaded angles in the diagram at right are corresponding angles. Note that if the two lines cut by the transversal are parallel, the corresponding angles are congruent. Conversely, if the corresponding angles are congruent, then the two lines intersected by the transversal are parallel. (p. 91); (b) Angles in two figures may also correspond, as shown at right. See corresponding parts for more information. (pp. 143 and 150)

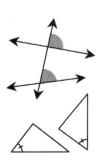

corresponding parts   Points, sides, edges, or angles in two or more figures that are images of each other with respect to a transformation. If two figures are congruent, their corresponding parts are congruent to each other. (p. 143, 150, 346)

cosine ratio   In a right triangle, the cosine ratio of an acute $\angle A$ is
$\cos A = \frac{\text{length of adjacent side}}{\text{length of hypotenuse}}$.   In the triangle at right, $\cos A = \frac{AB}{AC} = \frac{4}{5}$. (p. 241)

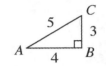

counter-clockwise   Counter-clockwise identifies the direction of rotation shown in the diagram at right. The opposite of counter-clockwise is clockwise. (p. 34)

counterexample   An example showing that a generalization has at least one exception; that is, a situation in which the statement is false. For example, the number 4 is a counterexample to the statement "All even numbers are greater than 7." (p. 238)

cross-section   The intersection of a three-dimensional solid and a plane. The cross-sections of a cone (and double-cone) are called "conic sections." (pp. 538 and 578)

cube   A polyhedron all of whose faces are squares. (p. 527)

cylinder (circular)   A three-dimensional figure that consists of two parallel congruent circular regions (called *bases*) and a lateral surface containing segments connecting each point on the circular boundary of one base to the corresponding point on the circular boundary of the other. (pp. 30 and 451)

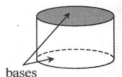

bases

decagon   A polygon with ten sides. (p. 393)

delta (Δ)   A Greek letter that is often used to represent a difference. Its uses include Δx and Δy, which represent the lengths of the horizontal and vertical legs of a slope triangle, respectively. (p. 47)

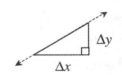

dependent events   Two events are dependent if the outcome of one event affects the probability of the other event. For example, assume you will randomly select two cards, one at a time, without replacement from a deck of cards. The probability that the first card is red is $\frac{26}{52} = \frac{1}{2}$ because 26 of the 52 cards are red. However, the probability of the second card now depends on the result of the first selection. If the first card was red, there are now 25 red cards remaining in a deck of 51 cards, and the probability that the second card is red is $\frac{25}{51}$. The second event (selecting the second card) is dependent on the first event (selecting the first card). (p. 207)

diagonal   In a polygon, it is a segment that connects two vertices of the polygon but is not a side of the polygon. (p. 400)

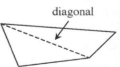

diagonal

diameter   A line segment drawn through the center of a circle with both endpoints on the circle. The length of a diameter is usually denoted d. Note that the length of a circle's diameter is twice the length of its radius. *See* circle. (pp. 341 and 485)

dilation   A transformation which produces a figure similar to the original by proportionally shrinking or stretching the figure. In a dilation, a shape is stretched (or compressed) proportionally from a point, called the point of dilation. (p. 138)

dimension   (a) Flat figures have two dimensions (which can be labeled "base" and "height"); (b) Solids have three dimensions (such as "width," "height," and "depth"). (pp. 98 and 452)

directrix   A line that, along with a point (called a focus), defines a conic section (such as a parabola). (p. 574)

dissection The process of dividing a flat shape or solid into parts that have no interior points in common.

dodecahedron   A polyhedron with twelve faces. (p. 529)

double cone   Two cones placed apex to apex so that their bases are parallel. Generally we think of the cones as extending to infinity beyond their bases. (p. 588)

Double cone

edge   In three dimensions, a line segment formed by the intersection of two faces of a polyhedron. (p. 527)

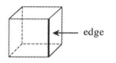

edge

distances from point *P* to foci

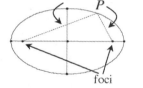

ellipse   A type of conic section. An example is shown at right. The sum of the distances between each point on an ellipse and two fixed points (called the foci) is constant. (p. 585)

foci

endpoints   See *line segment*.

enlarge   To enlarge something is to increase its size. For this course, an enlargement is a dilation of a figure whose result is similar to but larger than the original. (p. 140)

equator   If we represent the Earth as a sphere, the equator is the great circle equally distant between the North and South poles. The equator divides the Earth into two halves called the Northern and Southern hemispheres. The equator also marks a latitude of 0°. *See* latitude. (p. 549)

equilateral   A polygon is equilateral if all its sides have equal length. The word "equilateral" comes from "equi" (meaning "equal") and "lateral" (meaning "side"). Equilateral triangles not only have sides of equal length, but also angles of equal measure. However, a polygon with more than three sides can be equilateral without having congruent angles. For example, see the rhombus at right. (pp. 351 and 396)

exact answer   An answer that is precisely accurate and not approximate. For example, if the length of a side of a triangle is exactly $\sqrt{10}$, the exact answer to the question "How long is that side of the triangle?" would be $\sqrt{10}$, while 3.162 would be approximate answer. (p. 123)

expected value   For this course, the expected value of a game is the average amount expected to be won or lost on each play of the game if the game is played many times. The expected value need not be a value one could actually win on a single play of the game. For example, if you play a game where you roll a die and win one point for every dot on the face that comes up, the expected value of this game is $\frac{1+2+3+4+5+6}{6} = 3.5$ points for each play. (p. 516)

exterior angle   When a side of a polygon is extended to form an angle with an adjacent side outside of the polygon, that angle is called an exterior angle. For example, the angles marked with letters in the diagram at right are exterior angles of the quadrilateral. Note that an exterior angle of a polygon is always adjacent and supplementary to an interior angle of that polygon. The sum of the exterior angles of a convex polygon is always 360°. (pp. 403 and 407)

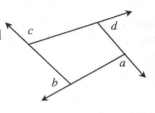

face of a polyhedron   One of the flat surfaces of a polyhedron, including the base(s). (p. 527)

fair game   For the purposes of this course, a fair game has an expected value of 0. Therefore, over many plays, a person would expect to neither win nor lose points or money by playing a fair game. (p. 510)

flowchart   A diagram showing an argument for a conclusion from certain evidence. A flowchart uses ovals connected by arrows to show the logical structure of the argument. When each oval has a reason stated next to it showing how the evidence leads to that conclusion, the flowchart represents a proof. See the example at right. (p. 167)

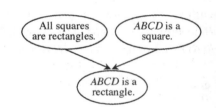

focus (plural: foci) A point that, along with a line (called a directrix), can be used to define all or part of a conic section (such as a parabola). (pp. 574 and 581)

fraction buster   "Fraction busting" is a method of simplifying equations involving fractions. Fraction busting uses the Multiplicative Property of Equality to alter the equation so that no fractions remain. To use this method, multiply both sides of an equation by the common denominator of all the fractions in the equation. The result will be an equivalent equation with no fractions. For example, when given the equation $\frac{x}{7}+2=\frac{x}{3}$, we can multiply both sides by the "fraction buster" 21. The resulting equation, $3x+42=7x$, is equivalent to the original but contains no fractions. (p. 512)

function   A relation in which for each input value there is one and only one output value. For example, the relation $f(x)=x+4$ is a function; for each input value (x) there is exactly one output value. In terms of ordered pairs (x, y), no two ordered pairs of a function have the same first member (x). (p. 589)

graph A graph represents numerical information spatially. The numbers may come from a table, situation (pattern), rule (equation or inequality), or figure. Most of the graphs in this course show points, lines, figures, and/or curves on a two-dimensional coordinate system like the one at right.

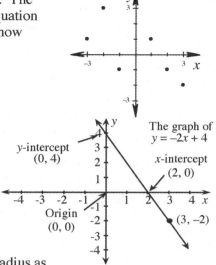

A complete graph includes all the necessary information about a line or a curve. To be complete, a graph must have the following components: (1) the x-axis and y-axis labeled, clearly showing the scale; (2) the equation of the graph written near the line or curve; (3) the line or curve extended as far as possible on the graph with arrows if the line or curve continues beyond the axes; (4) the coordinates of all special points, such as x- and y-intercepts, shown in (x, y) form. (p. 29)

great circle A cross-section of a sphere that has the same radius as the sphere. If the Earth is represented with a sphere, the equator is an example of a great circle. (p. 549)

golden ratio The number $\frac{1+\sqrt{5}}{2}$, which is often labeled with the Greek letter phi (ϕ), pronounced "fee." (p. 599)

height (a) Triangle: the length of a segment that connects a vertex of the triangle to a line containing the opposite base (side) and is perpendicular to that line; (b) Trapezoid: the length of any segment that connects a point on one base of the trapezoid to the line containing the opposite base and is perpendicular to that line; (c) Parallelogram (includes rectangle, rhombus, and square): the length of any segment that connects a point on one base of the parallelogram to the line containing the opposite base and is perpendicular to that line; (d) Pyramid and cone: the length of the segment that connects the apex to a point in the plane containing the figure's base and is perpendicular to that plane; (e) Prism or cylinder: the length of a segment that connects one base of the figure to the plane containing the other base and is perpendicular to that plane. Some texts make a distinction between height and altitude, where the altitude is the segment described in the definition above and the height is its length. (pp. 106, 110, 448, 534, and 547)

hemisphere A great circle of a sphere divides it into two congruent parts, each of which is called a hemisphere. If the Earth is represented as a sphere, the Northern hemisphere is the portion of the Earth north of (and including) the equator. Likewise, the Southern hemisphere is the portion of the Earth south of (and including) the equator. (p. 549)

heptagon A polygon with seven sides. (p. 393)

heptahedron A polyhedron with seven faces. (p. 529)

hexagon A polygon with six sides. (pp. 43 and 393)

hexahedron A polyhedron with six faces. A regular hexahedron is a cube. (p. 529)

HL ≅ (Triangle Shortcut) If the hypotenuse and one leg of one right triangle are congruent to the hypotenuse and corresponding leg of another right triangle, the two right triangles are congruent. Note that this congruence conjecture applies only to right triangles. (p. 299)

hypotenuse The longest side of a right triangle (the side opposite the right angle). (pp. 119 and 241)

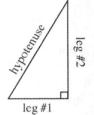

hypothesis A conjecture (or educated guess) in science.

icosahedron A polyhedron with twenty faces. (p. 529)

"If …, then …" statement A statement written in the form "If …, then …." Also known as a conditional statement. (p. 108)

image The shape that results from a transformation, such as a translation, rotation, reflection, or dilation. (p. 34)

incenter The center of the circle inscribed in a triangle. It can be found by locating the point at which the angle bisectors of a triangle intersect. The other points of concurrency studied in this course are the centroid and the circumcenter. (p. 193)

independent events If the outcome of a probabilistic event does not affect the probability of another event, the events are independent. For example, assume you plan to roll a normal six-sided die twice and want to know the probability of rolling a 1 twice. The result of the first roll does not affect the probability of rolling a 1 on the second roll. Since the probability of rolling a 1 on the first roll is $\frac{1}{6}$ and the probability of rolling a 1 on the second roll is also $\frac{1}{6}$, then the probability of rolling two 1s in a row is $\frac{1}{6} \cdot \frac{1}{6} = \frac{1}{36}$. (p. 207)

indirect proof *See* proof by contradiction.

inequality symbols The symbols < (less than), > (greater than), ≤ (less than or equal to), and ≥ (greater than or equal to).

inscribed angle An angle with its vertex on the circle and sides intersecting the circle at two distinct points. (p. 490)

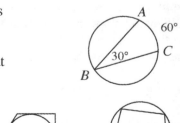

Inscribed Angle Theorem The measure of an inscribed angle is half the measure of its intercepted arc. Likewise, the measure of an intercepted arc is twice the measure of an inscribed angle whose sides pass through the endpoints of the arc. In the figure at right, if $m\overset{\frown}{AC} = 60°$, then $m\angle ABC = 30°$. (p. 494)

inscribed circle A circle is inscribed in a polygon if each side of the polygon intersects the circle at exactly one point.

inscribed polygon A polygon is inscribed in a circle if each vertex of the polygon lies on the circle. (p. 461)

⊙*B* is inscribed in the pentagon.   ⊙*C* circumscribes the pentagon.

integers The set of numbers { . . . −3, −2, −1, 0, 1, 2, 3, . . . }.

intercepted arc The arc of a circle bounded by the points where the two sides of an inscribed angle meet the circle. In the circle at right, $\angle ABC$ intercepts $\overset{\frown}{AC}$. (p. 489)

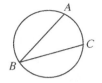

interior angle (of a polygon) An angle formed by two consecutive sides of the polygon. The vertex of the angle is a vertex (corner) of the polygon. (p. 402)

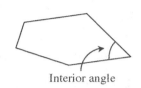

Interior angle

Interior Angle Sum Conjecture The sum of the interior angles of a polygon with n-sides is $180°(n-2)$. (p. 407)

inverse trigonometric functions When the ratio between the lengths of two sides of a right triangle is known, $\sin^{-1}$, $\cos^{-1}$, or $\tan^{-1}$ can be used to find the measure of one of the triangle's acute angles. (p. 248)

irrational numbers The set of numbers that cannot be expressed in the form $\frac{a}{b}$, where a and b are integers and $b \neq 0$. For example, π and $\sqrt{2}$ are irrational numbers. (pp. 115 and 467)

isosceles trapezoid A trapezoid with a pair of equal base angles (from the same base). Note that this will cause the non-parallel sides to be congruent. (pp. 77 and 371)

isosceles triangle A triangle with two sides of equal length. (p. 48)

Isosceles Triangle Theorem If a triangle is isosceles, then the base angles (which are opposite the congruent sides) are congruent. For example, if $\triangle ABC$ is isosceles with $\overline{BA} \cong \overline{BC}$, then the angles opposite these sides are congruent; that is, $\angle A \cong \angle C$.

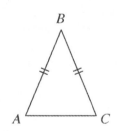

iteration The act of repeating an action over and over. (p. 598)

justify To give a logical reason supporting a statement or step in a proof. More generally, to use facts, definitions, rules, and/or previously proven conjectures in an organized sequence to convincingly demonstrate that your claim (or your answer) is valid (true). (p. 167)

kite A quadrilateral with two distinct pairs of consecutive congruent sides. (p. 353)

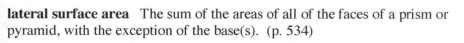

lateral surface area The sum of the areas of all of the faces of a prism or pyramid, with the exception of the base(s). (p. 534)

latitude An angular measure (in degrees) that indicates how far north or south of the equator a position on the Earth is. All points on the equator have a latitude of 0°. The North Pole have a latitude of 90°, while the South Pole has a latitude of -90°. (p. 549)

Law of Cosines For any $\triangle ABC$ with sides a, b, and c opposite $\angle A$, $\angle B$, and $\angle C$ respectively, it is always true that $c^2 = a^2 + b^2 - 2ab \cdot \cos(C)$, $b^2 = a^2 + c^2 - 2ac \cdot \cos(B)$, and $a^2 = b^2 + c^2 - 2bc \cdot \cos(A)$. (p. 267)

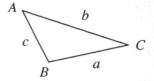

Law of Sines For any $\triangle ABC$ with sides a, b, and c opposite $\angle A$, $\angle B$, and $\angle C$ respectively, it is always true that $\frac{\sin A}{a} = \frac{\sin B}{b} = \frac{\sin C}{c}$. (p. 264)

legs The two sides of a right triangle that form the right angle. Note that legs of a right triangle are always shorter than its hypotenuse. (p. 119)

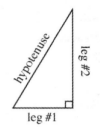

line A line is an undefined term in geometry. It is one-dimensional and extends without end in two directions. It is made up of points and has no thickness. A line can be named with a letter (such as l), but also can be labeled using two points on the line, such as $\overleftrightarrow{AB}$ below. (p. 81)

line of symmetry A line that divides a shape into two congruent parts that are mirror images of each other. If you fold a shape over its line of symmetry, the shapes on both sides of the line will match each other perfectly. Some shapes have more than one line of symmetry, such as the example at right. Other shapes may only have one line of symmetry or no lines of symmetry. (p. 5)

line segment The portion of a line between two points. A line segment is named using its endpoints. For example, the line segment at right can be named either $\overline{AB}$ or $\overline{BA}$. (p. 81)

linear scale factor (a) In the case of two similar two-dimensional figures, the linear scale factor is the ratio of the lengths of any pair of corresponding sides. This means that once it is determined that two figures are similar, all of their pairs of corresponding sides have the same ratio. The linear scale factor can also be called the *ratio of similarity*. When the ratio is comparing a figure and its image after a dilation, this ratio can also be called the *zoom factor*. (b) In the case of two similar polyhedra, the linear scale factor is the ratio of the lengths of any pair of corresponding edges. (pp. 140, 415, 457)

logical argument A logical sequence of statements and reasons that lead to a conclusion. A logical argument can be written in a paragraph, represented with a flowchart, or documented in a two-column proof. (pp. 10, 353, and 366)

longitude An angular measure (in degrees) that indicates how far west or east of the Prime Meridian a position on the Earth is. Lines of longitude (which are actually circles) are all great circles that pass through the North and South Poles. (pp. 549 and 551)

major arc An arc with measure greater than 180°. Each major arc has a corresponding minor arc that has a measure that is less than 180°. A major arc is named with three letters on the arc. For example, the highlighted arc at right is the major arc $\overgroup{ABC}$. (p. 485)

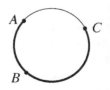

mat plan A top (or bottom) view of a multiple cube solid. The number in each square is the number of cubes in that stack. For example, the mat plan at right represents the solid at the far right. (p. 443)

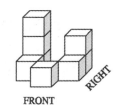

measurement For the purposes of this course, a measurement is an indication of the size or magnitude of a geometric figure. For example, an appropriate measurement of a line segment would be its length. Appropriate measurements of a square would include not only the length of a side, but also its area and perimeter. The measure of an angle represents the number of degrees of rotation from one ray to the other about the vertex. (p. 15)

median A line segment that connects a vertex of a triangle with the midpoint of side opposite to the vertex. For example, since D is a midpoint of $\overline{BC}$, then $\overline{AD}$ is a median of $\triangle ABC$. The three medians of a triangle intersect at a point called the centroid. (p. 471)

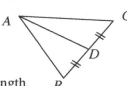

midpoint A point that divides a segment into two segments of equal length. For example, D is the midpoint of $\overline{BC}$ in $\triangle ABC$ at right. (p. 381)

midsegment A segment joining the midpoints of two sides of a triangle. (p. 371)

minor arc An arc with measure less than 180°. Minor arcs are named using the endpoints of the arc. For example, the highlighted arc at right is named $\overset{\frown}{AC}$. (p. 485)

Möbius strip A one-sided surface in a closed loop which can be formed by giving a rectangular strip of paper a half-twist and affixing its ends. (p. 8)

monomial An expression with only one term. It can be a number, a variable, or the product of a number and one or more variables. For example, 7, $3x$, $-4ab$, and $3x^2y$ are each monomials.

n-gon A polygon with n sides. A polygon is often referred to as an "n-gon" when we do not yet know the value of n. (p. 422)

net A diagram that, when folded, forms the surface of a three-dimensional solid. A net is essentially the faces of a solid laid flat. It is one of several ways to represent a three-dimensional diagram. The diagram at right is a representation of the solid at the far right. Note that the shaded region of the net indicates the (bottom) base of the solid. (p. 446)

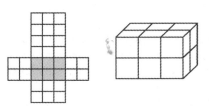

nonagon A polygon with nine sides. (p. 393)

nonahedron A polyhedron with nine faces. (p. 529)

non-convex polygon A polygon that is not convex. An example of a non-convex polygon is shown at right. *See* convex. (pp. 395 and 396)

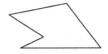

oblique   A prism (or cylinder) is oblique when its lateral surface(s) are not perpendicular to the base. A pyramid (or cone) is oblique when its apex is not directly above the center of the base. (pp. 451 and 538)

obtuse angle   Any angle that measures between (but not including) 90° and 180°. (p. 24)

octagon   A polygon with eight sides. (p. 393)

octahedron   A polyhedron with eight faces. In a regular octahedron, all of the faces are equilateral triangles. (p. 529)

opposite   In a figure, opposite means "across from." For example, in a triangle, an "opposite side" is the side that is across from a particular angle and is not a side of the angle. For example, the side $\overline{AB}$ in $\triangle ABC$ at right is opposite $\angle C$, while $\overline{AC}$ is opposite the right angle. (p. 241)

orientation   In this course, orientation refers to the placement and alignment of a figure in relation to others or an object of reference (such as coordinate axes). Unless it has rotation symmetry, the orientation of a figure changes when it is rotated (turned) less than 360°. Also, the orientation of a shape changes when it is reflected, except when reflected across a line of symmetry. (p. 241)

parabola   The graph of a quadratic function (any equation that can be written in the form $y = ax^2 + bx + c$) is a parabola. There are several other ways to find a parabola, including the intersection of a right circular cone with a flat surface parallel to an edge of the cone. (p. 574)

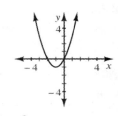

parallel lines   Two lines on a flat surface are parallel if they never intersect. Two line segments on a flat surface are parallel if the lines they lie on never intersect. There is a constant distance between two parallel lines (or line segments). Identical arrow markings are used to note parallel lines or line segments. (p. 47)

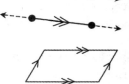

parallelogram   A quadrilateral with two pairs of parallel sides. (p. 361)

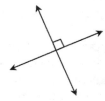

pentagon   A polygon with five sides. (p. 393)

pentahedron   A polyhedron with five faces. (p. 529)

perimeter   The distance around the exterior of a figure on a flat surface. For a polygon, the perimeter is the sum of the lengths of its sides. The perimeter of a circle is also called a circumference. (p. 15)

perpendicular   Two rays, line segments, or lines that meet (intersect) to form a right angle (90°) are called perpendicular. A line and a flat surface can also be perpendicular if the line does not lie on the flat surface but intersects it and forms a right angle with every line on the flat surface passing through the point of intersection. A small square at the point of intersection of two lines or segments indicates that the lines are perpendicular. (p. 47)

phi (ϕ) A Greek letter, pronounced "fee," that represents the golden ratio, $\frac{1+\sqrt{5}}{2}$. (p. 599)

pi (π) The ratio of the circumference (C) of the circle to its diameter (d). For every circle, $\pi = \frac{\text{circumference}}{\text{diameter}} = \frac{C}{d}$. Numbers such as 3.14, 3.14159, or $\frac{22}{7}$ are approximations of π. (p. 426)

plane A plane is an undefined term in geometry. It is a two-dimensional flat surface that extends without end. It is made up of points and has no thickness.

platonic solid A convex regular polyhedron. All faces of a platonic solid are congruent, regular polygons. There are only five possible platonic solids: tetrahedron (with four faces of equilateral triangles), cube (with six faces of squares), octahedron (with eight faces of equilateral triangles), dodecahedron (with twelve faces of regular pentagons), and icosahedron (with twenty faces of equilateral triangles). (pg. 529)

polygon A two-dimensional closed figure of three or more line segments (sides) connected end to end. Each segment is a side and only intersects the endpoints of its two adjacent sides. Each point of intersection is a vertex. At right are two examples of polygons. (p. 42, 393, and 396)

polyhedron (plural: polyhedra) A three-dimensional object with no holes that is bounded by polygons. The polygons are joined at their sides, forming the edges of the polyhedron. Each polygon is a face of the polyhedron. (p. 448)

postulates Statements accepted as true without proof. Also known as "axioms."

preimage The original figure in a transformation.

prism A three-dimensional figure that consists of two parallel congruent polygons (called *bases*) and a lateral surface containing segments connecting each point on each side of one base to the corresponding point on the other base. The lateral surface of a prism consists of parallelograms. (p. 448)

probability A number that represents how likely an event is to happen. When a event has a finite number of equally-likely outcomes, the probability that one of those outcomes, called A, will occur is expressed as a ratio and written as:

$$P(A) = \frac{\text{number of successful outcomes}}{\text{total number of possible outcomes}}.$$

For example, when flipping a coin, the probability of getting tails, P(tails), is $\frac{1}{2}$ because there is only one tail (successful outcome) out of the two possible equally likely outcomes (a head and a tail). Probability can be written as a ratio, decimal, or percent. A probability of 0 (or 0%) indicates that it is impossible for the event to occur, while a probability of 1 (or 100%) indicates that the event must occur. Events that "might happen" will have values somewhere between 0 and 1 (or between 0% and 100%). (p. 60)

proof A convincing logical argument that uses definitions and previously proven conjectures in an organized sequence to show that a conjecture is true. A proof can be written in a paragraph, represented with a flowchart, or documented in a formal two-column proof. (p. 10, 353, and 366)

proof by contradiction   A proof that begins by assuming that an assertion is true and then shows that this assumption leads to a contradiction of a known fact. This demonstrates that the assertion is false. Also known as an *indirect proof.* (p. 96)

proportional equation   An equation stating that two ratios (fractions) are equal. (p. 145)

protractor   A geometric tool used for physically measuring the number of degrees in an angle. (p. 22)

pyramid   A polyhedron with a polygonal base formed by connecting each point of the base to a single given point (the **apex**) that is above or below the flat surface containing the base. Each triangular lateral face of the pyramid is formed by the segments from the apex to the endpoints of a side of the base and the side itself. A tetrahedron is a special pyramid because any face can act as its base. (p. 533)

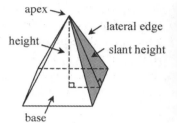

Pythagorean Theorem   The statement relating the lengths of the legs of a right triangle to the length of the hypotenuse: $(\text{leg } \#1)^2 + (\text{leg } \#2)^2 = \text{hypotenuse}^2$. The Pythagorean Theorem is powerful because if you know the lengths of any two sides of a right triangle, you can use this relationship to find the length of the third side. (p. 123)

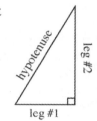

Pythagorean triple   Any three positive integers a, b, and c that make the relationship $a^2 + b^2 = c^2$ true. Commonly used Pythagorean triples include 3, 4, 5 and 5, 12, 13. (p. 260)

quadratic equation   An equation that can be written in the form $ax^2 + bx + c = 0$, where a, b, and c are real numbers and a is nonzero. A quadratic equation written in this form is said to be in standard form. For example, $3x^2 - 4x + 7.5 = 0$ is a quadratic equation. (p. 163)

Quadratic Formula   The Quadratic Formula states that if $ax^2 + bx + c = 0$ and $a \neq 0$, then $x = \frac{-b \pm \sqrt{b^2 - 4ac}}{2a}$. For example, if $5x^2 + 9x + 3 = 0$, then $x = \frac{-9 \pm \sqrt{9^2 - 4(5)(3)}}{2(5)} = \frac{-9 \pm \sqrt{21}}{10}$. (p. 163)

quadrilateral   A polygon with four sides.

radius (plural: radii)   Of a circle: A line segment drawn from the center of a circle to a point on the circle. (p. 341); Of a regular polygon: A line segment that connects the center of a regular polygon with a vertex. The length of a radius is usually denoted r. (p. 410)

random   An event is random if its result cannot be known (and can only be guessed) until the event is completed. For example, the flip of a fair coin is random because the coin can either land on heads or tails and the outcome cannot be known for certain until after the coin is flipped.

ratio A ratio compares two quantities by division. A ratio can be written using a colon, but is more often written as a fraction. For example, in the two similar triangles at right, a ratio can be used to compare the length of $\overline{BC}$ in $\triangle ABC$ with the length of $\overline{EF}$ in $\triangle DEF$. This ratio can be written as 5:11 or as the fraction $\frac{5}{11}$. (p. 60)

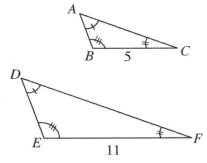

ratio of similarity The ratio of any pair of corresponding sides of two similar figures. This means that once it is determined that two figures are similar, all of their pairs of corresponding sides have the same ratio. For example, for the similar triangles $\triangle ABC$ and $\triangle DEF$ above, the ratio of similarity is $\frac{5}{11}$. The ratio of similarity can also be called the *linear scale factor*. When the ratio is comparing a figure and its image after a dilation, this ratio can also be called the *zoom factor*. (pp. 140, 415, and 457)

rationalizing the denominator Rewriting a fractional expression that has radicals in the denominator in order to eliminate them. (p. 252)

ray A ray is part of a line that starts at one point and extends without end in one direction. In the example at right, ray $\overrightarrow{AB}$ is part of $\overleftrightarrow{AB}$ that starts at A and contains all of the points of $\overleftrightarrow{AB}$ that are on the same side of A as point B, including A. Point A is the endpoint of $\overrightarrow{AB}$.

rectangle A quadrilateral with four right angles. (pp. 5 and 361)

reflection A transformation across a line that produces a mirror image of the original (preimage) shape. The reflection is called the "image" of the original figure. The line is called a "line of reflection." See the example at right. Note that a reflection is also sometimes referred to as a "flip." (pp. 34 and 38)

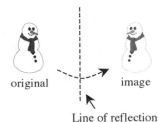

original   image

Line of reflection

Reflexive Property The Reflexive Property states that any expression is always equal to itself. That is, $a = a$. This property is often useful when proving that two triangles that share a side or an angle are congruent. For example, in the diagram at right, since $\triangle ABD$ and $\triangle CBD$ share a side ($\overline{BD}$), the Reflexive Property justifies that $BD = BD$. (p. 354)

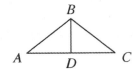

reflection symmetry *See* symmetry.

regular A polygon is regular if it is a convex polygon with congruent angles and congruent sides. For example, the shape at right is a regular hexagon. (pp. 42, 351, and 396)

REGULAR HEXAGON

relation An equation that relates two or more variables. For example, $y = 3x - 2$ and $x^2 + y^2 = 9$ are both relations. A relation can also be thought of as a set of ordered pairs. (p. 589)

relationship For this course, a relationship is a way that two objects (such as two line segments or two triangles) are connected. When you know that the relationship holds between two objects, learning about one object can give you information about the other. Relationships can be described in two ways: a geometric relationship (such as a pair of vertical angles or two line segments that are parallel) and a relationship between the measures (such as two angles that are complementary or two sides of a triangle that have the same length). Common geometric relationships between two figures include being similar (when two figures have the shape, but not necessarily the same size) and being congruent (when two figures have the same shape and the same size). (pp. 76, 91, 150, and 159)

reasoning *See* logical reasoning *and* proof.

remote interior angles If a triangle has an exterior angle, the remote interior angles are the two angles not adjacent to the exterior angle. Also called "opposite interior angles." (p. 397)

rhombus A quadrilateral with four congruent sides. (pp. 361 and 464)

right angle An angle that measures 90°. A small square is used to note a right angle, as shown in the example at right. (pp. 22 and 24)

right triangle A triangle that has one right angle. The side of a right triangle opposite the right angle is called the "hypotenuse," and the two sides adjacent to the right angle are called "legs." (p. 119)

rigid motions Movements of figures that preserve their shape and size. Also called "rigid transformations." Examples of rigid motions are reflections, rotations, and translations. Also called "isometries." (p. 34)

rotation A transformation that turns all of the points in the original (preimage) figure the same number of degrees around a fixed center point (such as the origin on a graph). The result is called the "image" of the original figure. The point that the shape is rotated about is called the "center of rotation." To define a rotation, you need to state the measure of turn (in degrees), the direction the shape is turned (such as clockwise or counter-clockwise), and the center of rotation. See the example at right. Note that a rotation is also sometimes referred to as a "turn." (p. 34)

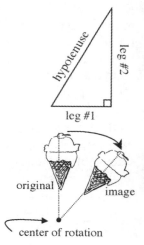

rotation symmetry *See* symmetry.

$r : r^2 : r^3$ **Ratios of Similarity** When a two-dimensional figure is enlarged (or reduced) proportionally, its lengths and area change. If the linear scale factor is r, then all lengths (such as sides, perimeter, and heights) of the original (preimage) figure is multiplied by a factor of r while the area is multiplied by a factor of r^2.

When a polyhedron is enlarged (or reduced) proportionally, its lengths, surface area, and volume also change. If the linear scale factor is r, then the surface area is multiplied by a factor of r^2 and the volume is multiplied by a factor of r^3. Thus, if a polyhedron is enlarged proportionally by a linear scale factor of r, then the new edge lengths, surface area, and volume can be found using the relationships below. (p. 457)

New edge length = $r \cdot$ (corresponding edge length of original polyhedron)

New surface area = $r^2 \cdot$ (original surface area)

New volume = $r^3 \cdot$ (original volume)

This principle also applies to other solids such cylinders, cones, and spheres.

same-side interior angles Two angles between two lines and on the same side of a third line that intersects them (called a transversal). The shaded angles in the diagram at right are an example of a pair of same-side interior angles. Note that if the two lines that are cut by the transversal are parallel, then the two angles are supplementary (add up to 180°). (p. 91)

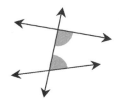

sample space The total number of outcomes that can happen in an event. The sample space for rolling a standard 6-sided die is the set {1, 2, 3, 4, 5, 6} because those are the only possible outcomes.

SAS ≅ (Triangle Congruence) Two triangles are congruent if two sides and their included angle of one triangle are congruent to the corresponding two sides and included angle of another triangle. Also referred to as "SAS Congruence" or "SAS ≅". (p. 299)

SAS ~ (Triangle Similarity) If two triangles have two pairs of corresponding sides that are proportional and have congruent included angles, then the triangles are similar. Also referred to as "SAS Similarity" or "SAS ~". (p. 171)

scale The ratio between a length of the representation (such as a map, model, or diagram) and the corresponding length of the actual object. For example, the map of a city may use one inch to represent one mile.

scalene triangle A triangle with no congruent sides. (p. 55)

secant A line that intersects a circle at two distinct points. (p. 557)

sector

sector A region formed by two radii of a central angle and the arc between their endpoints on the circle. You can think of it as a portion of a circle and its interior, resembling a piece of pizza. (p. 426)

semicircle In a circle, a semicircle is an arc with endpoints that are endpoints of any diameter of the circle. It is a half circle and has a measure of 180°. (p. 492)

side of an angle   One of the two rays that form an angle.

side of a polygon   *See* polygon.

similar figures   Two shapes are similar if they have exactly the same shape but are not necessarily the same size. The symbol for similar is ∼ . (pp. 136 and 155)

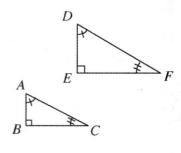

similarity statement   A statement that indicates that two figures are similar. The order of the letters in the names of the shapes determine which sides and angles correspond to each other. For example, if $\triangle ABC \sim \triangle DEF$, then $\angle A$ must correspond to $\angle D$ and $\overline{AB}$ must correspond to $\overline{DE}$. (p. 150)

sine ratio   In a right triangle, the sine ratio of an acute $\angle A$ is $\sin A = \frac{\text{length of opposite side}}{\text{length of hypotenuse}}$. In the triangle at right, $\sin A = \frac{BC}{AC} = \frac{3}{5}$. (p. 241)

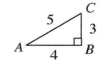

skew lines   Lines that do not lie in the same flat surface.

slant height   (a) Pyramid: The height of a lateral face drawn from the apex; (b) Cone: The distance from the apex of the cone to any point on the circular boundary of the base. (p. 534)

slide   See *translation*.

slope   A ratio that describes how steep (or flat) a line is. Slope can be positive, negative, or even zero, but a straight line has only one slope. Slope is the ratio $\frac{\text{vertical change}}{\text{horizontal change}}$ or $\frac{\text{change in } y \text{ value}}{\text{change in } x \text{ value}}$, sometimes written $\frac{\Delta y}{\Delta x}$. When the equation of a line is written in $y = mx + b$ form, m is the slope of the line. A line has positive slope if it slopes upward from left to right on a graph, negative slope if it slopes downward from left to right, zero slope if it is horizontal, and undefined slope if it is vertical. Parallel lines have equal slopes, and the slopes of perpendicular lines are opposite reciprocals of each other (e.g. , $\frac{3}{5}$ and $-\frac{5}{3}$). (pp. 47 and 190)

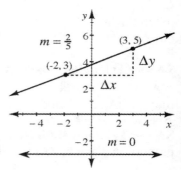

slope angle   See slope triangle.

slope-intercept form   A form of a linear equation: $y = mx + b$. In this form, m is the slope and the point $(0, b)$ is the y-intercept. (p. 123)

slope triangle   A right triangle with legs (parallel to the x- and y-axes) that meet the hypotenuse at two points on a given line or line segment. The lengths of the legs of the slope triangle can be used to find the slope of the line. The angle (θ) formed in a slope triangle by the hypotenuse and the horizontal leg is called the slope angle. (pp. 47 and 190)

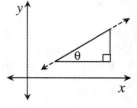

solid   A closed three-dimensional shape and all of its interior points. Examples include regions bounded by pyramids, cylinders, and spheres. (p. 443)

solve   To find all the solutions to an equation or an inequality (or a system of equations or inequalities). For example, solving the equation $x^2 = 9$ gives the solutions $x = 3$ and $x = -3$. The solution(s) may be number(s), variable(s), or an expression. (pp. 19, 87, and 163)

space   The set of all points in three-dimensions.

special right triangles   A right triangle with particular notable features that can be used to solve problems. Sometimes, these triangles can be recognized by the angles, such as the 45°- 45°- 90° triangle (also known as an "isosceles right triangle") and a 30°- 60°- 90° triangle. Other right triangles are special because the length of each side is an integer, such as a 3, 4, 5 triangle or a 5, 12, 13 triangle. (p. 260)

sphere   The set of all points in space that are the same distance from a fixed point. The fixed point is the center of the sphere and the distance is its radius. (p. 555)

Sphere

square   A quadrilateral with four right angles and four congruent sides. (p. 361)

Square

square root   A number a is a square root of b if $a^2 = b$. For example, the number 9 has two square roots, 3 and –3. A negative number has no real square roots; a positive number has two; and zero has just one square root, namely, itself. In a geometric context, the principal square root of a number x (written $\sqrt{x}$) represents the length of a side of a square with area x. For example, $\sqrt{16} = 4$. Therefore if the side of a square has a length of 4 units, then its area is 16 square units. (p. 115)

SSS ≅ (Triangle Congruence)   Two triangles are congruent if all three pairs of corresponding sides are congruent. (p. 299)

SSS ~ (Triangle Similarity)   If two triangles have all three pairs of corresponding sides that are proportional (this means that the ratios of corresponding sides are equal), then the triangles are similar. (pp. 155 and 171)

straight angle   An angle that measures 180°. This occurs when the rays of the angle point in opposite directions, forming a line. (p. 24)

180°

straightedge   A tool used as a guide to draw lines, rays, and segments. (p. 468)

statement   A recording of fact to present evidence in a logical argument (proof). (p. 459)

Substitution Method   A method for solving a system of equations by replacing one variable with an expression involving the remaining variable(s). For example, in the system of equations at righ t the first equation tells you that y is equal to $-3x + 5$. We can substitute $-3x + 5$ in for y in the second equation to get $2(-3x + 5) + 10x = 18$, then solve this equation to find that $x = 2$. Once we have x, we substitute that value back into either of the original equations to find that $y = -1$. (p. 87)

$$y = -3x + 5$$
$$2y + 10x = 18$$

Substitution Property The Substitution Property states that in an expression, one can replace a variable, number, or expression with something equal to it without altering the value of the whole. For example, if $x = 3$, then $5x - 7$ can be evaluated by replacing x with 3. This results in $5(3) - 7 = 8$. (p. 87)

supplementary angles Two angles a and b for which $a + b = 180°$. Each angle is called the supplement of the other. In the example at right, angles A and B are supplementary. Supplementary angles are often adjacent. For example, since $\angle LMN$ is a straight angle, then $\angle LMP$ and $\angle PMN$ are supplementary angles because $m\angle LMP + m\angle PMN = 180°$. (p. 74)

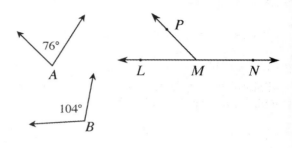

surface area The sum of all the area(s) of the surface(s) of a three-dimensional solid. For example, the surface area of a cylinder is the sum of the areas of its top base, its bottom base, and its lateral surface. (pp. 446 and 452)

symmetry (a) Rotation symmetry: A shape has rotation symmetry when it can be rotated for less than 360° and it appears not to change. For example the hexagon at right appears not to change if it is rotated 60° clockwise (or counter-clockwise); (b) Reflection symmetry: A shape has reflection symmetry when it appears not to change after being reflected across a line. The regular hexagon at right also has reflection symmetry across any line drawn through opposite vertices, such as those shown in the diagram. *See* reflection, rotation, *and* line *of* symmetry. (pp. 43, 44, 45)

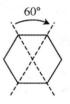

system of equations A system of equations is a set of equations with the same variables. Solving a system of equations means finding one or more solutions that make each of the equations in the system true. A solution to a system of equations gives a point of intersection of the graphs of the equations in the system. There may be zero, one, or several solutions to a system of equations. For example, $(1.5, -3)$ is a solution to the system of linear equations at right; $x = 1.5$, $y = -3$ makes both of the equations true. Also, $(1.5, -3)$ is a point of intersection of the graphs of these two equations. (p. 87)

$$y = 2x - 6$$
$$y = -2x$$

systematic list A list created by following a system (an orderly process). (p. 219)

tangent A line on the same flat surface as a circle that intersects the circle in exactly one point. A tangent of a circle is perpendicular to a radius of the circle at their point of intersection (also called the "point of tangency." (p. 496)

tangent ratio In a right triangle, the tangent ratio of an acute $\angle A$ is $\tan A = \frac{\text{length of opposite side}}{\text{length of adjacent side}}$. In the triangle at right, $\tan A = \frac{BC}{AB} = \frac{3}{4}$. (p. 200)

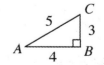

tetrahedron A polyhedron with four faces. The faces of a tetrahedron are triangles. In a regular tetrahedron, all of the faces are congruent equilateral triangles. (p. 533)

theorem A conjecture that has been proven to be true. Some examples of theorems are the Pythagorean Theorem and the Triangle Angle Sum Theorem. (p. 367)

theta (θ) A Greek letter that is often used to represent the measure of an angle. Other Greek letters used to represent the measure of an angle include alpha (α) and beta (β). (p. 190)

three-dimensional An the object that has length, width, and depth. (p. 340)

transformation This course studies four transformations: reflection, rotation, translation, and dilation. All of them preserve shape, and the first three preserve size. *See each term for its own definition.* (pp. 34 and 138)

translation A transformation that preserves the size, shape, and orientation of a figure while sliding (moving) it to a new location. The result is called the "image" of the original figure (preimage). Note that a translation is sometimes referred to as a "slide." (p. 34)

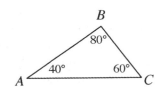
original   image

transversal A line that intersects two or more other lines on a flat surface (plane). In this course, we often work with a transversal that intersects two parallel lines. (p. 79)

trapezoid A quadrilateral with at least one pair of parallel sides. (pp. 107 and 361)

tree diagram A structure used to organize the possible outcomes of two or more events. For example, the tree diagram at right represents the possible outcomes when a coin is flipped twice. (p. 219)

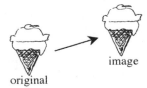

triangle A polygon with three sides.

Triangle Angle Sum Theorem The sum of the measures of the interior angles in any triangle is 180°. For example, in $\triangle ABC$ at right, $m\angle A + m\angle B + m\angle C = 180°$. (p. 99)

Triangle Congruence Conjectures Conjectures that use the minimum number of congruent corresponding parts to prove that two triangles are congruent. They are: SSS $\cong$, SAS $\cong$, AAS $\cong$, ASA $\cong$, and HL $\cong$. (p. 299)

Triangle Inequality In a triangle with side lengths a, b, and c, c must be less than the sum of a and b and greater than the difference of a and b. In the example at right, a is greater than b (that is, $a > b$), so the possible values for c are all numbers such that $c > a - b$ and $c < a + b$. (p. 119)

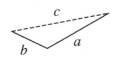

Triangle Midsegment Theorem The segment that connects the midpoints of any two sides of a triangle measures half the length of the third side is and parallel to that side. (p. 371)

trigonometry Literally, the "measure of triangles." In this course, this word is used to refer to the development of triangle tools such as trigonometric ratios (sine, cosine, and tangent) and the Laws of Sines and Cosines. (p. 192)

turn See *rotation*

two-column proof A form of proof in which statements are written in one column as a list and the reasons for the statements are written next to them in a second column. (p. 366)

two-dimensional A figure that that lies on a flat surface and that has length and width. *See* plane. (p. 340)

unit of measure A standard quantity (such as a centimeter, second, square foot, or gallon) that is used to measure and describe an object. A single object can be measured using different units of measure, which will usually yield different results. For example, a pencil may be 80 mm long, meaning that it is 80 times as long as a unit of 1 mm. However, the same pencil is 8 cm long, so that it is the same length as 8 cm laid end-to-end. (This is because 1 cm is the same length as 10 mm.) (p. 98)

Venn diagram A type of diagram used to classify objects. It is usually composed of two or more overlapping circles representing different conditions. An item is placed or represented in the Venn diagram in the appropriate position based on the conditions it meets. In the example of the Venn diagram at right, if an object meets one of two conditions, it is placed in region **A** or **C** but outside region **B**. If an object meets both conditions, it is placed in the intersection (**B**) of both circles. If an object does not meet either condition, it is placed outside of both circles (region **D**). (p. 51)

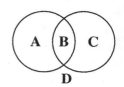

vertex (plural: vertices) (a) For a two-dimensional geometric shape, a vertex is a point where two or more line segments or rays meet to form a "corner," such as in a polygon or angle. (b) For a three-dimensional polyhedron, a vertex is a point where the edges of the solid meet. (c) On a graph, a vertex can be used to describe the highest or lowest point on the graph of a parabola or absolute value function (depending on the graph's orientation). (pp. 74 and 527)

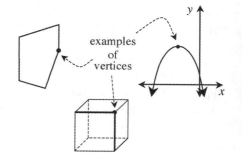

examples of vertices

vertical angles The two opposite (that is, non-adjacent) angles formed by two intersecting lines. "Vertical" is a relationship between pairs of angles, so one angle cannot be called vertical. Angles that form a vertical pair are always congruent. (pp. 75 and 91)

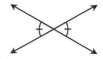

volume A measurement of the size of the three-dimensional region enclosed within an object. It is expressed as the number of 1x1x1 unit cubes (or parts of cubes) that fit inside a solid. (pp. 453 and 452)

weighted average In this course, weighted average is used to calculate expected value. The weighted average takes into account the relative probabilities of all possible outcomes and uses them to calculate the average win or loss of each game. *See* expected value *for an example.* (p. 508 and 516)

x-intercept   A point where a graph crosses the *x*-axis. A graph may have several *x*-intercepts, no *x*-intercepts, or just one.

y-intercept   A point where a graph crosses the *y*-axis. A function has at most one *y*-intercept; a relation may have several.

zoom factor   The amount each side of a figure is multiplied by when the figure is proportionally enlarged or reduced in size. It is written as the ratio of a length in the new figure (image) to a length in the original figure (preimage). For the triangles at right, the zoom factor is $\frac{8}{6}$ or $\frac{4}{3}$. See also "ratio of similarity" and "linear scale factor." (pp. 140 and 142)

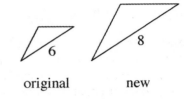

original   new

Index
Student Version

Many of the pages referenced here contain a definition or an example of the topic listed, often within the body of a Math Notes box. Others contain problems that develop or demonstrate the topic. It may be necessary to read the text on several pages to fully understand the topic. Also, some problems listed here are good examples of the topic and may not offer any explanation. The page numbers listed below reflect the pages in the Student Version. References to Math Notes boxes are bolded.

Symbols

α (alpha), **190**
β (beta), **190**
θ (theta), **190**
Δ (delta), **47**, 599

Number

30°-60°-90° triangle, **260**
30°-60°-90° triangles, 250
3-4-5 triangles, 255
45°-45°-90° triangle, **260**
45°-45°-90° triangles, 251

A

AA ~, **155, 171**
AAS ≅, **299**
Absolute value, 453, 575
Acute angles, **24**
Adjacent leg, **241**
Adjacent side, 236
Alpha (α), **190**
Alternate interior angles, 84, **91**
Angle Notation, **190**
  alpha, **190**
  beta, **190**
  theta, **190**
Angles, 22, **24**
  acute, **24**
  alternate interior, 84, **91**
  central, 382, 394, 488, **490**
  circular, 22, **24**
  complementary, 74, **76**
  congruent, **76**
  consecutive, 370
  corresponding, **91**
  equal measure, **351**
  exterior, 358, 403
  inscribed, 489, **490, 494**
  naming, **81**
  obtuse, **24**
  remote interior, 397
  right, 22, **24**
  same-side interior, 84, **91**
  slope, **190**
  straight, **24**
  supplementary, 74, **76**
  vertex, 74
  vertical, **91**

Apothem, **410**
Approximate, **123**, 240
Arc, 425, **426**, 430, 483, **485**, 488
  chord, 484, **485**
  intercepted, 489
  length, 488, **490**
  major, 484, **485**
  measure, 488, **490**
  minor, 484, **485**
  quarter circle, 405
  semicircle, 492
Area, **15**, 99
  of a triangle, 103
  of circle, **426**
  of parallelogram, **112**
  of regular polygons, **422**
  of trapezoid, **112**
  of triangle, **112**
  sector, **430**
  similar figures, 12
  surface, 446, **555**
Area model, 213, **219**
Argument
  proof, 365, 370
Arrow diagram, 84
ASA ≅, **299**
At Your Service Problem, 312
Average, weighted, 508

B

Base, 107
Base angles of an isosceles triangle, 90
Bases, 447, **448**
  lateral surface, 530
Beta (β), **190**
Bisect, 317
Bisector
  perpendicular, 459
Blood types, 214
Building a Kaleidoscope Problem, 21

E

Earth
  equator, 549
  great circle, 549
  hemisphere, 549
  latitude lines, 549
  longitude lines, 549, **551**
  prime meridian, 549
Edges, 527
  vertex, 527
Ellipse, 581, 583, **585**
  foci, **585**
Enlargement
  zoom factor, 140
Equality
  Reflexive Property, **354**
Equations
  graphing, **29**
  proportional, **145**
  Quadratic Formula, **163**
  solving linear, **19**
Equator, 549
  great circle, 549
Equiangular, **351**, 396
Equilateral, **351**
  polygon, **396**
Equilateral triangles, 11, 22
Equivalent, **512**
Euler, Leonhard, 595
Euler's Formula for Polyhedra, 595
Exact answer, **123,** 240
Examining, 129
Expected value, 507, **516**
  weighted average, 508
Experiment, 7
Exploration, **10**
Exterior angle, 358, 397, 403, **407**
  sum of, **407**

F

Faces, 527
  edge, 527
  lateral, 447, **448, 534**
  total surface area, **452**
Facilitator, 4
Factoring, **163**
Family Fortune, The Problem, 18, 170
Flipping a shape (reflection), 27, **34, 38**
Flowchart, 157, 167, 353
Focus (foci), 574, 581, **585**
  ellipse, 581
  hyperbola, 584
Focus-directrix paper, 576
Formula
  quadratic, **163**
Fraction busters, **512**
Function, **589**
  absolute value, 575

G

Geometry, 548
George Washington's Nose Problem, 147
Getting To Know Your Triangle Problem, 309
Golden ratio, 597, 598, **599**
  golden rectangles, 598
  golden triangles, 598
  spiral, 598, **599**
Golden rectangle, 598
Golden spiral, 598, 599
Golden triangles, 598
Graph
  focus-directrix, 576
Graphing an equation, **29**
Great circle, 549

H

Half-equilateral triangle, 40, 250
Half-square, 40
Height
  of pyramid, **534**
  slant, **534**
Hemisphere, 549
Heptagon, 393
Hexagon, 43, 393
Hinged Mirror Team Challenge, The Problem, 349
HL ≅, **299**
Horizontal change, **47, 190**
How Tall Is It? Problem, 202
Hyperbola, 584
Hypotenuse, **119, 241**

I

Icon
  Learning Log, 28
  stoplight, 88
  toolkit, 54
Image, 34
Incenter, **501**
Independent events, 207
Inscribed angle, 489, **490**
Inscribed Angle Theorem, **494**
Inscribed polygon, 461
Intercepted arc, 489
Interior angles, 402
  sum of, **407**
Interior Design Problem, 343
Intersecting chords, 498
Intersecting tangents, **560**
Intersections
  secant, 557
  tangents, **560**
Inverse, **248**
Inverse operations, 243
  trigonometric ratios, 243
Inverse trigonometric functions
  inverse cosine, **248**
  inverse sine, **248**
  inverse tangent, **248**

P

R

$r : r^2 : r^3$ ratios, **457**
Radius, **341**, 410
Rat Race, The Problem, 204, 217
Ratio, **60**
    cosine, 236
    golden, 597, 598, 599
    Law of Sines, **264**
    linear scale factor, 414, **415**
    of similar figures, **457**
    of similar solids, **457**
    of similarity, **142**
    proportion, **145**
    sine, 236
    slope, **47**, **190**
    zoom factor, **415**
Rationalizing the denominator, **252**
Ratios of similarity, **457**
Reasoning and justifying, 16, 180
Recorder/Reporter, 4
Rectangle, 5, **361**
    diagonals, **400**
Rectangular prism, 451
Reflection, 27, **34**, **38**
    line of, **34**, **38**
    of light, 85
Reflection symmetry, 3, **5**, 43, 44
Reflexive Property of Equality, **354**
Regular hexagon, 21, 43
Regular octagon, 402
Regular pentagon, 23
Regular polygons, **42**, 349, **351**, **396**
    apothem, **410**
    area of, **422**
    center, **410**
    central angle, 382
    radius, **410**
Regular polyhedra, 528
    dual polyhedron, 530
    platonic solids, 529
Relation, **589**
Relationship
    angles, 74, **76**, 84
    Law of Cosines, **267**
    Law of Sines, **264**
    Pythagorean Theorem, 122, 123
    similarity, 136, 139, **150**
Relationships
    angles, 84
Remote interior angles, 397
Representation
    solids, 443, 444
Reuleaux curves, 337
Reversal, **304**
Rhombus, 356, **361**, **400**, **464**
    diagonals, **364**, **400**, **464**
Right angles, 22, 24
Right pyramid, 538

Right triangle, **119**
    hypotenuse, **119**
    leg, **119**
    Pythagorean Theorem, 122
    special, **260**
Rotation, **34**
Rotation symmetry, 43, 45, 52
Rotation, center of, **34**
Rubber band, use of, 135

S

Same-side interior angles, 84, **91**
SAS ≅, **299**
SAS ~, **171**
Secant, 496, 557
Sector, 425, **426**
Segment, 38
Semicircle, 492
Shape bucket, 50
Shape Factory, The Problem, 40, 118
Shapes
    congruent, 140, **159**, **291**
    ratio of areas, **457**
    ratio of perimeters, **457**
    similar, 136, 139
    three-dimensional, 340
    two-dimensional, 340
Side
    face, 527
Side view, 444
Sides
    congruent, **351**
Similar figures
    area of, 12, **457**
Similarity, 136, 139, **171**, **415**
    AA ~, **155**
    congruent, 140, **159**, **291**
    proportional equation, **145**
    ratio, **142**
    SSS ~, **155**
    SSS ~, AA ~, and SAS ~, **171**
    statement, **150**
    zoom factor, 140, **142**
$\sin^{-1}$, 243, **248**
Sine ratio (sin), 236, **241**, **264**
Slant height, **534**
Sliding a shape (translation), **34**
Slope, 20, **47**
    negative, **47**
    of parallel lines, **47**
    of perpendicular lines, **47**
    positive, **47**
    triangle, **47**, **190**, **200**
    undefined, **47**
    zero, **47**
Slope angle, **190**, 202
    clinometer, 202
    common, **194**
Slope ratio, **200**, **241**
    common, **194**

Index of Symbols

$\geq$	"greater than or equal to"	$\measuredangle A$	angle with vertex A
$\leq$	"less than or equal to"	$m\measuredangle A$	measure of angle A
$>$	"greater than"	$36°$	"36 degrees"
$<$	"less than"	$\cong$	"congruent to"
$=$	"equal to"	$\tan \theta$	"tangent of theta"
$\sqrt{}$	square root or radical	$\sin \theta$	"sine of theta"
$\triangle ABC$	a triangle with vertices A, B, and C	$\cos \theta$	"cosine of theta"
		$\sim$	"similar to"
$X'Y'Z'$	"X prime, Y prime, Z prime"	$P:Q$	ratio of P to Q
$ABCD$	quadrilateral $ABCD$	$P(A)$	probability of event A
cm^2	square centimeter	π	"pi"
in^2	square inch	$\odot C$	circle C
$//$	"parallel to"	$\overset{\frown}{ABC}$	arc ABC
$\perp$	"perpendicular to"	$m\overset{\frown}{ABC}$	measure of arc ABC
AB	length of line segment $\overline{AB}$	α	alpha
$\overleftrightarrow{AB}$	line through points A and B	β	beta
$\overline{AB}$	line segment with endpoints at A and B	Δ	delta
$\overrightarrow{AB}$	ray starting at A and passing through B	θ	theta
		ϕ	phi

Equation Reference

$y = mx + b$	Slope-intercept form of a line	$x^2 + y^2 = r^2$	Equation of a circle with center at the origin $(0, 0)$, with radius r
$y = ax^2 + bx + c$	Standard form of a quadratic equation		

THIS BOOK IS THE PROPERTY OF:

Book No._____

ISSUED TO	Year Used	CONDITION	
		ISSUED	RETURNED

PUPILS to whom this texbook is issued must not write on any part of it in any way, unless otherwise instructed by the teacher.